Educational Linguistics - TESOL
University of Pennsylvania
Graduate School of Education
3700 Walnut Street/C1
Philadelphia, PA 19104

DELL H. HYMES

LANGUAGE IN SOCIETY

The Linguistic Revolution and Social Change

The science of language expresses man to himself; it shows him how he has constructed and perfected the most necessary instrument of civilization.

Bréal, Semantics

Language in Society

The Linguistic Revolution and Social Change

by

M. M. LEWIS

Director, Institute of Education
University College, Nottingham

SOCIAL SCIENCES PUBLISHERS
New York

Printed in the United States of America

CONTENTS

INTRODUCTION : The Linguistic Revolution .   1

PART ONE : LINGUISTIC INITIATION

1 The Infant 12
2 The Child at School 27
3 The Adult 45

PART TWO : LANGUAGE AND GROUP MIND

4 Language and Individual Mind . . . 71
5 Language and Group Behaviour . . . 94
6 Language and Group Consciousness . . 112

PART THREE : LANGUAGE IN MODERN
SOCIETIES

7 Language in Industry and Warfare . . 124
8 Language in Politics 147
9 Language and Social Integration . . . 173
10 Language and Social Conflict 199
11 Possibilities 221

APPENDIX : Changes in the Philosophy of
Language 231

REFERENCES 240

INDEX 245

TO
H W L
FOR
12 IV 46

LANGUAGE IN SOCIETY

INTRODUCTION

THE LINGUISTIC REVOLUTION

I

WE are in the midst of a Linguistic Revolution. During the last fifty years every major change in the lives of men in society has been affected by the growth of physical communication ; no less by the development of linguistic communication. We are only at the beginning of what must be vast changes in the functions of language for mankind ; to-day, for the first time in history, we see the possibility of universal literacy and the possibility that all men, at the same moment, may be listening to the same voice or reading the same words.

In the progress of man's command over language there have been four advances, all of great significance in the history of his life and thought ; the development of language itself, the advent of writing, the invention of printing, and now to-day the instantaneous transmission of speech and writing.

The Linguistic Revolution is the cumulative effect of all these four changes. It is the impact of the speech machines upon a world already profoundly affected by the printing machine ; a world the written word can span almost with the speed of thought. The new machines come to a generation more occupied with words than at any other time in the history of mankind. Universal literacy is within reach ; we take it almost as a matter of course ; yet how strange would it have seemed to Plato, perhaps even to Dr. Johnson. A world in which everyone reads is a new world. The newspaper, the cheap book, the free library—all these have brought the printed page into places where before there was none.

The magnitude of all this change must be grasped in order to understand its potential significance for men's thought and behaviour. Newspapers : each household in this country buys on the average ten newspapers a week.[1] Every year hundreds of thousands of copies of cheap books and reprints appear. The free libraries serve a vast public : nearly one-seventh of the total population of Great Britain and Ireland are borrowers, borrowing thirty books each every year.[2] More than this : the circulation of books and newspapers is no longer limited by national boundaries. Means of transmission and communication already in existence make possible " the simultaneous publication on five continents of a complete magazine forty-eight hours after the material has been written in a central editorial office in New York, London, Paris, Moscow, or Chungking. . . . It is now physically possible to make the most informative literature of all countries available to all who want to be informed, at less than the equivalent of twenty-five cents a copy." [3] For the first time in history a book may emerge into a world in which every person is a potential reader.

People read more ; they also write more. The extension of literacy, the introduction of the penny post, the invention of the telegraph, did something more than give men the means of communicating freely at a distance. They made writing more customary ; a change in social habits the effects of which on thought, behaviour, and on the structure of society may be profound.

Communities in which only a few could read and write have changed into communities in which only a few can not.

[1] PEP (For References, see end of book)
[2] Jast LC 199
[3] White PP 10. This is a sober report from the Commission on Freedom of the Press instituted by the University of Chicago.

2

In a society such as ours the illiterate man is fast becoming as much a social anomaly as in primitive societies the man who cannot work or fight, and may suffer penalties no less severe. It is held by careful observers that the anti-social behaviour of many delinquent children is the expression of emotional tension arising from their linguistic backwardness in school.[1]

Into this world, already literate, comes to-day a renascence of the spoken word, a change perhaps of even greater significance. The facts are familiar enough, their implications possibly not so obvious. In 1876 Bell invented the telephone, in 1877 Edison the gramophone ; twenty years later came Marconi's use of wireless for communication, and thirty years after that the talking film. Thus half a century brought us four machines, to-day so much the commonplaces of our lives that we may have ceased to reflect upon their personal and social meaning. But at the birth of this new era seventy years ago its possibilities struck men forcibly enough. A few months after the invention of the telephone *The Times* said, " A great change has come over the conditions of humanity. Suddenly and quietly the whole human race is brought within speaking and hearing distance. Scarcely anything was more desired or more impossible." [2]

To-day we see that the increase of the power of communication, whether in speech or in writing, is only the merest surface of the change. To speak instead of writing, to hear what is said instead of reading what has been written, to listen to the same words at the same time as uncounted multitudes of others, to speak at the same time to all men instead of writing for a few in each successive generation ; for the leaders of men to turn once again to the spoken word as a medium of communication after centuries of the growing use of the written word ; for the written word to be transmitted instantaneously throughout the world—these are more than the extension and acceleration of communication. They are transformations of human conduct, which must affect thought, feeling, and impulse as well as overt behaviour. They are much more than

[1] Burt YD 336 ; Schonell BS 507   [2] Leading article, November 19, 1877

a Linguistic Revolution. They are a part of vast changes—
only the beginnings of which we can as yet perceive—in the
social life of mankind.

2

We can understand the nature of the Linguistic Revolution
only if we recognize its relation to social change. Behind the
Linguistic Revolution lies the French Revolution. The extension of the franchise means the extension of literacy. In the
nineteenth century, for the first time since the ancient Greek
states, the broadening of the basis of government once more
gave discussion in the public forum a paramount place in
politics. It is a commonplace of the history of English education in the nineteenth century that the two major statutory
advances in the extension of the franchise were immediately
followed by advances in the extension of literacy : the Reform
Act of 1832 by the first Treasury grant for education in 1833,
the Reform Act of 1867 by the Education Act of 1870. It is
illuminating to observe the forces engaged on either side at
these two moments in a struggle that lasted throughout the
century and that is far from ended to-day.

On the one hand were the philosophical " reformers " who
advocated changes ; on the other the " practical men of affairs "
who brought them about. What were their intentions, on the
one side and on the other ? The denunciations of the social
prophets, and their utopias, survive for us in their writings ;
it is less easy to know what was in the minds of the legislators,
more closely constrained by the dominant forces of their day.
It is only in Plato that the philosophers are also the governors.
In nineteenth-century England the control of literacy was their
field of battle. Every demand of the reformers was—and then
only after a struggle—met by a compromise designed, by the
men of affairs, to concede as little as possible. Literacy for the
masses, certainly ; but only so much as would make them
the more fit to be governed.

The reformers fought on two fronts. They saw to it that
more books were made available for those who could already

4

read, and they pressed for legislation to abolish illiteracy. Brougham's *Practical Observations on the Education of the People* (1825) was followed by the foundation of the Society for the Diffusion of Useful Knowledge (1827), and the issue of the *Penny Magazine*, the beginning of a flood of " instructive " literature. Thirty years later it was estimated that one publisher alone, John Cassell, issued between 25 and 30 millions of copies of penny publications each year.[1]

While this steady enlargement of adult education was going on, the reformers were also pressing forward to their goal of universal literacy. In all this they were impelled by two motives not wholly compatible with each other. As social philosophers, disseminators of cheap books, promoters of free libraries, they were moved by a humanitarianism that recognized education as a good in itself, and demanded therefore that in egalitarian justice it should be denied to no man. But as members of the governing classes they also saw that the extension of literacy could be a means of government. It could be the chief instrument in the betterment of social conditions, in civilizing the masses degraded by industrial life, in rendering them amenable to control. The art of government, Bentham had said, was the art of education ; more education, fewer crimes.[2]

But in the hands of the practical men of affairs the extension of literacy was a tool with a sharper edge and a narrower range of application. When in 1833 they conceded the first Treasury grant in aid of education, no doubt this had been made inevitable by the unceasing agitation of the philosophical Radicals ; but its urgency was due to recent political change. As soon as the Reform Act of the previous year had become law, it was evident that an illiterate electorate would be a danger to those who intended to remain their governors. The Radical reformers lost no time in pressing the attack at this moment of fear. It was during a Commons speech in support of the Treasury grant that Roebuck—a Benthamite—said, " The hitherto subject many are about to become paramount in the State " ; at once

---

[1] *Trans. Brit. Assoc.* 1862, 174   [2] Bentham PM (ii) 236, PL (i) 569

a warning of the perils of government by the illiterate and a reminder that literacy, skilfully controlled, may well be a means of ensuring docility. And it was in keeping with the competitive industrialism of the day that this beginning of State responsibility should take the form of a subsidy in aid of private enterprise and mass production—the monitorial system of Bell and Lancaster.

Thirty years passed ; the annual grant of twenty thousand pounds had swollen to a cumulative total of nearly four and a half millions ; it was natural for an industrial community to inquire whether the commodity so heavily subsidized was both " sound and cheap." The Newcastle Commission of 1861 reported that the investment had in fact been far from profitable. One of the most enlightened of the commissioners, James Fraser, afterwards Bishop of Manchester, pointed out that in aiming at education rather than literacy, the schools had frequently achieved neither. In rural districts where boys must finish their schooling at ten or eleven, what at the most could be hoped for ? This : to spell the words that the boy will have to use, read a common narrative or newspaper paragraph, write a legible and intelligible letter, make out or test a shop bill, have some notion where foreign countries lie on the globe, be sufficiently acquainted with the Bible to follow a plain sermon, and remember enough of the Catechism to know his duty to God and Man. Fraser was bold enough to maintain that so much was feasible ; in aiming at more, most schools had achieved far less.[1]

It was an allowance of literacy just sufficient to stabilize the existing social and economic structure of a community dominated by ideals of private enterprise and competitive industry. And the method of securing it was in keeping with these ideals ; Lowe's system of " payment by results "—payment only when tested samples showed that the goods were up to standard.[2]

---

[1] *Newcastle Commission Report* 1861 (ii) 46

[2] The " standards " of the " New Code " of 1862 embodied the specifications of Fraser : Adamson EE 231

But the system also tended to widen the gap between literacy and education. It gave the subsidized schools the single task of equipping the worker with so much command of the written language as would enable him to do his work efficiently and live in obedience to his economic and political masters ; but at the same time it cut off this command of language from its natural sequel in education—personal growth, culture and development, the mastery of knowledge, and the cultivation of taste. It was as though the governors had taken heed of Roebuck's aphorism by allowing the subject many only so much literacy as would *prevent* their becoming paramount in the State.

The philosophers, however, were not silenced. The " New Code " had been carried through only in the face of their vigorous protests ; in a very short time a further change in political structure gave them the opportunity of bringing the problem of literacy once more to the front. The Reform Act of 1867 in doubling the number of the electorate, made mere literacy not only inadequate but dangerous. Lowe's warning to the Commons, " we must educate our masters," [1] was ammunition borrowed from the enemy—Roebuck's earlier admonition now repeated as an alarm to those in power, that if they had to submit to be ruled by the many it would be better for them if their rulers were civilized.

The Act of 1870 attempted to balance the extension of the franchise by the extension of education ; it probably created more problems than it solved. Just so much literacy as will make a man more readily subject to economic, political, and ethical control—this is a clear, perhaps even a feasible object ; but the ideal of education for all opens unending vistas of difficulty. To-day we see the results of this double allegiance of our grandfathers.

They themselves were far from unaware of the dangerous complexity of the problem. The philologists and metaphysicians

---

[1] This was the phrase broadcast throughout the country. His actual words were less epigrammatic : " I believe it will be absolutely necessary that you should prevail on our future masters to learn their letters."

7

of the day saw with increasing clarity that the nature of language is only to be understood if we take account of its functions in society.[1] If, therefore, we inherit the problems bequeathed by their politicians, we also inherit the understanding of them suggested by their philosophers.

3

The problems are the same throughout the world to-day because they arise from changes in the social functions of language characteristic of our day. The extension of literacy and the development of linguistic communication, instead of freeing the mind and spirit of the common man, may commit him more deeply into the hands of the few. First the written word and then the spoken—the press and the radio—although potentially the means of bringing every man within the circle of communication, and so making him a self-determining member of the community, may in fact make him subject to anyone who succeeds in capturing the source of communication. Yet while the word binds, it frees. Make a man literate in order to govern him, you may make him more able and more urgent to govern himself.

The practical recognition of this truth was immediate and far-reaching in the new polities that were born between the two wars. The outstanding instance is the U.S.S.R., where the liquidation of illiteracy has taken its place as a major goal of planning side by side with the development of industry, of transport, and of armament. "Without literacy no politics ; but only rumours, small talk, and prejudices "—the words are Lenin's.[2]

There the leaders of the State have purposively undertaken to add a new tool to the equipment of every one of its members. Those whose only means of communication was speech will now read and write as well. It is as though an organ already long in use were now taught a new function, as though a man

[1] see Appendix p. 231   [2] Webb SC 891

who can walk and run now listens to music for the first time and learns to dance. For those who first become literate when already adult this must be an overwhelming experience—we can catch something of its meaning in the delight that the Soviet masses show in the mere patterns of words, in the gigantic letters that sprawl across their banners.

Words which so long as they were only spoken and heard were floating and evanescent, like a gesture or a frown, now are given a body, are fixed, can be seen. And even for the second generation—the children of these men and women—general literacy may still be something that sits not quite naturally ; they live in a world of elders for whom the written word yet remains something of a wonder.

All this, however, is the impact upon the surface. The fuller effects penetrate deeply into the thought, feeling, and action of men as members of a society. In acquiring the instruments that at first may make them more readily amenable to political, social, and industrial control, they acquire the means of resisting control. The common language that makes possible the unity of thought, feeling, and action throughout a vast federation of republics may also make their members more aware of their real differences. A common language may provide conflict as well as community of thought, feeling, and action.

A somewhat similar pattern, though with characteristic differences, showed itself in Nazi Germany. Hitler at once recognized that in our day authority is with him who can command the dissemination of words. " Leadership," he said, " is the art of moving the masses." [1] But to move men and women in whom generations of literacy have bred a distrust of the written word, the Leader must have the power of giving new life and vigour to the spoken word. Here, therefore, it is the spoken word that becomes of supreme importance ; the radio booming out its message in every street and home. " I know that men are to be won over less by the written word than by the spoken, that every important movement in the

[1] " Denn Führen heisst : Massen bewegen können."—Hitler MK 650

world owes its growth more to the great speakers than to the great writers." [1]

In his time and place Hitler was probably right. The written word, to the man just made free of it, has an almost magical force ; with greater familiarity there grows, in a few, some power of critical discrimination ; in many more distrust, disbelief, even complete negativism. For these, for whom reading has become a drug, continued recourse to which has numbed the first keenness of response, a new stimulant is necessary—the orator, the vibrations of his personality magnified by the loud-speaker.

But it need hardly be said that although all men may listen at the same moment to the same words, and although their acts and even their uttered words may be uniform, there is no control of the unuttered words that shape themselves. And the more the life of a community is permeated by words, the greater the likelihood that thoughts and feelings that might otherwise remain unspoken will come to utterance. The increase of centrally controlled communication arouses responses that elude control. Once more we have the potentiality of conflict.

Finally, in the democracies a similar pattern, again with characteristic differences, also appears. The press and the radio, while making men more open to control by those who command these sources of power, at the same time provide readers and listeners with the munitions of resistance to control. Freedom of speech may be the source not of unity but of disunity in a society.

In every form of society, because language is so closely related to the thoughts, feelings, and actions of men, we cannot change the extent, nature, functions of language without setting in motion further, perhaps unintended, changes. Language is so fundamental and pervasive throughout human

---

[1] " Ich weiss, dass man Menschen weniger durch das geschriebene Wort als vielmehr durch das gesprochene zu gewinnen vermag, dass jede grosse Bewegung auf dieser Erde ihr Wachsen, den grossen Rednern und nicht den grossen Schreiber verdankt."—Hitler MK pref.

conduct, both in the life of man as an individual and in his social life, that changes as great as those that make up the Linguistic Revolution must produce stresses and strains, tensions, and conflicts in thought, feeling, and action.

Our task in the chapters that follow is to examine the Linguistic Revolution in its context of social life. We are to consider how language, in the world of to-day, works in society and between societies ; its effects on both social unity and social conflict. We begin with a survey of the linguistic initiation of the individual into society, from infancy to manhood. Then we pass to an analysis of the functioning of language in a community and its relation, therefore, to group thought, feeling, and action. Finally, we turn to some concrete instances of these group functions of language in and between modern societies ; the mutual effects of economic, political, and social changes and the Linguistic Revolution.

PART ONE

LINGUISTIC INITIATION

CHAPTER I

THE INFANT

I

THE constant intention of every society is to socialize its members. In a primitive community social behaviour is largely physical action ; the history of civilization is the story of the intervention of language into all social behaviour. To-day language is the primary means of the socialization of the individual. As he becomes increasingly a member of a lingustic community, language plays a larger and larger part not only in his social life but in his personal behaviour, feeling, and thought. His effective membership of his society directly depends upon his ability to communicate with his fellows ; in turn his power of communication is a primary factor in his development as an individual. We must begin therefore with a survey of the process by which the individual is initiated into the linguistic community ; the beginnings of language in the child, its further development in school, and the slow but un-ceasing education in language that goes on throughout adult life.

The socialization of the individual is a process of constant tension between convergent and divergent forces. The child growing up in society is impelled, if not by innate tendencies then at least by early training, to seek the support of others, to converge towards the group ; at the same time he seeks to maintain his individuality in face of others, to diverge from them. These others, for their part, seek to absorb him into the group, to make him one of themselves, but in the very act of doing so they elicit and develop those powers by which he is able to assert his individuality with greater strength and diverge from the group.

The initiation of the child into a society of speakers, since it is the chief means of socialization, falls into this pattern of tension between convergent and divergent forces. At the outset the roots of language are already present in the infant, but they are individual, non-conventional, non-social ; purely expressive cries and noises, they are not at first in any way directed towards others. The group takes heed of these unformed rudiments of speech and shapes them into language, moulds individual utterance into conventional forms, directs and defines its functions so that it comes to serve as the medium of social intercourse. But at every moment in this ceaseless process of socialization, the child's speech still remains deeply rooted in himself and expressive of himself.

This is not, of course, to say that either the child or the group is conscious of these forces. The child may for long be unaware of any of the intentions that impel him to the mastery of speech : and again it is only highly sophisticated groups who will be fully aware of their purposes in developing the language of their children. Our understanding of the psychological motives impelling the individual and the group to the cultivation of language must therefore largely come from observing how these motives express themselves in overt behaviour. We see that for the child the primary functions of speech are to communicate with others as well as to assert himself ; so that while communication brings him more certainly under the control of others, it also adds greater strength to his individuality, for it opens up channels through which the resources of the group may flow to him and sustain him. For the group, on the other hand, the primary function of language is to enable them to deal more readily with the new-comer among them ; yet in giving each of its members language, the group not only makes him one of themselves but make him more himself. The greater his command over language as a means of social communication, the greater his command over language as a means of self-expression.

It is evident that this process of development continues as long as an individual is a member of a group ; linguistic initiation is a life-long process. In infancy, at school, and at work everyone is constantly learning to communicate with his fellows. Hardly has the child entered the world when he begins to acquire the rudiments of the mother tongue. In three years or so he achieves sufficient mastery over the repertory of its sounds, the system of its structure, and its vocabulary, to make himself intelligible in expressing his immediate needs and to respond appropriately to the demands of others in relation to these needs. All this preliminary phase of linguistic initiation proceeds in the home with the minimum of conscious direction from those surrounding the child.

Then follows the period of directed education, when society, through the specialized instrument of the school, seeks of set purpose to develop the child's powers of communication and expression. The third stage of linguistic initiation begins when schooling has ended : this is the life-long acquisition of language, the constant enlargement and refinement of the powers of linguistic intercourse. It is a process obviously slower and slighter in some members of society than in others ; it may be so slow and so slight as to be barely apparent, but it is probably never entirely absent. At this moment in history the process, in the lives of all men, is more rapid than for a very long time past ; this speeding-up and expression of life-long education in language is indeed one aspect of what we have called the Linguistic Revolution.

Let us now look a little more closely at each of these three stages.

2

The first stage of language—the initiation that begins at birth—is a process of growth rather than of instruction. The child does not learn his mother tongue as one might learn a foreign language in later life ; as he grows, language grows in him.

The basis of all language lies in the child's earliest expressive sounds. Within a few hours after birth he begins to utter a cry when discomfited—the characteristic cry of all children, the bleat of the human infant. And in a few weeks another kind of expressive utterance begins to appear : sounds expressive of comfort, again characteristic and more or less alike in all infants.[1]

The child cries and makes his characteristic sounds like any other vocal animal. Like any other vocal animal, too, his mother responds to him. It is reasonable to postulate that in us, as in other animals, both the utterance of cries and the response to them are innate tendencies. What is certainly clear is that both tendencies are greatly modified and developed by life in society. Because the mother lives in a society of speakers, her response owes much to tradition—the social heritage half-consciously gained in the course of her development. It is a result, therefore, of her joint biological and social heritage that her child's cries have power to rouse her to attend to him. She comes to him, soothes and alleviates his discomfort if he is in distress, shares and increases his pleasure by smiling and playing with him if he is pleased. These responses of hers at once give the child's utterance a fuller *meaning* for him. As his cry of discomfort or gurgle of pleasure is regularly followed by a specific sequel of experience, he comes to anticipate this sequel, which becomes for him a part of the meaning of the vocal noise that he utters. For the child, therefore, the meaning of a cry or gurgle is complex ; the sound comes to stand for the child's experience at the time when he makes the sound, together with his experiences of the sequel to his sound—his mother's response to it. From the very outset, then, the meaning of language for the individual

[1] The sounds tend to be alike in all children because their physiological origin is the same ; they are expressive in Darwin's sense (Darwin EE). There is a detailed discussion of the facts in Lewis IS.

not only arises from within himself, but is also determined from without, by his social environment.

Ultimately the child's utterance will become intentional : he will use words, more or less articulate, to mean that he is, for instance, uncomfortable ; and intend them to mean that he wishes his mother to do something about this for him. He will use other words to express pleasure, with the intention of securing some response from those around him. But before this development of intention in the use of language, two other factors have begun to operate, both showing the interplay of the convergent and divergent social and individual forces characteristic of all linguistic growth. These two factors are imitation and babbling.

3

Imitation, like expression, is a form of behaviour characteristic of many other animals than man, but if it is innate in man, this is true only of its rudiments. The power of imitating language which we find in the infant in his earliest months is very crude ; imitation is itself an art to be acquired, and its acquisition is socially determined.[1] The adults around the child constantly encourage him to imitate them ; they show approval when he is successful and correct his errors. A perhaps even greater aid to his development is their constant imitation of him—they use his " baby words " as a means of approximating their language to his and so of getting into touch with him, very much as European traders in China once used " pidgin English." The child's progress in imitation is thus an inevitable accompaniment of his growing up in a community of speakers, urged by the necessity of bringing him, the infant, the speechless one,[2] as rapidly as possible within the pale of human intercourse. Until the child begins to

---

[1] The social determination of imitation in general is discussed by Miller SL ; in children's behaviour by Guillaume IE ; and in relation to language by Lewis IS.

[2] Latin *infans* : unable to speak

speak he is not quite one of us ; to the young mother whose child's speech is retarded, the most terrifying thought is that perhaps he may never speak and so will remain something less than fully human. And since the child is felt to be speaking only when he uses words recognizably like our own, there is a constant urgency in the group to accelerate the growth of imitation.

Observations suggest that progress in imitation of language normally falls into three stages. From about the age of three months a child will frequently respond to the speech of others with sounds of his own, and then usually improve in his approximation, especially if those around him take the trouble to make sounds like his. Then there comes a time—often in the later part of the first year—when this primitive imitation dies down : the child's responses are increasingly to the *meaning* of what he hears. After a lapse of some months, there is a renewal of imitation ; but now the child is concerned not so much with sounds themselves as with these sounds in relation to their meaning. His imitation is now directed towards both the forms and the functions of heard and uttered speech.

It is far from true, therefore, that imitation is an inevitable response, innately determined, to heard sounds. The child improves in his imitation of sounds by practice ; and the chief incentive to practice is that the sounds he hears have important meanings for him. In this way his own personal repertory of sounds is brought into close relation with the language spoken around him ; his own speech is socialized. For a long time, however, he may continue to assert his individuality—unconsciously and perhaps even consciously—by resisting as well as he can the socialization of his speech ; many children persist in using " baby language " far into later childhood, a few even into adult life.[1] Thus imitation is marked by the typical tension between the individual and the group ; the fact that all this goes on with the minimum of awareness reminds us how

---

[1] Boys appear to be more resistant than girls ; they are more frequently retarded in speech, and stammering and other speech defects are more common among them. See, for instance, Seth SC 117, 177. One is tempted to regard this as one instance of a characteristic male tendency to resist socialization.

deeply rooted in human conduct is the process of linguistic initiation. In everyday life it can go on without any of the participants being aware that it is happening.

The second important factor in the child's initiation is the socialization of his own babbling. While he is learning to imitate he spends much of his time in babbling. He plays with sounds ; at first sight nothing could seem more individual, less social ; but in the end this too is brought under social influence and made to contribute to the growth of language.

By babbling we mean the child's utterance of sounds not to express his discomfort or his pleasure, but for the sake of the satisfaction this utterance itself brings. It seems to occur in all children alike and consists of strings of " meaningless " sounds, repeated in rhythmical patterns and with characteristic tunes.[1] The child is playing with sounds ; psychologically the sources of babbling are of the same kind as of other forms of play in children. These psychological features of babbling, and its relation to the aesthetics of literary expression and enjoyment, we need not discuss here ; it is enough to point out that, like other aspects of language, babbling arises primarily as non-social behaviour, and that it is at once seized upon by the group and socialized—brought in to swell the growing current of communication between the group and the child.

That babbling is primarily non-social is evident when we observe that all children, even the deaf, spontaneously babble. It is sustained in the child's life and becomes habitual to him in the same way as other forms of play, furnishing an end in itself, in the satisfaction which its exercise brings. And in most of us it remains one of the incentives to the utterance of language—few people wholly outgrow the pleasure of hearing themselves speak. There, at that level—as a form of play, of self-stimulation, of narcissism—it might remain. But the group does not allow it to remain at that level. As soon as the child is heard to babble, those around him begin to intervene ; they break into his streams of babbling with words of their

[1] Lewis IS chapter v

18

own, many of which he comes to imitate and make the starting-point of further babbling. In this way he is led to practise not only his own " meaningless," personal, non-social sounds, but also the sounds, words, phrases, intonations of the mother tongue. So even his linguistic play is socialized and made to serve the purposes of communication ; and again all this happens with the minimum of awareness in himself and in the group.

4

So the child acquires the rudiments of speech ; but for this to become a means of communication between him and the group there must of course be an approximation both of form and of function. The forms of speech which the child uses, and the meanings that he gives to these forms, must be brought as near as possible to those of the language spoken around him. This approximation is a necessary condition of any development of communication ; but the growth of communication in its turn results in approximation between the child's language and that of his social environment. The process of communication, and the approximation of form and function influence each other.

Let us take as one example the history of the word that is usually the most important in the early life of a child—*mama*. The great majority of children utter this, or something very like it, in the course of their earliest cries ; most of them use it as one of their earliest "words." We have therefore many records of its development, by numerous observers, and can describe its typical course with some exactness.[1]

In general, sounds like *ma . . . ma* occur in the course of expressive cries at some time during the first six months, and towards the end of his first year a child will generally be found using a " word " of this form with some definite meaning—that is, he begins to use it in specific circumstances with specific intentions, and to respond to the sound of it in specific ways. At this stage, of course, overt behaviour is our only guide to

[1] Lewis IS ; Index, *mama*

meaning ; the only way to understand what a child of ten months " means " by *mama* is to observe what he does when he hears it and his accompanying acts when he himself utters it.

In a typical case (K) the main stages of development were as follows. In the sixth month he was heard to say *m . . . m . . .m* during a chain of babbling ; three months later he was saying *mama* when uncomfortable or lacking something. In his twelfth month he said *mama* when looking at his mother and stroking her face ; two months after this with reference to a woman visitor ; and at the age of eighteen months on seeing a picture of a woman not his mother. In the meantime he had also come to respond to the word in characteristic ways. The first observed instance of this child's overt response to the word was when at the age of twelve months he held up a crust on being told, *Give Mummy crustie* ; but soon after this he would, at these words, hand the crust as frequently to his father as to his mother. A month later he nestled his head on his mother's shoulder at the words, *Love Mummy* ; at sixteen months he sometimes went to her when she said, *Come to Mummy* ; at eighteen months, asked, *Where's Mummy?* he usually pointed in the right direction.

The nature of our central topic in this book forbids our going into greater detail or giving further examples ; this brief outline must serve to illustrate the general lines of development which emerge from numerous observations.

It is clear that at first this fragment of speech " means " for the child his own affective and conative behaviour,[1] and that only gradually does a definitely cognitive meaning for it grow up. At the outset *mama* is, with its varied intonations, expressive for him of varied affective stirrings and conative strivings ; then it begins to have a vague and loose cognitive reference to some of the objects bound up with these affective and conative experiences—the child's food, his playthings, or

---

[1] British psychologists—particularly Aveling, Flugel, and Spearman—have suggested the term " orectic " as an equivalent of " affective-conative," to mark the fact that affect and conation are normally closely intermingled. Here we shall use *orectic* and the corresponding noun *orexis* where convenient.

his mother. Slowly the influence of the community of speakers around the child—in their responsive behaviour to him, and as they speak to him—gives the meaning of the word a bias in the direction of his mother, so that it begins to have a cognitive reference to her rather than to other things. But the looseness and vagueness of the reference is still evident from the child's attachment of the word to his experience of persons other than his mother. He uses it himself as little more than an accompaniment of action towards a person ; and when he hears it, it is little more than an incentive causing him to perform some action. After this, it is only gradually, and under long-continued social pressure, that the child comes to use and respond to the word with its conventional cognitive reference to the one specific person, his mother. And at the same time, as the scope of the word's meaning is narrowed for him in this direction, it gains in richness of content. He learns by much trial and error that other women whom he spontaneously would name *mummy* must be referred to in such other ways as *granny, auntie, lady* ; he learns, too, that another child or even his puppy has a *mummy*—or *mother* ; for sooner or later instead of his own baby word he adopts the social, adult form. By the age of six or seven he has some notion of the relationships that this word names ; by the age of fourteen he has further enlarged its meaning in such concepts as *mother-country* and *Mother Nature*.

If, as we may, we take this as a typical picture of what occurs, two things are clear : first, that the child's language from the beginning is rooted in physical action and is inseparable from it ; and second, that language is at first mostly expressive of affect and conation, becoming progressively more cognitive, as a means of referring to objects and situations.

At the outset the child's cries are among the many varied ways in which he behaves in the effort to satisfy his needs— his cries are a part of his total physical reaction to a state of discomfort. His gurgles of satisfaction, again, are closely linked up with his physical reactions when his needs have been satisfied.

If then we ask what are the meanings of the child's earliest utterance we must say that both his cries and his gurglings express orectic states closely connected with physical behaviour. For him speech is not yet a means of naming the objects he perceives ; and it will be a long time before he can use it as a means of formulating judgments or engaging in reasoning. Gradually his language acquires these cognitive functions, partly no doubt by the mere maturation of his intellectual power, certainly in the main as a result of his increasing command of communication itself. To the expression of feeling and desire language gradually adds the power of communicating thought.

Throughout all this development there is both convergence and divergence in his relations with his social group. There is convergence ; he seeks to attract their attention and they his. He learns how to use speech so as to secure physical help, or an affective response ; or both. At the same time he learns to respond in both these ways to the speech of others. There is convergence too in the forms of speech. The child imitates the sounds of the language of those around him, while they approximate their speech to his baby language. Meanwhile there is also divergence both in the functions and in the forms of language. The child will often persist in using "words" that bear little or no resemblance to any he hears ; or he persists in extending the use of accepted words in "unconventional" ways. Sometimes these personal usages are tolerated by the group, but sooner or later it is the child who conforms. An instrument of communication is gradually fashioned.

Our recognition of the truth of this picture of development is of the first importance if we are to understand the functions of language in society. The meaning of language remains throughout life rooted in action and expressive of affect ; the cognitive functions of language—its use as a means of analysing and synthesizing a cognitive picture of the world around and as a means of formulating thought—these are slowly hammered out through constant interchange between the individual and the group.

5

Let us now look a little more closely at the incentives that impel the child to communicate with others, and so to engage in that special form of social behaviour that we call language. The incentives appear to be of two main kinds, which we may name the "manipulative" and the "declarative."

The child uses speech manipulatively when it is an instrument to secure the satisfaction of his primary needs : to remove discomfort, to obtain pleasant experiences or to prolong these once they have begun. At the beginning the child in discomfort vaguely strives to rid himself of it ; the contortions of his body, the thrusting out of his arms and legs, and not least his cries—these are all of them different ways in which his striving shows itself.[1] Then, as he comes to recognize that the possession of a particular object, for instance food, relieves his discomfort, his vague striving may change into a directed reaching-out to secure this object. In the same way, catching sight of some plaything, for instance a bright ball dangling from his cot, he gurgles with pleasure and reaches out towards it. But it is of course a long time before he is physically capable of achieving his intention ; this is where the group intervenes to help him. His cry is heard and food is brought to him. Or his mother hears his gurgle of delight, and her sympathetic hand swings the ball towards him. Thus his utterance becomes the instrument of achieving his intention, an instrument used blindly and fumblingly at first, but with a clearer understanding of its use as time goes on. It is a social instrument —a means by which, instead of directly manipulating his physical environment, the child manipulates his social environment, which in turn manipulates his physical environment for him.

In its declarative function language plays a different part. Often it is evident that the child is not so much attempting

[1] This is Darwin's account of the origin of expression in *Expression of the Emotions* (1872).

23

to seize hold on some portion of his physical environment as simply to express its effect on him, and that his satisfaction comes from securing an appropriate expressive response from someone else. For instance, the child lying in his cot and gurgling with pleasure at the dance of light and shade on the ceiling becomes happier still when his mother points to the dancing pattern and also expresses her delight. Soon it is clear that he is intentionally trying to secure this response from her, that he declares his pleasure in order to enhance it by affective communion with her. In this declarative use of speech the child seeks to obtain from others, not some manipulation of his physical environment, but simply an expressive response. Speech is still a social instrument, but now it is directed, not to secure some change in the physical environment, but social response as an end in itself.

If we are to understand the functions of language in society it is important to recognize these two incentives of communication ; not only social manipulation but also social declaration. It is easy to see that communication is constantly manipulative ; it is perhaps not so obvious that it is just as often declarative. But observation of the infant and consideration of the everyday uses of language in society make it at once clear that the manipulative and the declarative are the twin incentives by which the development of language is fostered in the child, and remain the essential functions of language in society.

The manipulative function, in its most fully developed forms, serves what we may call the practical activities of society as a whole and of its individual members. The range of these practical activities is very wide ; they include the immediate everyday business of satisfying economic needs, the political organization of the group to preserve its identity in a warring world, as well as the application of science with the intention of controlling the physical universe. For all these purposes, the individual is by means of language able to call on the resources of the group, and the group to organize the behaviour of its individual members.

The declarative function when fully developed ranges from

everyday conversation to the highest levels of aesthetic communication and expression. A good deal of everyday conversation is an end in itself, a species of social play—what Malinowski in describing primitive communities called " phatic communion." [1] We say Good-morning, or How are you, or talk about the weather, as a means of getting into touch with the other person. The telephone, a machine originally devised to serve " practical " needs, a machine to facilitate the manipulative use of language, becomes also a means of extending the range—and the duration ?—of phatic communion. All this everyday conversation is largely declarative rather than manipulative.

Higher forms of the declarative function are seen in aesthetic expression. The whole of the literary art, in so far as it is moved by an aesthetic intention, is declarative : verse, fiction, belles-lettres, and the drama. The communication of scientific thought often has also an aesthetic function ; when the mathematician, for instance, is concerned not with any practical application of his work, but with the beauty of ordered thought in itself, an appreciation of which he is moved to share with others. Hogben is certainly taking an unbalanced view of the place of mathematics in society when he over-emphasizes its practical origin and functions. Mathematics, he says, is chiefly important in society in order to arrive at the truth about such things as social statistics, population trends, man's hereditary make-up, the balance of trade. [2] A more comprehensive view is that of Whitehead ; he points out that while some parts of mathematics—for instance, trigonometry—have taken their rise from practical problems, others—for instance, conic sections —have begun as an interest in the theory itself. [3] A mathematician writing under such an impulse would be using the language of mathematics declaratively. In all the higher developments of the declarative function, language has the effect of establishing a community of thought or feeling, or both, rather than of organizing the group for action in relation to the physical or social environment.

[1] Ogden MM 315   [2] Hogben MM 28   [3] Whitehead IM 174

Thus the society into which the child is initiated is constantly using language with manipulative and declarative functions. The child himself, because language is for him a means of communication with others, is also impelled to use it in both these ways. His early utterances, as we have seen, receive responses of two kinds : people do things for him, and also respond affectively to his own expressions of affect. His own responses to the speech of others also come to be of both these kinds. Thus more and more the linguistic communication between the child and his society takes on both functions.

One of the chief effects of the child's education in school is the progressive socialization of his language in both these directions. By the time he is ready to leave the narrow circle of the home and enter upon the more systematic education of the school, he has already acquired a considerable command over language as an instrument of communication. He can express thought, feeling, and impulse with both manipulative and declarative intentions, and he has learnt how to respond to these intentions in the language of others. Education in school is largely the further development of these functions of language and of the systematic socialization of the child's behaviour—physical, cognitive, and orectic—through language.

CHAPTER 2

THE CHILD AT SCHOOL

I

WE have seen how language begins and how it develops in the home ; what happens next, when the child goes to school ? The main business of the school is to carry further the child's initiation into language, for it is through language that the child will be brought within reach of the ways of thought and feeling current in the community. Modes of thought and feeling are embodied in the vocabulary and structure of the vernacular : traditional modes that have developed in the community as its members, generation after generation, have striven with one another and with the world around them ; and new modes of thought and feeling, which as they arise find their appropriate means of expression.

To begin with the socialization of the child's thinking : the school, through language, develops in the child the modes of thinking current in his society, as well as acquainting him with the body of knowledge which is the outcome of these modes of thinking. The fact that the structure of knowledge is shaped by the necessities of language is a commonplace, but probably it has been so only since the time of Locke. It was new enough for him to give it a special emphasis. Men, he said, classify things and arrange their ideas of them in orderly fashion, not only on the basis of their real character-istics, but in order to be able to talk about them with one another. " Nature makes many particular things, which do agree one with another in many sensible qualities, and pro-bably too in their internal frame and constitution ; but it is not this real essence that distinguishes them into species ; it is men who, taking occasion from the qualities they find united in them . . . range them into sorts, in order to their naming, for the convenience of comprehensive signs." [1]

[1] *Essay* bk. 3 ch. vi

Since Locke wrote it has become increasingly evident that we must carry his emphasis a stage further. If language determines thought, it is action that determines language. This has been brought home to us with great force by the work of the ethnologists ; such observers as Malinowski and Hocart have shown in detail that the vocabulary of a community reflects, in its classification of things, the practical activities of the group in dealing with these things. " Language is essentially rooted in the reality of the culture, the tribal life and the customs of a people, and cannot be explained without constant reference to these broader contexts of verbal utterance." [1] And as practical interests vary from group to group and from age to age, the forms and functions of language vary ; and with these the fundamental assumptions underlying thought, even the logical procedures used in thinking. The laws of logic may be universally true ; but the emphasis on some assumptions and procedures rather than others varies with time and place.

This is one of the main themes of Pareto in *The Mind and Society*, but it hardly needs the elaboration of his treatment and the wealth of his illustrations to convince us of its truth. Take, for instance, witchcraft. In 1580 the great jurist Bodin wrote his *Démonomanie* to prove by logical analysis that the reality of the phenomena of witchcraft must be accepted by every person prepared to reason impartially and strictly. To-day the procedure of a jurist of equal calibre would differ in a number of ways from that of Bodin ; he would not accept Bodin's fundamental assumptions, such as the unquestionable accuracy of every statement in the Bible and Aristotle ; he would require the testimony of trustworthy witnesses to corroborate the confessions of witches ; above all, he would probably reason inductively from the evidence rather than deductively from first principles.

Now it is through communication that characteristic ways of thinking become current in a society. Not only linguistic communication ; pictorial symbols and ritual acts also play

[1] Malinowski in Ogden MM 305 ; Hocart *Brit. J.Ps.* 1912

their part. But while these latter forms of symbolization tend to express and to shape affect and conation, it is language that is the chief means of communicating and so influencing cognition : the recall of the past by the individual and the group, their awareness of the present, and their anticipation and foresight of the future.

Through language, then, the individual acquires the ways of thinking current in the society in which he is growing up. Initiation into language is necessarily initiation into ways of thinking. The child at school, in acquiring the current language, is acquiring the current modes of thought ; the fundamental hypotheses that lie at the bases of our thinking as well as the inductive and deductive procedures that the development of the sciences during the last three centuries has brought into currency.

2

What is the work of the school in this process ? There are obviously two factors here : the nature of the child and the character of the school. The work of the school is always influenced, on the one hand, by the psychological features of the child's development ; and, on the other, by the traditions of its historical past and by its present functions as a social institution. There are general features of psychological development common to most children growing up in modern societies ; and also special features arising from the fact that the child is growing up in a particular society with traditions of its own. We shall consider these two factors in turn, illustrating the effects of tradition and social function from the circumstances of British schools.

What are the psychological features of the child's development towards logical thinking ? It is surprising that in spite of unending work in recent years on the psychology of children, we should know so little in detail of this important aspect of their growth. Probably the most illuminating account, open to criticism though it may be in particulars, is still that of

Piaget,[1] who has attempted to bring some of the findings of ethnology and general psychology into relation with his first-hand observations of children. His picture of what occurs gives us much insight into the processes by which, during the school years, the child's ways of reasoning are moulded by his acquisition of the means of communication. He shows us how the child learns to think as he learns to communicate.

The main features of Piaget's account are that the development of the child's powers of logical thinking falls into four stages : up to the age of three thinking is " autistic " ; from then to the age of seven " egocentric " ; from seven to eleven marked by the need for " logical justification " ; and only after eleven truly logical. The first two stages, of autism and egocentricity, together make up the " pre-logical " phase— a conception that Piaget owes to sociologists of the school of Durkheim, particularly Lévy-Bruhl, who interpreted the modes of thought current in some primitive communities as being not so much illogical or contrary to logic, as precedent to the development of true logic.

By autistic thinking Piaget means thinking that is wholly determined by the child's needs and that takes little or no cognisance of the reality of the world external to the child ; it is thinking of which the child himself is hardly aware and in which his rudimentary cognitive behaviour is guided not by a conscious purpose but by unconscious needs ; it is thinking that uses pictorial rather than verbal imagery and that is therefore not readily communicable by language. It is evident that autistic thinking is very similar to unconscious mental processes, as described by Freud ; [2] Piaget himself acknowledges his borrowing of the term autistic from the psychoanalytic studies of Bleuler.[3]

As autism changes into egocentricity the child's thinking is still dictated by affective needs, but he begins to be aware of his thought and to direct it. In the course of growing communication with others, and in the effort to make himself intelligible to them, he begins to fit his thinking to the facts

[1] Piaget LP and his subsequent works   [2] see page 90 below   [3] Piaget LP 59

of his environment and to adapt it to the thought of these others. So long as this double adaptation is rudimentary and sporadic, the child's thinking is still pre-logical in character. Where the adult uses logical inference, verbally expressed and determined by objective reality, the child uses visual, pictorial schemas, linked together vaguely in broad "syncretic" associations, and unified by personal feelings and needs.

In the next stage, during the years from seven to eleven, the child seeks "logical justification" for his thinking. His growing social awareness, his reliance upon social guidance, and his need to communicate, all force him to seek criteria of truth which are not merely personal to himself. But since he has not yet reached the stage of objective, self-sufficient, logical judgment, he accepts instead principles and explanations at second hand from adults, without seeking further verification. He also makes independent inferences from his own experiences, but these continue to be intuitive rather than logical, and he is rarely concerned to test their objective validity.[1]

Finally, after the age of eleven, truly logical thinking, characterized by accurate observation and inductive and deductive inference, begins to play its part in the child's life.

The interest of this account of Piaget's for us is his strong conviction that the development of the child's thinking is intimately bound up with the progressive socialization of his language. First he learns to do things, then to speak about them and so to think logically about them. In the earlier stages his skill in dealing with things is of course far in advance of his power of thinking logically about the same things ; for instance, a child of seven well able to ride a bicycle and even to adjust it, may find it quite impossible to give an ordered description of it, that is, to analyse and synthesize its structure in verbal terms.[2] But as time goes on he talks about it with others, asks and answers questions about it ; and so ultimately his thought about it falls into a logical orderly pattern. It is in the process of communication that he learns how to think logically.

[1] Piaget LP 256   [2] the same 105

The main criticism of Piaget's formulation has come from British observers, principally Burt, Isaacs, and Hazlitt.[1] Their contention—based also on first-hand observation of children—is that Piaget imposes far too rigid a form on what is in fact a much more fluid process. The child's thinking in the early stages is less exclusively " pre-logical " than Piaget suggests. A child of three may be quite capable of accurate logical thinking so long as he is dealing with familiar experiences and the logical processes required are not too involved. Further, the chronological ages marked out by Piaget cease to have much validity when children of a wide range of intellectual ability and social condition are taken into account ; it is in fact a characteristic of the highly intelligent child that he is capable of logical thinking at an early age.

But allowing the truth of all this does not affect the accuracy of the main outlines of Piaget's picture of the child's development. Some children certainly develop faster than others, and at any one moment in a child's life his thinking—as indeed the thinking of adults—may show traces of autism, egocentricity and " logical justification " side by side with valid logical thinking. But all the evidence goes to show that the course of development is in the main as Piaget has described it ; and in particular that it is in the effort to deal verbally with what he can already deal with physically that the child acquires the art of logical thinking. And since this logical thinking arises in the course of verbal communication, and is expressed in verbal terms, it is shaped by the modes of thought current in the community in which the child grows up. The work of the school consists very largely in making language an effective means of socializing the child's thought.

3

It is, however, important to recognize that the work of Piaget—and the work of his critics on this point—deals only

[1] Burt Appendix to *The Primary School Report* (1931) ; Isaacs *Intellectual Growth in Young Children* (1930) ; Hazlitt *Brit. J. Ps.* (1930)

with one side of the child's mental development ; the growth of his powers of cognition. Nothing has so far been said about the socialization of his oretic development. Psychologists seem hardly to have concerned themselves with the relation between the child's linguistic growth and his orectic behaviour. In the absence of detailed evidence one would surmise that this has something of the pattern of cognitive development. One would suppose that in the early stages the child's emotions, largely because they are unverbalized, are subjective and chaotic : they are subjective in the sense that they are mainly aroused by situations closely connected with the child's immediate orectic needs ; and they are chaotic in that they do not bear any ordered relation to one another. Then, under social pressure, largely mediated by language, the child acquires the patterns of orexis current in the society about him. His emotions come to be aroused in the same situations as arouse them in other people ; they become organized into " senti-ments," " attitudes." The child's emotional idiosyncrasies are shaped into socially acceptable patterns.

But it is necessary to realize also that in relation to language there are important differences between cognitive and orectic development. Society socializes orexis, i.e. brings individual orexis into the service of the group, by encouraging the symbolization of some of its aspects and denying this to others. It is a process that we shall examine in detail later ; [1] here we can say that its effect upon the individual is that orexis remains much more unverbalized than cognition. The un-conscious mind, in Freud's picture of it, is made up of " com-plexes " rather than of logical thought ; and a complex may be described as a sentiment—a pattern of orexis—of which the subject is unaware to the extent that he does not verbalize it.

The unverbalized aspects of orexis, in so far as they become socially communicated, tend therefore to use non-linguistic means of expression : gestures, inarticulate sounds, pictures ; those very modes of expression that cognitive thinking leaves behind as it progressively develops with the use of language.

[1] see chapter 9

Even in adult life, where language is used for the expression and communication of orexis, it tends also to be pictorial. To-day social life is dominated by the power of the newly developed machines for the communication of pictures in conjunction with words ; the broadcasting of pictures—on the hoardings, in the press, and on the cinema and television screens—increases the pictorial content of the accompanying language. This is especially true where, as in the cinema and radio, the associated word is spoken, and therefore enriched by the orectic symbolisms of intonation. The consequent permeation of social life by group imagery, through communicated words and pictures—to an extent unprecedented in human history—brings with it social effects of great importance.[1]

As yet, we know little or nothing of the manner in which the constant experience of words and pictures affects the development of orexis in the individual child. All that we can say is that as his cognitive development is socialized through language, his orectic development remains relatively unsocialized. If socialized at all, it is through pictures and the more pictorial forms of language.

4

To turn now from the psychology of the child to the traditions of the school, the community that receives him from the home. It is a community with intentions, forms of behaviour, and in fact a language different in many respects from those of the community in which he has hitherto lived. Within the family the child has normally been understood even though his language has been imperfect—his half-spoken words, his gestures, even his silences have been correctly interpreted. But the community of the school is unfamiliar— different from the family : there are new locutions, pronunciations, intonations, gestures, for the child to interpret ; unfamiliar persons for whom his customary language and

[1] see chapter 10

gestures may fail to have their customary meaning. Thus the child enters what is really a new community, and if its atmosphere and way of life are such as to encourage him to develop his growing need to communicate, the school will succeed in performing one of its major functions : the initiation of the child into the ways and thought and feeling of the larger society.

This in fact has always been implicit in the conception of school : the traditional centre of all school education and its characteristic achievement is the initiation of the child into language. It is true of every civilized society of whose educational system we have records ; of ancient Greek and Roman education, of Hebrew education throughout the Middle Ages and later, of Chinese education, almost wholly linguistic for more than twenty-five centuries. And it has been the tradition of modern education since the Renaissance. To recognize this enables us to understand some of the difficulties of education in our schools to-day. The linguistic tradition is one of the chief clues to the history of education in the modern world and therefore to some of its strange aberrations, particularly to that oddity in European societies —the persistence of an apparently inordinate attention to the study of two ancient obsolete languages, often at the expense of the cultivation of the living mother tongue. Throughout all the changes that have taken place in education, the school is still influenced by its heritage of the linguistic tradition.

Let us look back therefore and ask what was the value attached to the study of the classics at the inception of modern education during the Renaissance. The answer is beyond doubt ; it was held that through the classics the thought, feeling, and behaviour of the boy would be shaped in accord with desired ethical and social aims. Through the classics the boy was initiated into a community extended behind him through time and extending around him in space. He became a member of a community of thought and feeling reaching from the classical writers up to his own day, a community whose continued existence seemed to be the safeguard of the existence

35

of civilization itself. He became also a member of the community of all civilized men living in his own day, the community whose medium of intercourse was Latin. Not to know Latin was to be incompletely human : the Greek and Latin literatures were the humanities. For the leaders of humanism the classics were not an end in themselves but an instrument of ethical and social education. This was the fully explicit conception of such leaders of humanist education as Vittorino da Feltre in the fourteenth century, of Erasmus in the fifteenth and of Vives in the sixteenth. " To Erasmus antiquity was not a subject of liberal study alone, but partook of the nature of a working ideal of social order, to be adjusted to modern conditions." Elyot, whose book *The Governor* (1531) was the first manifesto of the ideal of liberal education in England, was a close disciple of Erasmus, and it was in following Elyot that the tradition of classical education grew up in the English grammar school.[1]

It is not surprising, therefore, that the study of language should have remained the centre of education, or that successive additions to the classical curriculum, almost up to our own day, should have been linguistic in nature or given a linguistic bias. Thus the two major developments of human enterprise in the centuries following the Renaissance—the growth of nationalism and the growth of inductive science—brought into the schools of this country not additions to the content of the curriculum so much as an extension of linguistic education. It is as though it were felt that as the society moved out towards new provinces of action and of thought, the first necessity was to initiate the young into the uses of new instruments of communication. In both cases—nationalism and science—one of these instruments was the vernacular, which thus for the first time took its place in the grammar school.

The growth of nationalism was reflected in the curriculum by an increase of attention to the cultivation of the mother tongue. At first, as by Vives in 1523, the vernacular was brought into the school mainly as a useful instrument in learn-

[1] Woodward ER (iii) 13, 186, 289

ing the classical languages, but only twenty years later it was establishing its own right to a place in education. Ascham wrote his *Toxophilus* (1545) in English, he tells us, because many of the gentlemen for whom he intended it were ignorant of Latin. In another thirty years Mulcaster, in his *Elementarie* (1582), was demanding full attention to the mother tongue as the indispensable medium of growing nationalism and a growing national literature. Another forty years and, with nationalism beginning to expand into imperialism, we find Brinsley urging the need for establishing English as an international language to meet the needs of a growing empire. An enterprising schoolmaster, he must surely be one of the first advocates of English as the language of Empire, English for imperial preference. 1621 is the date of his tract, *A Consolation for our Grammar Schools*, " and all ruder countries and places . . . for Ireland, Wales, Virginia with the Sommer Islands, and for their more speedie attaining of our English tongue . . . that all may speak one and the same language." The settlement of the Somers Islands (the Bermudas) made more urgent an already growing attention to the linguistic problems of colonization. *The Tempest* (1611)—said to have been suggested by this settlement—reflects something of this same preoccupation. Prospero anticipates Locke in explaining to Caliban that in giving him language he had at the same time given him the means of becoming aware of his own behaviour :

> when thou didst not, savage,
> Know thine own meaning, but wouldst gabble like
> A thing most brutish, I endowed thy purposes
> With words that made them known.

Caliban's reply is in the manner of those who are doubtful of the blessings that civilization brings to primitive societies :

> You taught me language ; and my profit on't
> Is, I know how to curse.

A few years later problems of communication arose to meet

the needs of inductive science, a new province, this time of the mind. In addition to refinements and extensions of the symbolism of mathematics, attention was given to the adaptation of the vernacular as a means of communicating scientific concepts with exactness—there was a movement towards what the founders of the Royal Society termed " mathematical plainness of language." As to mathematics, the historians tell us that when modern applied mathematics began with Newton, at once the problem arose of an appropriate notation, a question to which such thinkers as Leibniz devoted much attention.[1] And as to the relation between science and the vernacular, one of the first enterprises of the Royal Society was to appoint a committee (1664) to inquire into the use of English as the language of scientific transactions and communications ; as a result it became a principle of the Society to " reject all amplifications, digressions, and swellings of style. . . . They have exacted from their members a close, naked, natural way of speaking . . . bringing all things as near the mathematical plainness as they can." [2]

It is significant also that when eventually the " real " subjects were added to the curriculum—history, geography, the sciences—they were at first largely taught in a linguistic fashion, and with the traditional methods of linguistic study. In the Public Schools history and geography are still sometimes called " English subjects " ; in teaching the sciences, experimental and inductive methods—introduced in the Dissenting Academies towards the end of the eighteenth century—hardly became common until after the publication of Armstrong's *The Heuristic Method* in 1890.

5

With the extension of literacy in the nineteenth century the teaching of the mother tongue showed a confused compromise between ancient linguistic traditions and new social, political, and economic needs, permeated throughout by the

[1] Bell DM 144 ; Cajori HM 211   [2] Sprat RS

assumption that there must be a stratification of education according to social classes. As a result, attention was confined to the two extremes of the normal functions of the vernacular. " Secondary " education for an élite should endeavour to cultivate the declarative values of literature and literacy expression, while " elementary " education for the masses was to be concerned with its primary manipulative uses : the rudiments of reading and writing. Inevitably, perhaps, there could as yet be hardly any notion that the mother tongue has fundamental manipulative and declarative functions for the community as a whole. Even Matthew Arnold and Ruskin could see no further than the possibility that the lower classes might be trained to appreciate those declarative qualities of language that hitherto had been the prerogative of the few. When Arnold, impatient of the narrowness of the elementary school curriculum in English, sought to enlarge its scope, it was the study of *literature* that he emphasized. The topic recurs regularly in his reports as an inspector of schools. For instance (1871) : " What is comprised under the word literature is in itself the greatest power available in education ; of this power it is not too much to say that in our elementary schools at present no use is made at all." The social conscience of Ruskin, vigorous though it certainly was, roused him only to the pitch of urging that every man could educate himself to appreciate Milton.[1]

These demands upon the mother tongue in both elementary and higher education meant that at any rate it had found a place for itself in the curriculum. Its unique importance in education had by now become so obvious that—in theory at any rate—it was held to have changed places with the classical languages. These were now often justified as being instrumental to the cultivation of the mother tongue ! [2]

To-day we inherit the ancient linguistic traditions of educa-

[1] Arnold ES 82 ; Ruskin SL
[2] " It must never be forgotten that the main object for which boys learn the dead languages is to teach them to use their own."—*Clarendon Report* on the Public Schools, 1868 (i) 15

tion, modified by their passage through the nineteenth century.
. In the meantime social, political, and economic changes have
taken place which make further demands upon the cultivation of
the mother tongue. It is to the variety and the incompatibility
of the old traditions with the new conditions that we owe the
complex and confused conception of education in the mother
tongue which characterizes our schools to-day. There is
primary education in English—its instrumental uses for everyday needs and for the rest of the school curriculum ; higher
education in English—the study of literature. Added together
these do not, however, make up a conception of linguistic
education adequate to meet the overwhelming social and
political changes of our generation—not least those transformations of communication which make up the Linguistic
Revolution.

In a word, what has been neglected is what we may call
the social manipulative and declarative functions of the mother
tongue : English as a means of promoting the more complex
technical activities of the individual in a society, and of the
integrative activities of the society itself—English as a means
of social integration.

6

Confused as much of our practice is to-day, there are,
however, clear signs of a fuller understanding of these important social functions of the vernacular. Perhaps the most
striking evidence of this is seen in the change of attitude in
two official reports separated by almost exactly twenty years :
the *Report on the Teaching of English*, 1924, and the *Report* of
the Norwood Committee, 1943. The earlier report, expressing views well in the forefront of educational opinion at that
time and since, was certainly fully alive to one aspect of the
social significance of the mother tongue : the disruptive effects
of unequal linguistic education. " Two causes at present distinguish and divide one class from another in England. The
first of these is a marked difference in their modes of speech. . . .

The second . . . is the undue narrowness of the ground on which we meet for the true purposes of social life. . . . The English people might learn as a whole to regard their own language, first with respect and then with a genuine feeling of pride and affection. . . . Such a feeling for our own native language would be a bond of union between classes. . . . Even more certainly should pride and joy in the national literature serve as such a bond." [1]

In this Report the value of a common speech and a common literature is thought to be that they are the great levellers between classes. It takes one step beyond Matthew Arnold in recognizing the growing importance of the spoken word. The social dangers of the absence of a common speech are emphasized ; but it is noteworthy that the emphasis is on the more superficial characteristics of speech : those differences of dialect forms, of enunciation, and of intonation, which widen and perpetuate social distinctions. Attention must therefore, it urges, be given to the cultivation of those features of speech which mark the privileged classes ; it is in this sense that there must be a raising of the standards of speech.

Twenty years later, in the Norwood Report, the emphasis has changed. There is an almost revolutionary recognition of the functions of the mother tongue. It is seen to be the chief instrument of the development of thought in the individual, and of the integration of thought and feeling in a society. In an otherwise conservative and even timorous report the following passage is quite outstanding for the depth of its insight. The cultivation of the vernacular is declared to be one of the three *essentials* of all education ; the other two being moral and physical development. " There are three elements essential to a good education. . . . These elements, which in our view are more than subjects, because in one form or another they run through almost every activity, intellectual and other, which a school fosters, are (i) training of the body, (ii) training of character, (iii) training in habits of clear thought and clear expression of thought in the English language." [1] It is this permeative function of the mother tongue, its indispensable use as the medium of all individual and social behaviour, that the conditions of our time have forced upon our attention.

As a result the Norwood Report urges the fullest cultivation of the power of communication, both in speech and in writing. The school must not only cultivate the aesthetic qualities of speech and its social graces, but must above all develop in children skill in using spoken language as a means of communication. Manner of approach, ease of address, choice of vocabulary, clarity of thought—all these are at least as important as the use of some sounds rather than others, or the art of interpreting verse or the drama. In the terms we have used here, the Committee are demanding more attention to the manipulative and declarative uses of spoken language as a means of communication within a society.

" It happens too often that little stress is laid upon oral expression as a means of developing ease in social relationships ; by oral expression we do not mean speech training, though that may be a necessary ingredient, but such practice and facility in expressing thoughts aloud in the presence of others as will lead to some degree of confidence and at least the appearance of ease of manner." [2] This is a long step ahead of the earlier Report, but notice the tentativeness of the last phrase : for many children the *semblance* of ease in social intercourse is as much as can be hoped for.

The same emphasis on communication is seen in the Norwood Committee's views on the teaching of written expression and of the art of comprehension. The committee voice what they feel to be a widespread dissatisfaction with the standards reached by boys and girls leaving secondary schools. " In the course of our enquiries we have been furnished with much evidence on the results of English teaching in secondary schools. . . . This evidence comes from many varied quarters ; it is backed with authority and experience, and is entitled to very serious consideration. . . . Briefly the criticism is this,

---

[1] *Norwood Report* 1943, 66   [2] the same 94

that too many boys and girls after leaving the secondary schools show themselves deficient in ability to master the thought of a passage and to express their ideas in writing or orally with precision and clarity." [1] Notice that the Committee is not concerned with failure to write literary English or show "appreciation of literature." On the contrary ; the Report maintains that training in the use and understanding of the mother tongue is too much in the hands of specialist teachers ; undue weight is therefore given to essay-writing and the study of literature. In a word, they deplore over-emphasis on some of the very aims that the 1924 Report had wished to foster.

To bring out these implications of the Norwood Report we may say that the arts of reading and writing, because they have been thought of as the rudimentary instruments of education, or, on the other hand, have been too closely identified with the aesthetic and cultural values of language, have been kept somewhat remote from the personal and social needs of children—their need to express themselves with clarity for everyday social purposes and for the purposes of technical skills, and their need to be able to read not only literature but those publications that subserve social action. The emphasis of the Norwood Report is on maintaining a due balance between what we have called the declarative and the manipulative functions of language. We must add that the need for this balance is recognized and given practical application in many schools to-day. [2]

Another and very important indication of the same recognition of the social and therefore personal importance of language is to be seen in the increased attention paid to the linguistic training of " backward " children—not only those who are dull, but those of moderate and normal general ability who nevertheless show specific linguistic retardation. Much time and thought is being given to the observation and

[1] *Norwood Report* 1943, 92
[2] A fuller statement of these tendencies in the teaching of the mother tongue will be found in Lewis LS.

analysis of their disabilities, and detailed guidance, based on experiment, provided for teachers. The standard general work on the subject in this country is Burt's *The Backward Child* (1937) ; backwardness in writing and reading is analysed, and practical remedial work suggested by Schonell in *Backwardness in the Basic Subjects* (1942). The speech defects of children are, over a large part of the country, in the hands of speech therapists who work under the Local Education Authorities, in close co-operation with the schools. In 1944 these therapists were constituted into the College of Speech Therapists, recognized as "medical auxiliaries" by the General Medical Council. In all this work the intention is certainly not to concentrate on the aesthetic functions of speech, reading, and writing : the aim is rather to bring retarded children to a level of skill in communication so that they will no longer be hampered in their social intercourse.

It is evident that all these tendencies in education show a clear recognition of the necessity of directing and extending linguistic training in the school so that it shall be adequate to the manipulative no less than the declarative needs of every member of society ; his technical needs in his daily occupation and his social needs in relation to his fellows. The function of the school in linguistic education is seen to be the development of the powers of communication of each individual as a member of a society.

It would seem, therefore, that our schools are beginning to free themselves from some of the hampering traditions of linguistic education, and to direct the education of children in the mother tongue towards their personal and social needs. This education, however, is no longer confined to the school. It goes on throughout life : the continued linguistic education of the adult.

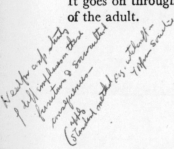

CHAPTER 3

THE ADULT

I

IN a modern society everyone is always learning language. In a primitive community, once adult status is reached, the range of adult experience is relatively fixed and unchanging : the language of the adult likewise remains static. But the complexity of civilized life prolongs the period of linguistic initiation and also extends the need for this prolongation throughout the society. Linguistic initiation is prolonged as the society becomes more literate : the prolongation is extended throughout the society as communication within the society develops. It is obvious, for example, that the villager of to-day is subject to a much more varied linguistic experience and a longer linguistic education than his forbear of the eighteenth century. Not only does he come into closer contact with the townsman, so that those changes in language which reflect the changing life of society reach him at no great interval ; in addition to this, the agencies of adult education seek him out in his own village and add their quota to the extension of his vocabulary and the general transformation of his means of expression. The newspaper, the radio, and the cinema are constant influences in the same direction. In the eighteenth century it was probably only the " educated " man, the highly literate person, and the man who travelled abroad, whose linguistic initiation was prolonged beyond childhood : to-day this is the experience of every man.

The complexity of civilized life means also that the organization of society is characterized by a multiplication of group techniques : the division of labour in industry, commerce, politics, and warfare. In each group performing its special techniques there will tend to grow up a special form of language with both manipulative and declarative functions : mani-

45

pulative, as a technical instrument immediately serving the practical purposes of the group ; declarative, as integrating the affect and conation of the group, partly for fostering its joint work, partly as an end in itself. Technical terms, " terms of art," slang, professional jargon—all these are aspects of the special languages that grow up in the various sub-groups within the larger society.

Finally, the complexity of modern life also demands more highly developed means of communication between societies, while at the same time it provides these means. Language is an article of export. To-day, as never before, inter-communication means that no society is wholly uninfluenced by the language of other societies. In particular, our own language is increasingly influential beyond our shores and influenced by other languages. The mother tongue of the Englishman is now the tongue of many millions in relatively alien communities in distant parts of the globe. Daily, too, the forms of American speech are moulding the language of Englishmen ; obvious enough in the effects of the radio and the cinema upon the speech of the young, it is no less powerful in the more subtle Americanization of the language of the popular newspaper.

The speed and range of modern communication also bring the language of the ordinary person within the influence of still wider fields of influence. Borrowings from foreign languages, daily encountered in the press and on the radio, rapidly become current terms ; many become naturalized in everyday English speech and are no longer thought of as immigrants.

These tendencies in our own language are only special instances of a much more general movement in the modern world. Intercommunication between societies is increasingly both necessary and possible. First let us notice that the four Great Powers—the British Commonwealth, the U.S.A., the U.S.S.R., and China—are all of them confederations of societies, and are therefore faced with the problem of a single common language that will be current throughout the confederation. And secondly, we must observe that there is a growing urgency for a common language of even wider range, a universal world language.

The linguistic initiation of an adult is to-day correspondingly complex ; at the least, potentially so. He is a member of one or more sub-groups : of a trade or profession, with its association or union ; of clubs that serve his leisure ; of committees for social or political action. He is also a member of the national society, with its mother tongue, visibly changing within the span of a lifetime, and in the conditions of our day demanding of everyone a greater command of both the spoken and the written word. And we may even detect the beginning of a still wider demand upon the ordinary man : that he shall begin to acquire a language whose scope transcends the national society, the means of intercommunication between societies.

What are the factors at work in the continued linguistic initiation of an adult ? We happen to be in a good position to answer this question, for in time of war the normal processes of linguistic initiation are intensified and accelerated. The military and economic exigences of modern warfare give birth to new groups within the framework of the larger society, each group having a tendency to develop its own specific group language. At the same time there are more frequent and more rapid changes within the mother tongue, arising from the new forms of activity which everyone is called upon to undertake during a war ; new techniques and the increased urgency for social co-operation. Finally, the needs of war, as well as those of the readjustment following war, also demand the development and organization of international communication.

Let us consider briefly each of these tendencies, strengthened and intensified as they are in time of war : the growth of special languages in special groups within a society, the development of communication throughout the society as a whole, and the organization of communication between societies—all as they affect the linguistic initiation of the adult members of a society.

2

The development of special languages for special groups organized within the framework of the larger society is a phenomenon common in the social history of language. Whenever men are organized into groups for the purposes of specific action, they tend to develop a language foreign in some measure to the language of the larger society in which they move. The jargon of tramps and the slang of thieves, the terminology of the medieval schoolmen and the secret language of Freemasonry are obvious instances.[1] In time of war this tendency for group action to give birth to a special group language receives a sudden impetus. There is a luxuriant growth of jargon and slang in the workshop, the camp, and the airfield. And where, as in the case of air warfare, numerous forms of action are new, the growth of new language is the more vigorous.

The first point worthy of notice here is that since warfare to-day is the immediate concern of every member of the community, almost everyone undergoes the experience of initiation into group slang. In time of peace the grocer, the joiner, or the clerk learns the terms of his special trade, but possibly no other specific group language—unless it be the vocabulary of such a hobby as photography, fly-fishing, or rock-climbing. In war-time, however, the grocer is in the army, the joiner in a munitions factory, and the clerk in the R.A.F. ; each learns the language of his new task.

Let us notice what happens to a young recruit to one of the services or to industry, faced with the lingo of the new group into which he is suddenly precipitated. It is worth our attention, because it enables us to see at close quarters and at greatly increased speed much of what normally occurs in

---

[1] We may note also the international character of such specific languages where the groups concerned are international : this is true in some measure of all four examples given above and more markedly in such special languages as Romany and Yiddish.

the slow life-long acquisition of language ; it is a rapid-motion film of the patterns of growth.

In the initiation of a new-comer into the language of a special group we find those factors that characterize the beginnings of language in the infant, modified of course by the effects of maturity and experience. We find the twin functions of language—the manipulative and the declarative—determining the whole process of linguistic initiation. We find also the characteristic conflict between the resistance of the individual to socialization—absorption by the group—and his need to enter into membership of the group. And we find that the extent and the depth of initiation vary with differences of temperament and upbringing, and so therefore with sex.

It is clear that the recruit at once becomes subject to those two linguistic needs—the manipulative and the declarative—which arise wherever men are formed into groups for the purpose of organized action. Slang begins as the language of a gang. On the one hand there are the terms needed to make organized action speedy and effective ; on the other, the need to sustain unity of emotion and social experience. Slang, then, is partly an instrument of effective common action and partly the means and symbol of group loyalty ; in the end it is zealously fostered as the outward expression of the unity of thought, feeling, and action in the group.[1]

Resistance : the infant, as we have seen, tends to resist innovations in his rudimentary language as the same time as he welcomes them ; there is constant conflict. Both tendencies —resistance and acceptance—persist throughout life ; they are stronger or weaker, more or less conscious, according to circumstances and the temperament and upbringing of the individual. In the case of the young recruit to a group every-

---

[1] A comprehensive collection of group slang of the War is Hunt and Pringle, *Service Slang* (1943). Of 860 locutions, 240 are neologisms, the rest existing words with a new meaning. One example to illustrate the raciness of R.A.F. idiom and its defiance of the conventions of the mother tongue : " *Elsan Gen*—news which cannot be relied upon. Literally ' news invented in the gentlemen's toilet,' Elsan being the trade name of the chemical lavatories with which bombers are equipped." (*Gen* is a common R.A.F. term for news.)

thing serves to weaken resistance to innovation. His initial bewilderment and social unease in the face of new words, still more in the face of familiar words used in a new way, combine to draw him into the language of the group—as in Shakespeare's day, he returns home on leave "full of strange oaths," and proud of them. The vocabulary of service slang gives more than one indication of this initial bewilderment [1] : the need to escape as quickly as possible from a state of social embarrassment is of course a very powerful incentive to the mastery of a new language.

But individual characteristics play their part in hastening or retarding the process. The young man who by nature and upbringing is ready to fit into a new group, who tends to be enterprising in social relations, who is willing to "try everything once"—this is the recruit who will soon be at home in the new language.

There are also characteristic differences with sex : in young women the whole process is probably more complicated than in young men. Women, on the whole, appear to have stronger impulses towards social conformity than men, but in the special social situation we are considering these impulses do not show themselves in a simple tendency to accept slang. For one thing a young woman is commonly rather more socially mature, more strongly socially conditioned than a young man of the same age, more settled in her social habits, and therefore more resistant to change when she enters a new group. Thus even her general tendency to social conformity works in the direction of resistance in this special case : she is less ready than a man to depart from the behaviour—including the linguistic behaviour—of the larger society. She is also moved more strongly by the need to remain socially respectable, to preserve standards of personal conduct and "distance," to guard against behaviour that suggests a cheapening of personal

---

[1] "*Goon :* the West country name for recruit, apparently given because new arrivals are prone to walk about with a dazed expression until they have accustomed themselves to their surroundings." "*Comedian :* commandant. Men referred to the 'Camp Comedian' have sometimes spent hours searching for an Entertainments Department."—Hunt SS

value. Women in organized groups, therefore, are less likely to grow a special language than men.[1]

On the other hand women are more attracted than men by the social prestige of those who use a special form of language ; the fact that a locution or accent is " fashionable " will give it a title to acceptance.[2] As a result the language of the officers and that of the rank and file in the women's services tend to approximate ; in the men's services, however, a word current among officers will tend to be taboo among the men.

Another primary factor is age. The infant, as we have seen, tends for a time to be resistant to new forms of speech : in a new situation he prefers to extend the use of his limited repertory. It is only when he realizes the great increase of social power that a wide vocabulary brings him that he becomes avid of new experiences in language. This avidity commonly grows throughout childhood, and may be very marked in adolescence, the verbomania of which may be very amusing to those who view it from the complacent distance of adult maturity. Now in time of war most recruits to new groups are only just beyond adolescence ; this certainly helps to increase the fecundity of war-time slang.

In spite, therefore, of linguistic conservatism and resistance to innovation, war in our day means a luxuriant growth of group languages and slang, which will certainly leave their traces upon the mother tongue.

3

Meanwhile the linguistic education of the ordinary adult is also being reinforced and accelerated by his participation in the war-time tasks of his society as a whole. The needs of technical training in the Forces, in Civil Defence, and in industry bring into the lives of many people new forms of language with

[1] Of the 860 locutions in *Service Slang*, only three seem to have arisen in the women's services.

[2] The factors at work here are very much the same as in women's behaviour with regard to dress (Flugel, *The Psychology of Clothes*).

manipulative functions : those who enter these new fields of activity have to acquire the " terms of art " of their new tasks. A more complex organization demands an increase of communication. Professional firemen, for instance, when they were organized into the National Fire Service, soon observed, " We've never done so much writing in our lives." Rationing makes similar demands on the citizen. Those whose linguistic skill is unequal to these may find it necessary to avail themselves of help ; during the War a not uncommon notice in the windows of back street houses read, " Ration books filled up here."

At the same time the attempt to achieve a fuller unification of thought and feeling throughout the society also develops language in a declarative direction : the Army Educational Service, the Army Bureau of Current Affairs, the discussions and lectures organized in Civil Defence groups and in the factories, and the overwhelming popularity of the radio " Brains Trusts "—all these give currency to new forms of language with a speed and to an extent unknown at more stable periods of history.

As a result universal literacy became indispensable in the Second World War. But this was only the last phase of a movement that had already been gathering force for many years. From the beginning of the century, in fact, there had been in every society in the world an urgent need to extend the area of literacy ; to-day nothing less will do than that every society shall be wholly literate. All over the world, campaigns for the " liquidation " of illiteracy : in the United States, in the Soviet Union, in China, in India, and in Africa.

It is a measure of the distance we have moved in this direction that we now take it for granted that universal literacy is feasible and within reach ; it is only a question, we feel, of applying on a large scale the means already at hand. No-one concerned in the campaign appears to be daunted by the size of the problem. How large this is can hardly be known with accuracy. Probably the estimates of the British and Foreign Bible Society are as good as any : illiteracy to the extent of 90 per cent. in China and India, 98 per cent. in non-Christian

Africa, 99 per cent. in Afghanistan, Iran, Irak, Turkestan, and Arabia.[1]

But the size of the problem is matched by the optimism of those who are determined to solve it. The same Report quotes with assent the words of Laubach, a pioneer in the present movement : " We can expect within fifty years that five hundred million new readers will step out of the silent ranks of illiteracy." There would seem to be good grounds for this optimism in what is said to have been already achieved. In China, for instance, it is claimed that of 165 million adult illiterates, 25 million became literate in the two years 1938 to 1940.[2] In the Soviet Union, beginning with a more literate population, the speed has naturally been slower ; for the attempt to liquidate illiteracy completely must mean reaching out into those remoter backwaters of civilization which have the strongest traditions of illiteracy. Nevertheless, we are told, 35 millions in the Union learned to read in the twenty years following the Revolution ; [3] so that by 1939 it was possible to say that " within the limits of the age-group between 10 and 25 the proportion of illiterates is now swiftly approaching zero," while over the whole population the proportion had sunk to 22·6 per cent., just one-third of the pre-revolutionary level.[4]

What does this liquidation of illiteracy involve ? In the first place, it is clear that illiteracy of the read and written word is by no means the same thing as lack of skill in language. A man unable to read or write may yet be a master of the spoken word. This no doubt was true of the ancient civilizations, and its tradition is not yet wholly lost : it is likely that some of the societies most illiterate in the read and written language are distinguished by their cultivation of the finer graces of speech. On the other hand, in our own society at this moment there is a danger that linguistic education, both of the child and of

[1] *Report* 1944. Another estimate : " Of the more than a billion adults in the world, only about one out of four can read more than a few words or characters in his own tongue."—White PP 4
[2] *Times Educ. Suppt.* June 10, 1944
[3] Epstein in *Year Book of Educ.* (London) 1937, 785
[4] Steinberg in Cole SA 169

the adult, may be too narrowly directed upon the written word at the expense of education in speech ; at this moment, when as never before speech is gaining ground over writing as the primary form of communication.

We must recognize further that the " liquidation " of mere illiteracy may have comparatively little effect on thought, feeling, and action. A man may be called literate when he is just able to read and to sign his name, but until he can write a simple letter and make out the meaning of a paragraph in a popular newspaper, he is still functionally illiterate. And even at this higher level his literacy may yet fail to provide him with a working instrument of communication closely related to his personal and social life.

The War has reminded us of this with disconcerting clarity. The needs of warfare demanded that every man and woman in the Forces had to be able to read and write ; [1] and so much do we take for granted universal literacy in a society such as ours that we were shocked to find that between one and two per cent. of the men in the army were totally illiterate. It is, however, of much greater importance that between fifteen and twenty per cent. were functionally illiterate. [2]

Something had to be done ; classes were instituted to teach the rudiments of reading and writing to the totally illiterate ; at the end of a six-weeks course up to two-thirds had learnt to " read and understand " a newspaper and up to five-sixths to " write letters unaided." [3] This was also an unprecedented opportunity to investigate the nature of illiteracy in adults.

It was found that the majority of men and women fully illiterate were probably below the average in general intelligence ; [4] many of them had been backward at school. But

[1] This is discussed in detail later ; page 143 below.
[2] Burt, *Br. J. Ed. Psy.*, 1945 ; he concludes that of the adult population of England and Wales two or three hundred thousand are completely, and about three millions functionally, illiterate.
[3] *Times Educ. Suppt.* December 23, 1944
[4] This needs a good deal of further investigation. The evidence given by Burt (as above) and Wall (*Br. J. Ed. Psy.* 1944, 1945) is based on tests that themselves are largely *verbal*.

it is clear that although this may be an important contributory factor, it is by no means the only one. Their level of ability in reading was lower—sometimes considerably lower—than is to be expected even at their level of intelligence. There must be other factors at work. Even in time of peace these men and women need to be literate ; yet their initial lack of literacy had persisted and had often deteriorated further. Frequently they appeared to offer a certain resistance to the removal of their disabilities.

Deterioration is no doubt partly due to the fact that even in modern life it is still possible for many men and women to dispense with literacy and yet conceal their disability. In general this may be truer of women, whose everyday life in the home makes fewer demands on the read and written word than men's work even in the lower ranks of industry.[1] And the increase of spoken communication may have an immediate—though hardly an ultimate—effect in the same direction.

But in addition to this persistence of illiteracy and the progressive deterioration of literacy through disuse, there is also a positive resistance to the improvement of literacy. Burt found that in the young men and women studied by him there was an aversion " from anything of a sedentary, bookish or literary nature. . . . During the adolescent stage it appears to develop almost into a protective mechanism, half unconsciously built up, not merely by the individual, but by the group to which he belongs." This is, in part, a further example of resistance to change in linguistic habits. It is also, in part, a certain bibliophobia, which not only has roots deep in the past—the ancient fear of the written word—but also draws some nourishment from a more recent tradition of inverted

---

[1] Although girls are linguistically more apt than boys, yet in a partially literate population, more men than women will be literate, because of the greater everyday urgency of the *manipulative* functions of language in men's work. For the U.S.S.R. the comparative figures are (percentages of literates) :

	1917	1939
Men . . .	50	88.2
Women . .	15	66.6

Steinberg in Cole SA 169

class-snobbery. Since the "upper" leisured classes are traditionally literate, bookish, the "lower" classes may take a certain pride in their ignorance and contempt of books.

How then, in the presence of these factors, are wholly illiterate adults made literate in six weeks? The methods found to be most successful are those which recognize that progress in literacy depends on incentive, the most powerful incentive being the realization of the learner that reading and writing have something of value to offer him in his everyday life.

The beginning must therefore be with what we have called the manipulative functions of language. "Throughout," says Burt, " the instruction should be linked up, so far as possible, with the practical activities of the man's everyday work at home, in the factory, or in the army. At first it may be wise to dissociate the idea of reading from the idea of books. To stress the more practical uses of reading will be far more effective—advertisements, film announcements, racing news and football results, signs, tickets, and announcement seen in shops and streets, or official notices and papers." So too the strongest incentive to learning to write was the experience that a letter home brought in return cigarettes or pocket-money at the least. But more than this, the letters were a link with home ; the declarative value reinforcing the manipulative.[1]

It is evident that the development and maintenance of literacy throughout a society are more complex than may at first appear. Deterioration through disuse, the traditions of the customary behaviour of the group, and resistance therefore to change, all work in opposition to the incentives—strong though these may be—of the functions of reading and writing for the individual in society.

---

[1] " Many relatives of men have written to thank the instructors. One woman wrote, ' It has made such a difference to us since George has been able to write home. Now, when the postman comes, the kiddies run to the door and see if there is a letter from Daddy.' "—*Times Educ. Suppt.* December 23, 1944

4

Some of these same factors are seen to be at work in another aspect of the linguistic education of the adult : his acceptance of changes in his mother tongue, both in vocabulary and in style. These are processes as old as language itself ; here again in war-time we see reinforcement and acceleration. Technical terms, at first confined to a limited group of workers, gain a wider currency : for instance, *embody* (in the sense of *mobilize*, itself an innovation of the First World War), *utility* (clothing), *point* (rationing), *decontaminate* (gas). Existing terms are quite given wider meanings : *evacuate, fuel target, black-out.* Side by side with these manipulative terms introduced in the service of techniques are terms whose main function is declarative, having the effect of arousing and organizing orexis in the society ; for instance, *Vansittartism, refugee, squander-bug.* From abroad, new locutions are imported in response to the same technical and orectic needs : *jeep, blitz, Gestapo, totalitarian, Nazi,*[1] *quisling.*

There are also changes in the style of English. In writing, an approximation to the spoken language ; in speech, a greater informality. It is not easy to demonstrate these changes without a good deal of detailed evidence. But there is an impression among many students of language that if we were to compare the leading articles of *The Times* of, say, 1900 with those of to-day, we should find a marked change in the direction of simplicity, an approximation to the style of spoken language. And there can be little doubt that there is an increase of informality in speech itself ; many people would no doubt call it a lowering of standard. *Punch* records the change in manners ; the young woman in slacks (milieu : " middle-class ") : " Really, mother, if I can't say ' coo ' *or* ' blimey,' civvy street's going to be a bit of a bind ! "[2] Certainly the enormously increased impact of the spoken word on our daily

[1] The symbolic functions of *Nazi* are analysed more fully later, page 189 below.
[2] *Punch*, January 3, 1946

lives during the Second World War must have greatly accentuated the tendency towards informality in both the written and the spoken language.

But the extent to which such changes in vocabulary and style are fully taken up into the language of the adult depends upon the final adjustment of the two mutually opposed forces of resistance and acceptance. The adult member of society is moved—by manipulative and declarative needs—in the direction of acceptance of new modes of language ; at the same time he is resistant to innovation, although this resistance is rarely so strong as to halt his linguistic education completely. He reaches a stage of comparative stability where innovations, if not actively rejected, are at any rate far from welcomed. There is a kind of linguistic xenophobia : the foreign word is felt to threaten the unity of the linguistic community. When therefore the range of experience of a society widens and new forms of language become necessary the immediate tendency —as in infancy—is to use the existing resources of the language before seeking new inventions. It is the case of the skilled workman, confronted with a novel task, who will prefer to use to their fullest extent the tools already as his command before consenting to experiment with a tool specially devised for the new purpose.[1]

It must be observed that resistance to innovation does not of itself mean that the linguistic community is decrepit ; on the contrary it may be a sign of linguistic health. Too ready an acceptance of innovation might in fact result in the disintegration of the community, for there is no institution that gives the members of a society so strong a sense of its being as language. The efficiency of intercourse within the contemporary community and therefore the maintenance of its identity, the conservation too of its identity through the passage of time, alike depend upon the strength of reluctance to modify the forms of language. Thus we find both in the Elizabethan time and in our own day—two periods of heightened activity

[1] This is true to some extent even of slang. Note the comparatively small proportion of neologisms in *Service Slang* (page 49, footnote).

and of rapid change—a constant battle between the need to preserve the traditions of the language and the need to admit innovation.

We have in fact an interesting example here of conflict between the conscious beliefs of a community and their behaviour, determined as this is by motives of which they are often unaware. At the present moment those people in Great Britain who are concerned about innovation in language—teachers in schools and universities and laymen who write to the newspapers and the B.B.C.—are most strongly opposed to what they would term the corruption and Americanization of English ; and if they do not openly object to Service slang it is because they are willing to extend an amused toleration to the young who serve the community with such devotion. If therefore we were to judge of the possibility of change in contemporary English by the strength of the expressed resistance of these theorists, we might conclude that our language has become static. But in fact, as we have seen, there has been considerable innovation both in the locutions and the style of the mother tongue since the beginning of the present century. Each of the two world wars has brought its quota of change ; the Second, with its impacts setting wider circles in motion throughout the community, probably more than the First.

Teachers who are aware of this constant conflict between conservatism and creation in language are sometimes concerned as to which side of the balance to weight with their influence : should children be allowed to use slang in speech and writing ? The truth probably is that it hardly matters. Change in language will go on and linguistic initiation will extend through life whether we encourage it in school or not. If the adolescent ceased to learn language on the day he left school, the responsibility of the teacher would certainly be heavy ; but the fact is that changes in language are rarely brought about by directed schooling. They are the work of the home before schooling begins and the cumulative effects of everyday experience throughout adult life.

5

So much for what the Second World War has taught us of the factors at work in the continued linguistic initiation of the adult. Before the War this process of initiation was perhaps a minor problem of language in society. To-day it has taken on a new importance, for over a large part of the world men are being called upon to learn a new language in addition to their mother tongue. We have seen the adult as a member of one or more sub-groups within his national society as well as a member of this society as a whole. Now we must notice his linguistic education as it is determined by the relation of his society to other societies ; the growth of international communication.

First there is the development of a single language in each of the great confederate Powers. In the British Commonwealth, English is the common language in virtue of the manner in which the Commonwealth has grown up. As Brinsley foresaw at its birth,[1] the expansion of empire has meant the expansion of the mother tongue of the pioneers. The colonists carried their language with them, and with them it took root in the foreign soil. Where, on the other hand, the Empire grew by conquest not colonization, so that English, as in India, came to a land with a highly developed linguistic civilization of its own, even here it inevitably acquired a special function of inter-communication. To-day, although the number who speak English in India is still small, for them it is a *lingua franca*, perhaps the only one. And it is these few who are the leaders in their own societies and who count for most in the relations between India and the rest of the Commonwealth : " Indian nationalism is almost entirely the product of English education ; the medium of all political discussion is necessarily English." [2] As Orwell tells us in a collection of talks broadcast by the B.B.C. to India during the War, it is those people who speak English who are the likeliest to have access to short-wave radio sets ; they thus become

[1] page 37 above   [2] Marriott EI 18

active members of the linguistic community of the whole British Commonwealth.[1] This need for a general means of communication received official recognition when in 1944 the government decided to promote the use of Basic English as an international auxiliary language within as well as beyond the British Commonwealth.[2]

In the United States the problem of a single common language is, of course, somewhat different, but no less urgent. English was the language of the pioneers : but successive groups of immigrants, instead of attempting to acquire a new language, have often shown the usual resistance to change. Within the greater American society there are huge communities speaking, reading, and writing the varied languages of their original homes. Only twenty years ago it could be said that in the heart of Pennsylvania 60 per cent. of the inhabitants could speak German, and that 30 per cent. used it constantly. In 1930 there were 130,000 persons whose language was Dutch, with ten weekly papers in this language and two in Flemish ; there were 600,000 speakers of Swedish, with 27 weekly papers ; 1,200,000 speakers of Yiddish, with 12 daily and 25 weekly papers ; and no fewer than 1,800,000 speakers of Italian, with 8 daily and more than 100 other periodicals.[3] As a result, there must be a great deal of functional illiteracy in English.[4] Yet obviously it is only in the presence of a single common language functionally effective in thought, feeling, and action that it is possible for the United States to be an integrated society in the face of military, economic, political, and social needs.

In the Soviet Union we find again the same need of a common language, again with specific differences. At the Revolution the attempt was made to establish Russian as the one language of all the constituent republics, but this policy was abandoned as soon as local resistance made itself felt ;

---

[1] Orwell SI 7
[2] Mr. Churchill in Parliament, March 9, 1944 : Cmd. paper 6511
[3] Mencken AL 616, 623, 627, 633, 647
[4] In 1940 there were 10 million illiterates in the U.S.A.—*Report* (1946) of Nat. Educ. Assoc. of U.S.A., cited in *Times Educ. Suppt.* 18 January 1947

another instance of linguistic conservatism. The official doctrine then changed to a recognition of the traditional vernacular in each republic as the indispensable medium of primary education ; and this is the policy in practice throughout the Union. But although Russian could not be imposed as a first language, it has readily been accepted as a second, to serve the purposes of a common means of inter-communication. In 1938 all the republics in which Russian was not already the vernacular decided to make this the compulsory second language in secondary schools.[1]

The problems of linguistic education in the Soviet Union are many and complex. There are republics which before the Revolution lacked a written language, and for which, therefore, an alphabet had to be created ; others with a language fitted only for primary education ; others whose language was adequate only for secondary education, but no further ; only in the Russian, Ukrainian, White Russian, Georgian, and Armenian languages can education of university standard at present be given.[2] It is clear that if thought, feeling, and action are to be integrated throughout the Union, many of its citizens will, for a long time to come, be bilingual, learning Russian as a second language ; and that there will long be a serious problem of how to achieve adult functional literacy in this one common language, Russian.

China, the fourth of the great confederate units, has also its own problem of a single common language. Here the special difference is that for centuries there has been a common written language throughout China, but no common speech. The common language is " an esperanto, but exclusively a written one," the pronunciation of the words varying with the dialect of the reader. " Thus an edict issued in Peking can be read and understood everywhere in this vast country, but the Cantonese read it aloud in a way that sounds utter nonsense to the Pekingese." [3]

The main problem in China is therefore the establishment of a common spoken language where a common written

[1] Maynard RP 293 ; also p. 53 above   [2] Maynard, as above   [3] Karlgren SS 38

language already exists ; and here again this was one of the tasks to which the leaders of the Revolution immediately addressed themselves. In the very first year of the Republic a conference of philologists began to devise a common phonetic script, which was officially adopted in 1918 and embodied in a national phonetic dictionary. Two years later the Ministry of Education opened an institute at Peking to train teachers of this national language. But it was soon found that an artificial language so devised by scholars was too bookish and too remote from any living dialect to be readily acceptable as functionally effective speech. It would be interesting to know what headway has since been made with a common spoken language.

At the same time the problem of general literacy, read and written, had also to be faced. The traditional written language, though current throughout China, was again a language of scholars, too complex and too difficult for the everyday purposes of the ordinary citizen. A simplified form of the written language—a sort of Basic Chinese—was therefore devised ; text-books in this simplified language were written, and schools everywhere set up to use them.[1]

In all four of these large confederate units there would, then, seem to be the same problem : the need to establish general literacy in a common spoken and written language. The immediate result of any approach to the solution of this problem must be bilingualism for many of the adult members of the constituent societies within these confederations. This means a doubling of functional literacy. The adult must be able not only to speak, read, and write his first language, the language of his childhood, so as to satisfy his immediate needs, but also to speak, read, and write a second language in order to be an effective member of the greater society.

6

Beyond this there looms a still wider possibility : the development of a common world language, supplementary to

[1] All these facts about China from Chuang EC 58, 155-163

national and to confederate languages. Perhaps we are witnessing the beginning of the fulfilment of an ancient dream : one tongue in which all men may converse—debabelization, as Ogden calls it. Like so much else in our contemporary world, this dream first began to take on its present pattern in the seventeenth century. And this, as we have tried to show, is not merely a happy coincidence. New developments in the thought and action of societies demanded modifications of language, the chief technique of social thought and action. The one international language of the Middle Ages had been adequate enough as a means of inter-communication among the leaders of the societies of Western Europe, and up to the middle of the seventeenth century it was still the international language not only of the arts and the sciences but also of politics—as Milton's office under Cromwell reminds us.

But now Latin was becoming inadequate to serve the wider needs that physical and mental exploration were creating : the needs of colonial expansion and of science. For the former it was thought, as by Brinsley, that the linguistic needs of a growing empire would be served by the natural expansion of the language of the imperial power ; for the needs of scholarship, such men as Leibniz thought it necessary to devise an artificial language on logical and philosophical principles.[1]

The history of the attempts, during the three centuries since then, to devise and promote a universal language is largely a history of failure ; [2] but if to-day we see the first faint stirring of future promise, this is in part the cumulative effect of those unceasing experiments. Converging upon this in our day are at least two other forces, also the slow product of the same three centuries. Through the machines of communication, the physical means by which a universal language may grow and live lies at last in our hands. And, above all, the need for a world language has become inescapable.

· First, the constant preoccupation of linguists with the problem of a universal language, together with the closer study

[1] Brinsley ; see p. 37 above ; Leibniz NE bk. 4 ch. vi sect. 2
[2] As recounted, for instance, by Bodmer LL

of language in general, has taught us that a world language is, even in its beginnings, likely to be ineffective unless it has some declarative power for its speakers. A world language, if it is to be fully a language, must perform the functions of any language for the society that uses it—that is, a world language must be able to satisfy both the manipulative and the declarative needs of mankind as a world society. Obviously the language must be an efficient means of political, scientific, and economic inter-communication ; but since these manipulative functions are inseparable from the declarative, there is no hope of success for any projected world-language that does not in some measure engage the feelings and the will, as well as the thought and action, of those called upon to use it.

Side by side with this growth of insight into the essential nature of a world language has been the development of the machines that can make it effective. It would be unnecessary to emphasize this once again, were it not for the fact that it is ignored by those who contend that a world language is an idle dream, because inevitably the curse of Babel means the disintegration of any widespread language into mutually un-intelligible dialects. They bring in evidence the history of language. But true as it is that dialects become increasingly differentiated where the groups that use them are isolated from one another, this also means that with the growth of inter-communication dialects become smoothed down toward uni-formity. At the end of the sixteenth century the grammarian Richard Mulcaster could still say, " The English tongue is of small reach, stretching no further than this island of ours, nay not there over all." [1] The machines that broadcast the written and the spoken word have made our whole world a smaller island than Mulcaster's.

But above all, the promise of a world language lies in the urgency of our need of it. Before the War it was still necessary to demonstrate this need ; now it has become a commonplace. It is an everyday assumption that the future of mankind depends on the enlistment of all men, both in understanding

[1] Mulcaster E 271

65

the problems of the world and also in support of the action necessary to meet them. It is coming to be taken for granted that communication between societies can no longer be confined to their leaders, speaking Latin or some other language of diplomacy. The establishment of UNO rests upon the assumption that there will be intercommunication among the members of all nations. At the first session of its assembly Mr. Attlee said, " I think that at the present time the ordinary men and women in every nation have a greater realization of what is at stake. To make this organization a living reality we must enlist the support not only of Governments, but of the masses of the people throughout the world." [1]

7

Certainly the need for a world language is increasing in urgency : what are the possibilities ? Undoubtedly a very strong factor in retarding its development will be that resistance to linguistic innovation which we have so often been obliged to notice in the course of this survey. It is probable that the immediate future will see a common bilingualism. For, as many observers have pointed out, concurrently with the growth of international communication, there is a striking increase in the preservation and cultivation of national languages.

Throughout the world nations cling with increasing tenacity to their indigenous languages and seek to foster patterns of culture in these native idioms. As a result Mumford, for example, believes that no single language can ever come to dominate the world, " for unless an international language can be made relatively fixed and lifeless, it will go through a babel-like differentiation in precisely the same fashion as Latin did." [2]

Although his analysis is somewhat confused, we can accept his prognosis of an imminent era of bilingualism. For the manipulative needs of intercommunication supra-national languages are inevitable ; but for declarative needs the

[1] London Times January 11, 1946   [2] Mumford TC 295

mother tongue of infancy will, for most men, and for a long time to come, remain the dominant language ; the mother language, the matrix in which all the subsequent linguistic education of an individual is fashioned. For a long time to come, therefore, bilingualism, if not trilingualism, may be necessary for many of us. Superimposed upon the language of infancy there will be a second or even a third language, acquired in adolescence or adult life.

Under these conditions the promotion of general adult literacy in a common language is hopeless, unless it takes account of the causes of potential linguistic resistance. Men will not change their linguistic habits unless they are moved by the anticipation of the satisfaction of needs, or by the desire for declarative communion. A supra - national secondary language will not make much headway unless those who are called upon to learn it are convinced that it will contribute to their desired ends.

Failure to recognize this must retard the development of adult literacy in a supra-national secondary language. But we must recognize, on the other hand, that conditions to-day are favourable, as never before, to the spread of such languages. The needs of political, economic, and scientific security are driving men to gather into large confederacies, and therefore to learn languages that will enable them to speak together for the purposes of confederate action. At the same time the machines of communication make this immeasurably more feasible than ever before. By making intercourse rapid and frequent they concentrate groups scattered over a wide area into a single linguistic community, so that even a secondary language acquires declarative force. As this happens, the secondary language begins to show the promise of becoming the primary language. May not Russian, for instance, ultimately become the one mother tongue throughout the Soviet Union, or a single language the mother tongue throughout China ?

Here, then, are possibilities ignored by Mumford as by others. The development of bilingualism may be a step on the way to a world language. Perhaps the time is at hand when a world language will be the secondary language of everyone ; perhaps the time may come when it is even the primary language of all. The history of our day suggests that this is something more than a fantastic dream. The hope of a world language is not, as Mumford appears to think, that it shall be " fixed and lifeless." On the contrary, it must be fluid and alive. The essential conditions are that the language shall satisfy the needs of action, feeling, and thought, and that it shall command resources of communication. For although the history of language has always been the story of the persistence and even the further differentiation of dialects, the two chief factors have certainly been the difficulty, if not the impossibility, of physical communication and the absence of incentive to engage in communication. Where there is no effective linguistic community there can of- course be no common language. But to-day the machines of language by binding mankind into a single linguistic community begin to make a single common speech possible. When New York and Moscow can speak daily to each other, and even, through television, face to face ; can read the same books and newspapers and see the same films, does it seem beyond possibility that at some future time one language may become their common mother tongue ?

Still more powerful than the machines is the incentive to world communication. Beyond doubt there will be false starts and setbacks before this incentive is at least fully effective. But if the war has been world-wide, " peace is indivisible." A world society can exist only in the presence of a world language. Without communication there can be no community.

By the convergence of all these forces, what form is a world language likely to take ? Here our task is not to plead a cause, but to observe what is happening around us. And freeing ourselves as much as we can from partiality, it would seem that we can record a likelihood that the first world language will be English. It is probable that no language is

understood by a larger number of people.[1] English is the
language of two of the four Great Powers ; behind it stand
the all-pervading influences of American film and British radio ;
and in its modified form as Basic English it is the official
auxiliary language of the British Commonwealth for external
as well as internal communication. Basic English has been
devised to satisfy the political, economic, and scientific needs of
international communication, and it also has the declarative
force of a language with traditions and a literature ; a force
that no wholly artificial language can well have. And although
it is primarily a modification of a natural language, its inventor
Ogden has taken account of the experimental artificial languages
of three centuries. It is therefore at once a natural and an
artificial language, carrying something of the prestige and the
declarative tone of a natural language, while yet logically
devised to perform the manipulative functions of international
communication.

At this moment, it would of course be foolish to attempt
to predict what will be the world language of the future. It
may not be Basic English ; it may not even be English. The
history of the coming century may shift the centre of world
influence from the English-speaking peoples. But there can be
little doubt that a world language is on its way.

8

So far we have been considering the facts and the possibilities of linguistic communication in modern societies. We
have seen the individual growing up from infancy to manhood
into a society permeated by language and other forms of
symbolic communication ; becoming initiated into membership of the society as he is initiated into its language.

We have now to consider the deeper implications of these
facts. What are the prevailing circumstances of our time—
the economic, military, political, and social tasks of our

[1] Richards BE 17, estimates that only English and Northern Chinese are
understood by as many as 200 millions.

societies—that have made necessary the great developments of symbolic communication that we have witnessed, and with them the recognition of the importance of linguistic initiation ?

To answer these questions we must first consider a more fundamental problem. What is the relation of communication to group thought, feeling, and action ? It is a complex relationship, which is likely to be misconceived unless we make a somewhat close analysis of what is involved. Generalities will not serve us. We need to consider in detail the nature of group behaviour, including group thought and group feeling, permeated and determined as these are by the complex working of group communication.

PART TWO

LANGUAGE AND GROUP MIND

Chapter 4

LANGUAGE AND INDIVIDUAL MIND

I

WHAT is the function of language in group mind? This is certainly the central problem of our study of the place of language in society. At once it raises the question of the nature of group mind itself. Is there anything in the behaviour of groups of which it is reasonable to use the term " mind " ? This, however, is a question that is only to be answered by considering the functions of language in group behaviour. We shall attempt to show that group mind and group language are only to be understood in relation to each other and to group behaviour as a whole.

Throughout the history of philosophy the notion of group mind has repeatedly appeared and has constantly been challenged—perhaps never so strongly as at the present time. But even to-day it is an uneasy challenge, as if the doubters are still sometimes haunted by what one of them calls the " group ghost." [1] And the warmth of the discussion betrays the fact that something more than a purely metaphysical entity is at stake. It becomes clear that there are two fundamental issues : the nature and existence of individual mind, and the political and ethical corollaries that might follow upon any one conception of group mind.

Every discussion of group mind naturally begins by asking whether there is anything in a group corresponding to mind in

---

[1] Cohen RN 387. Malinowski calls it " the phantom of collective soul : " AP 327.

an individual. We are brought face to face with such problems as the existence of mind as a substantial entity, the nature of mind, the relation between mind and brain. And it is easy —perhaps suspiciously easy—to demolish the notion of group mind by showing its incompatibility with one conception or another of individual mind. For instance, if by mind we mean soul, or a part of the soul—an entity attached to the body and capable of surviving it—then certainly we are unable to point to any such corresponding entity attached to and surviving a group. Or if again we say that a mind cannot exist apart from a brain, or even if we regard mind as the functioning of a brain, it is just as easy for the sceptic to ask to be shown the group brain.

Scepticism of this kind is reinforced by the apparently dangerous corollaries that would appear to follow upon the admission of any conception of group mind. " It is easy to show," says Ginsburg, " that the use of the term social mind is exceedingly dangerous, or carries with it implications of far-reaching importance. In the first place, the use of the term Mind or Person to designate society has led to the ascription to the latter of a fictitious unity which it does not possess, to the consequent belittlement of individuality and of minor groupings, and to a mischievous antithesis between the good of society and the good of individuals." [1]

But the dangerous implications of facts do not absolve us from facing the facts. Ginsburg himself asserts that groups " clearly are unities of mind, since they consist of minds in inter-relation, and the relations themselves are dependent upon mental factors." He immediately adds, " Nevertheless it seems mistaken to regard a community as a mind." [2] It is perhaps as mistaken to speak of a community as a mind as to speak of a man as a mind ; but it would be even more misleading to refuse to recognize that there is something in the behaviour of groups that can only be called group mind. In considering group behaviour we find certain phenomena—very important phenomena—that stand exactly in the same relation to the group as

[1] Ginsburg PS 48   [2] the same 66

72

individual mind does to the individual. We should attach the name mind to these phenomena because their functions in a group are exactly of the same kind as those of mind in an individual ; the name, and the comparison that underlies it, helping us to a clear understanding of these facts of group life.

It is therefore first of all necessary to consider what we mean by individual mind. We must consider the problem in some detail, for undoubtedly much of the vagueness in discussions of group mind is directly due to an inadequate picture of individual mind. And we must do so in the terms and within the field of the conceptions current in our own day, for it is in these terms and within this field that we are observing and considering the facts of group behaviour.

In the present chapter, therefore, we shall attempt to find, in the statements of those psychologists and metaphysicians who concern themselves with the nature of mind, the points of agreement or at any rate convergence. This is not a departure from the main topic of our study, language in society, for there is no current concept of individual mind which does not take account of the individual and social functions of language.

There are three points of agreement among the many and diverse attempts, within the present century, to describe the nature of mind. These are : first, that mind is a form of behaviour, an activity ; second, that the individual is himself largely unconscious of his own mental activity ; third, that the essential characteristic of this activity is the use of symbols, principally language. After the present chapter, in which we survey the trend of modern thought in emphasizing these three attributes of individual mind, we shall attempt to show that in group behaviour exactly parallel features exist, to which we must therefore give the name of group mind.

2

Mind is the name that we give to an activity, a mode of behaviour ; on no point are metaphysicians and psychologists to-day more in agreement than on this. It is particularly striking in what we may call the modern reaches of the main stream of thought in this country—the work of Ward, Stout, and Alexander ; it is no less central in the Hormic psychology of McDougall, in Behaviourism, and in the psycho-analytic doctrine of Freud and Jung. Perhaps it is the point on which the several schools of psychology most readily agree. For centuries—certainly since Descartes—it was the remoteness of mind from body that had been emphasized. Thinking, especially the deductive thinking of philosophers, had been regarded as something quite different from all other human behaviour. The last fifty years have made us recognize the biological context of thinking, as of all other mental behaviour.

Current psychology in Britain begins with James Ward, the first, as he tells us, to teach the subject in Cambridge. In 1885, in the first draft of the book that for a generation was to be the standard work in English, he asserts that thinking is best understood if we remember that it is an activity ; it is one of the chief purposive activities of man, for it is " primarily undertaken as a means to an end." [1] What is the nature of this means and what are its ends ? These are the questions to which he and his successors devoted themselves.

Ward's pupil, Stout, makes a close analytical scrutiny of the mind as an activity. In emphasizing the fact that mind is purposive—an activity of the organism striving to achieve its goals—he shows that thinking arises in the service of feeling and will. In more exact psychological terms, cognition arises as a differentiation of affect and conation. It is in striving to achieve its ends that the organism thinks. Thus even attention, which at first sight might seem to be essentially cognitive, is in fact essentially conative. " Attention is simply conation, so far as it requires for its satisfaction fuller cognizance of its object without any other change in it. It is thus a subsidiary phase of conation in general, from which it can only be abstractly distinguished." [2]

Alexander carries this a stage further. With Stout he sees mind as essentially conative activity ; and thinking as this

[1] Ward PP 303   [2] Stout MP 158

conative activity when directed towards the knowing of things. But he brings thinking into even closer relation with the general behaviour of the organism by reminding us that thinking may be of two kinds : " practical " as well as " theoretical." [1] A man is engaged in theoretical thinking when—as in Stout's description of pure attention—his mind is satisfied to obtain " fuller cognizance of its object without any other change in it." The man is contemplating the object, considering it, studying it, but not attempting to change it. On other occasions, however, he may be engaged in getting to know things precisely in order to change them. This is practical thinking, which is at least as important as theoretical thinking.

The significance for us of this line of development from Ward through Stout to Alexander is that it brings mind into relation with human behaviour in general. So far from mind being that part of man most remote from his everyday practical life, it is the central activity by means of which he lives this life. And instead of regarding thinking as the activity of the mind when most abstracted from practical behaviour, we must recognize that thinking is the characteristic activity of the mind when practically engaged with the world around. " Mental life," says Alexander, " is practical through and through. It begins in practice and it ends in practice." [2]

This biological conception of mind is given its most striking and popularly acceptable form in the Hormic psychology of McDougall. Defining psychology alternatively as the study of behaviour and as the science of mind, he implies that mind is a form of behaviour. And since the essential feature of this behaviour is its purposiveness, all processes of the mind may well be named " hormic," a term which includes all the forms of striving of the organism, unconscious as well as conscious. Conative processes are, then, those hormic processes of which the organism is conscious.[3] In this way, by relating conation to the wider concept of " horme," McDougall comes within the " conative " school of Ward, Stout, and Alexander. Through his concept of mind as behaviour he joins hands

[1] Alexander CP 245   [2] the same 245   [3] McDougall OP 73

with the Behaviourists on the one side ; and through his recognition of the unconscious, with the Psycho-analysts on the other.

As to Behaviourism, this certainly did not begin with its chief protagonist Watson : it goes back at least as far as William James. Already in 1890 James had felt that the best description of mind was a " stream of consciousness." [1] In the course of the next twenty years, in trying to make this conception more explicit to himself, he was led to the conclusion that consciousness is nothing but a stream of *activity*. By 1912 his answer to his own question, " Is there such a thing as consciousness ? " is, No, there is no such thing, no such entity. " Let me explain that I mean only to deny that the word stands for an entity, but to insist most emphatically that it does stand for a function."[2] Startling as this may have seemed to some at the time, it is only a more graphic way of stating Alexander's view that mind is a continuum of activity.

If consciousness is no entity but a function, what sort of function is it ? In other words, what kind of behaviour is mental behaviour ? This is the question asked by the Behaviourists. Their answer that it is only inner speech is no doubt much too crude, but we shall see that a modified form of this doctrine, as expounded, for instance, by Bertrand Russell, has become widely accepted to-day. Russell's *Analysis of Mind*, beginning with James's view that consciousness is not an entity but a function, goes on to show that the essential characteristic of this function is that it operates through the use of words and other symbols.[3]

Meanwhile, at the other extreme from the Behaviourists, the Psycho-analysts insist no less strongly on the dynamic nature of mind. Thus McDougall, a link between the extremes, is able to point out that his *horme* and the *libido* of psycho-analysis are but two names both intended to emphasize this same dynamism.[4] Libido, central to the doctrines of both Freud and Jung, is defined by an approved exponent of the latter in these terms : " Jung conceives the total psychic system as being

[1] James PP (ii) 239   [2] James RE 3
[3] Russell AM 25, 29   [4] McDougall OP 73

in continuous dynamic movement. By psychic energy he means to be understood the *totality* of that force which pulses through and combines one with another all the forces and activities of this psychic system. This psychic energy is called *libido*." [1] It is probably the Psycho-analysts who have given the widest currency to the modern picture of the mind as a dynamic system rather than a static entity. It is certainly to the Psycho-analysts that we owe the modern recognition of the fact that mind is a dynamic system of which the individual himself is largely unconscious.

3

The unconscious mind : this is commonly regarded as a discovery of modern psychology. But it is not so much a discovery as a part of the general movement we have just described, towards the concept of mind as an activity. Nor can it be regarded as a discovery of our own day. Freud, as is well known, was much indebted to Von Hartmann's *Philosophy of the Unconscious* (1868) ; but the concept of unconscious mind is much older than that. Even if we do not trace it back to Plotinus, we certainly find it present at the inception of modern psychology in the seventeenth century. Locke had regarded mind and conscious mind as synonymous terms, insisting in the *Essay* that " thinking consists in being conscious that one thinks " ; but Leibniz had at once objected : " It does not follow that because the thought is not perceived it ceases for that reason," and had brought examples to show that mental activity may go on without the individual being aware of it. [2]

It is this that remains the central conception of the doctrine of unconscious mind : that every man engages in a great deal of mental activity of which he is unaware. But this clear conception has unfortunately been much over-clouded by the vaguer and more mystical notion of the Unconscious with a capital U, as elaborated by Von Hartmann, and it is around

[1] Jacobi PJ 50   [2] Leibniz NE 112

this notion that discussion—often trivial and sometimes acrimonious—has raged during the present century. Here it is important to distinguish between that part of Von Hartmann's doctrine which he derived from Leibniz, and for which there is much empirical evidence, and those metaphysical implications that he and others have been unable to resist. Recognition of the fact that we may be unconscious of much of our mental activity adds clarity to our picture of mind ; but the metaphysical hypotheses of an Unconscious Self in the individual and of the Unconscious Absolute in the universe only bring vagueness and confusion into the picture.

Von Hartmann's starting-point is that there is a great deal of mental behaviour of which the individual is unconscious while it occurs. Behaviour of this kind he called *unbewusst*—strictly, that of which one is unconscious. He proceeded to demonstrate the validity of this view by a close inductive analysis of a multitude of empirical data. He showed that any form of mental function—conative, affective, or cognitive—may go on without the awareness of the individual being directed upon it, and that functioning of this kind is of profound importance in behaviour ; indeed the more important any behaviour is for the individual the more likely is it to proceed without his awareness. The vital functions of the individual, his sexual behaviour, his social relations with his fellows—all these tend to be unconscious functions in this sense, that they may not be consciously directed and not within awareness while they occur. Thus at any moment in a man's life his mental activity may be said to be partly conscious, partly unconscious ; more of it being unconscious than conscious. Von Hartmann concluded that mental behaviour is by its nature unconscious, becoming conscious only in special circumstances.

It is clear that all this provided an excellent point of departure for Freud when he applied himself to consider the psychological implications of disorders in any of the more important functions of man. Von Hartmann, for instance, had seen the profound significance of Kant's remark that the clue to sexual behaviour lies in the unconscious ; [1] in the hands of Freud and his pupils—both Jung and Adler were his pupils—this was elaborated into the doctrine of the *libido* as we know it to-day. Varied and even opposed as the diverse schools of psycho-analysis may be, there is no doubt that on two fundamentals they agree : the concepts of the libido and of the unconscious.

Corroboration of the general concept of the unconscious has come from what might be regarded as unexpected quarters. Ward, Stout, Alexander, Spearman, approaching the problems of mind in the English tradition of introspective analysis —an approach certainly very different from Freud's—all insist that there is mental activity of which the subject himself may not be conscious. Ward and Stout follow Leibniz in demonstrating the fact that one may engage in cognitive activity of which one is not aware.[2] Alexander urges that our awareness of our own mental life is of a different kind from our awareness of any other thing, suggesting that we should speak of " enjoying " our own mental activity as contrasted with " contemplating " other things. He implies that there is some mental activity that is not " enjoyed " ; that is, mental activity of which we are not conscious.[3] And Spearman, in the course of his attempt to formulate the primary principles of cognition, is " obliged by the facts," he tells us, to range himself with Leibniz, Von Hartmann, and Freud ; by " the facts " he means the experimental evidence that a great deal of mental activity operates " below the level of introspective awareness." [4]

Even the Behaviourists, in spite of their jibes at the mysticism of psycho-analysis, do not deny the existence of the unconscious ; they merely give it another name. Watson tells us that the " Freudian unconscious " is nothing but the " unverbalized." In infancy and throughout life, he says, we build up many habits of skill and much emotional organization (he calls it " visceral "), without putting them into words. " This unver-

[1] Von Hartmann PU 22   [2] Ward PP 90 ; Stout AP (i) 24
[3] Alexander CP 243   [4] Spearman NI 60, 167

balized organization makes up the Freudian unconscious." [1] This may be an explanation—it is certainly not a refutation —of the unconscious. But even the explanation is Freud's. Quite explicitly he had already pointed out that an essential difference between unconscious and pre-conscious mental behaviour is that the latter has been brought into relation with verbal images.[2] Mental behaviour emerges from the unconscious to the pre-conscious, and so becomes available for consciousness by being put into words.

What Watson has done is to emphasize one way in which behaviour may lie beyond awareness : there are thoughts, feelings, and desires that have never been verbalized. But Freud has given much greater breadth and depth to our conception of mind by demonstrating that behaviour, especially orectic behaviour, may at first be conscious and then become repressed into the unconscious. There is thus no impassable barrier that divides the unconscious from the rest of mental life ; there is constant interflow between the conscious, the pre-conscious (subconscious), and the unconscious. Freud's greatest achievement here has been to draw attention to the transformations that unconscious mental life undergoes when it emerges into consciousness ; the phenomena of " condensation " and " displacement " which are so closely related to language and other symbols.

Not all of this is accepted as valid by all schools of psychology. But the agreement that remains in spite of the differences gives us a picture of the mind that may be described in the following terms.

4

Mind in the individual is an activity of which he is unconscious, subconscious, or conscious. Broadly speaking, unconscious mental activity arises in two ways. There is behaviour of which the individual is primarily unconscious ; this is the field to which, with varying degrees of acceptance, the term " instinct " has been applied. Then there is that

---

[1] Watson UB 279   [2] Freud EI 85

behaviour of which in the first instance the individual is conscious but of which he may subsequently become subconscious or even unconscious. These characteristics of individual mental life are, as we shall see, exactly paralleled in group behaviour.

Of the behaviour of which the individual is primarily unconscious little need be said here ; it is a field often explored and described, but which to-day is rapidly shrinking. Where Von Hartmann devoted a large part of his book to the discussion of instinct and McDougall twenty-five years ago made it the centre of his doctrine, to-day the evidence seems to suggest that much of what might have been ascribed to innate tendencies is in fact the impact of " culture-patterns " upon the individual growing up in a society. If agreement may be said to emerge from the controversy still raging,[1] it is this : there may be a few innate patterns of behaviour ; but in general, behaviour that is common to all the members of a society consists of habits that have grown up unconsciously or with the minimum of consciousness and now function beyond consciousness.

We are on more certain ground when we come to those transformations of behaviour which can actually be observed : behaviour that at first functions under the direction of consciousness, then becomes subconscious or unconscious, and subsequently on occasion again emerges into consciousness. Of these transformations rather more must be said here because of the importance of the parallel processes in the life of a group. Let us look at the transformations first of the cognitive aspects of behaviour and then of its orectic aspects.

Cognitive behaviour becomes unconscious when habits of skill are set up, concerned with manipulating or exploring environment. The individual first of all learns these habits consciously, guiding his actions by means of what Alexander calls practical thinking. In time these habits may come to function unconsciously or subconsciously ; but the direction of them may become conscious again at a moment of difficulty.

[1] e.g. symposium in *Brit. J. Ed. Psych.* 1942–3

Take, for example, a very familiar practical action that goes on in most people without the direction of consciousness : the use of knife and fork at table. The setting-up of this habit—or hierarchy of habits—has demanded in its day a great deal of awareness ; in time the habits became unconscious and for the most part remain so. When, if ever, is consciousness again turned upon these habits ? Only when some novel feature appears in the familiar situation, so that the stock pattern of action ceases to be adequate. In a hotel abroad, for instance, our customary table manners may embarrass us ; we turn upon our own behaviour and become conscious of it.

A more complicated but essentially similar case is that of a hunter stalking his prey. He threads his way through the forest noiselessly and yet with the greatest agility ; all the time having the minimum of awareness of the trees, of his movements, or of himself. How much of this behaviour might be " instinctive " no one can say ; certainly a good deal has been consciously learnt since childhood. Now most of it goes on with the lowest degree of consciousness, some of it without any at all.

There comes a moment, however, when an unaccustomed feature springs up in the familiar situation. The spoor suddenly disappears or a fallen tree blocks the path. Now consciousness begins to intervene ; the hunter begins to " attend " to what he is doing, to " remember," " imagine," " think." All these are terms used by us to indicate that the hunter is conscious of his mental behaviour.

The most important instance of the same process in modern life is the acquisition and application of a skilled technique, a craft involving the use of tools. A craftsman is at his bench ; much of what he does demands little or no conscious control by him— it is a hierarchy of reflexes and acquired habits. The movements of his arms, hands, and fingers as he grasps and guides a tool, all the series of complicated acts that make up the skilled task—applying the tool, directing it, adjusting the pressure—all this may go on with the minimum of his awareness.

But there comes a moment when the hitherto familiar situation takes an unfamiliar turn : something goes wrong with the tool or there is a flaw in the material. If the usual technique will answer, the intervention of consciousness may be slight ; but if his habitual behaviour fails him in his attempt to deal with the new problem, the craftsman begins to " think."

In all these three instances we see the initial development of a process under the partial or total guidance of cognitive consciousness, the gradual withdrawal of consciousness from it so that it comes to function unconsciously, and finally the intervention of consciousness at moments of stress. What is the nature of this intervention ? This we shall consider in the next section.

In the meantime there remain the corresponding transformations of orectic mental activity, the processes that above all others Freud has illuminated for us ; in particular the development of " complexes." In the course of every person's life the things that matter most to him become the centre of strong feelings ; in the terms given currency by McDougall there is the growth of sentiments for particular objects, in Freudian terms there is cathexis of the libido by these objects. A man's life and behaviour are permeated by a network of sentiments towards himself, the persons, things, and places familiar to him, the things and ideas he has heard and read about. But a sentiment or cathexis of this kind may come into conflict with his leading sentiments or habits of thought or behaviour—in other words, the sentiment may not be " approved " by him, although he himself may be unaware of either conflict or disapproval. In such a case the sentiment itself may be lost to consciousness : there is " repression " ; a complex is formed. A complex may therefore be defined as a sentiment of which the individual is unaware but which nevertheless determines his behaviour. The degree of awareness will of course vary with the complex ; it may range from a light subconsciousness from which a complex readily emerges, to a deep unconsciousness from which a complex is brought to light only through the help of clinical techniques such as word-association, hypnosis, or dream-analysis.

Again we have to ask, what is the nature of this emergence into consciousness ? The answer, as also in the case of cognitive activity, depends upon a recognition of the functions of words and other symbols in mental life.

5

Consciousness is behaviour that uses symbols : this—like the unconscious—might be called a modern discovery except that again the Greeks thought of it first. The often-quoted remark that Plato puts into the mouth of Socrates : " When the mind is thinking, it is talking to itself," [1] embraces all the implications that to-day we are making explicit and that provide the chief key to the understanding of group mind.

After Plato, nothing so explicit as this until the seventeenth century, except that the medieval pre-occupation with the alternatives of nominalism or realism was in effect largely a problem of the relation between language and thought. But after Plato, nothing so explicit until Hobbes when, with the beginning of inductive science and modern mathematics, it became urgent to consider how language could serve the new techniques of thought. As his present-day disciple Colling-wood tells us, it was one of Hobbes's greatest achievements to recognize that without language, knowledge could never have come into existence.[2] Hobbes said that language, with which man is endowed by nature, has two functions : not only communication but thinking as well. Language enables us " to register what by cogitation we find to be the use of anything. . . . Understanding is nothing else than conception caused by speech. . . . Reason is nothing but reckoning of the consequences of general names agreed upon, for the marking and signifying of our thoughts. . . . Children therefore are not endued with reason at all, till they have attained the use of speech." [3]

---

[1] *Theat.* 189 ; in Cornford PT 118   [2] Collingwood NL 43
[3] Hobbes L 25, 31, 33, 37

A generation later, as we have seen,[1] Locke took the next step. Man is not simply endowed with language by nature, but it is the need of communication that is the source of language, and language that in turn breeds thought. " Knowledge . . . has greater connexion with words than is commonly suspected. . . . Men, in making their general ideas, seeking more the convenience of language . . . than the true and precise nature of things as they exist, have in the framing their abstract ideas, chiefly pursued that end, which was to be furnished with store of general and variously comprehensive names." [2] In other words, the process of abstract thinking is determined by the needs of communication : the necessity of language is the mother of thought.

Leibniz, critical of Locke though he was, on this point fully agreed with him.[3] But during the one hundred and fifty years that ensued, the bold conception of these three thinkers, Hobbes, Locke, and Leibniz, was accepted only by a few others of the same calibre. Throughout the whole of the eighteenth century and well into the nineteenth Hobbes and his followers were stigmatized as "materialists," and there was a constant fear and hatred of the religious and ethical implications of their doctrines. The common attitude in the middle of the nineteenth century may be seen in the work of Stoddart (1849), one of the few writers of his day with insight into the nature of language, but violently opposed to what he considered the subversive doctrines of the " materialists." He quotes the opinion of Horne Tooke that what are called the operations of the mind are really the workings of language, and the allied view of Condillac, " On ne pense pas sans le secours des langues " ; such men, he says, pervert the true doctrine of Locke that thinking depends on sensation. See now where this has led them, he exclaims ; the materialism of Hobbes, Gassendi, Hartley, Priestley, Erasmus Darwin, D'Alembert, Diderot, Condillac, Condorcet " has at length attained its climax in the public atheistical lectures of M. Comte." [4] With the material-

---

[1] page 27 above
[3] Leibniz NE 287
[2] Locke E 84
[4] Stoddart PL 21, 65

ists able to muster such a roll of names, it is no wonder that Stoddart took himself seriously as a David confronting an army of Goliaths.

It was into this arena that Max Müller, with more courage than discretion, burst with his battle-cry, " No thoughts without words ! " (1861). Perhaps a better battle-cry than a scientific hypothesis ; confronted by such doughty opponents as Galton, Romanes, and Whitney, Müller though never routed, had to retire to a less vulnerable position. By 1887 he was saying, " All I maintain is that thought cannot exist without signs, and that our most important signs are words." [1]

To-day this position has become a stronghold reinforced from all sides by allies not otherwise on particularly good terms with one another, but united in the determination to advance in the direction first pointed out by Hobbes. From the main English school of psychology as expounded by Ward and Stout, from the metaphysics of Bergson and Croce, from Behaviorism, from psycho-analysis—from all these diverse directions come different forms of the same central principle, that symbols, verbal or pictorial, are indispensable to consciousness. Some would go the whole way and concede nothing from the position that consciousness *is* the use of symbols.

Ward's *Psychological Principles*, although not published in its final form until 1918, was already drafted while Müller was yet writing, and shows signs that the psychologist could not ignore the current controversy. Ward mentions Müller, but is unable to give him full support. But what support he gives is clearly indicative of the trend of opinion. While it is certain, he says, that thought begins without language, just as arts begin without tools, yet language enables us to carry the thinking process enormously further.[2] If we give full weight to Ward's qualification we see that he has said almost everything ; thinking without language is as rudimentary as an art without tools.

Taking so much for granted, Stout attempts a closer analysis. What, he asks, is the special function of language in our think-

[1] Müller ST 58   [2] Ward PP 296

ing ? The answer is that language has the function that he would call " expressive " ; a word is an instrument for thinking about the *meaning* that it expresses. Thus he emphasizes the semantic functions of language.[1] And, as so often in the history of thought, it is not simply a coincidence that the same year that saw the publication of his book saw also the appearance of Bréal's *Essai de Semantique*, where the word *semantic* is first used ; the beginning of the modern preoccupation of the linguist with all the problems of meaning. " Language is a product begun and continued with a practical goal in view," says Bréal.[2] " Mental life," Alexander was soon to say, " is practical through and through." [3] The paths are converging. The psychologist concerned with mental activity and the linguist concerned with the functions of language find that at many points they are dealing with the same thing.

6

From that moment at the turn of the century, a great deal of thought has been given to the problems implied in this convergence. The metaphysicians, the Behaviourists, and the Psycho-analysts are in their different ways all preoccupied with the same question of the relation between mind and language, and from their different directions make their varied contributions to its solution.

Bergson, concerned primarily with evolution as creative of mind, sees language as one of the principal means by which intelligence is able to free itself from the bondage of instinct. Everywhere except in man, consciousness has remained the captive of instinct. But " Language furnishes consciousness with an immaterial body in which to incarnate itself, and this exempts it from dwelling exclusively on material bodies, whose flux would soon drag it along and finally swallow it up." [4] In other words, in the course of evolution it is language that makes thought possible, particularly abstract thought. Language is

[1] Stout AP 192
[2] Bréal ES 2
[3] page 75 above
[4] Bergson CE 279

the means of the transition from instinctive to intelligent behaviour.

Croce would go further : " It seems clear that if man does not speak, he does not think. This presupposition we accept." [1] And as it is one of Croce's chief principles that all symbols are forms of language, we may take his statement to mean that it is only by virtue of symbols that man thinks. In the words of Henri Delacroix : " Toute pensée est symbolique. Toute pensée construit d'abord des signes qu'elle substitue aux choses." [2]

It was at this time, when psychology and metaphysics were already moving in the same direction, that Behaviourism came to birth. In 1919 Watson announced as fundamental to his new doctrine the principle that there is no consciousness : what we call thinking is only silent talking.[3] It is not to belittle his achievement if we point out that instead of battling, as he thought, against the stream of modern psychology, he was in fact swimming with one of its main currents. In appearing to echo Max Müller in making language the one necessary condition of thought, he was doing himself less than justice. His conceptions of thought and of language are much wider and more fruitful. So far from merely identifying thought with language, he at once makes the important qualification that what we call thinking includes not only all " implicit language activity," but also all " other activity substitutable for language activity." [4] And when he adds that the thought processes must not be abstracted from " their general setting in bodily integration," we see at once the conformity of his views with those of the other thinkers we have named.

In going further than most of them, however, and saying things more emphatically, Watson startled many into a closer reconsideration of the functions of language in thought, sometimes to the full recognition that thinking *is* symbolic activity. But his main influence has been indirect ; it is the less crude formulations of Behaviourism that have had the greater effects.

---

[1] Croce L 4
[3] Watson PB 344
[2] Delacroix LP 64
[4] the same 346

Bertrand Russell, for instance, was saying in 1921 that although not of the Behaviourists, he was prepared to go a long way with them. He was prepared to go as far as this : " Almost all higher intellectual activity is a matter of words, to the nearly total exclusion of everything else." And more generally : " The whole essence of the practical efficiency of ' thought ' consists in sensitiveness to *signs*. . . . Of these, words are the supreme example." [1]

The contribution of psycho-analysis to this trend of modern thought is to bring sharply into focus the relation between language and consciousness. Mental behaviour, says Freud, becomes conscious mental behaviour to the extent that it is mediated by verbal images. This gives us a clue as to the way in which the unconscious mind probably became conscious in the course of evolution. " It is probable that thinking was originally unconscious . . . and that it became endowed with further qualities that were perceptible to consciousness only through its connection with the memory-traces of words." [2] The same transformation takes place in the individual ; unconscious mental activity moves towards consciousness, by being verbally symbolized. " The question, ' How does a thing become conscious ? ' could be put more advantageously thus : ' How does a thing become pre-conscious ? ' And the answer would be : ' By coming into connection with the verbal images that correspond to it.' " [3] The similarity of this with Bergson's picture of evolution is evident ; Freud goes further when he makes clear that the transition from unconscious to conscious mental activity is also the transition from pictorial symbols to the use of words. The essential means by which we become conscious of our mental activity is that we symbolize it in words. Consciousness therefore is verbally symbolized mental activity.

Here then is the modern answer to the ancient question, What is consciousness ? Man's behaviour towards the world around him is often carried on by means of symbols ; this symbolizing behaviour we call mental behaviour. He can

---

[1] Russell AM 29, 211, 293   [2] Rickman SF 48   [3] the same 248

then become conscious of this mental behaviour by symbolizing it.   So he acquires the power of " turning round upon "
his own behaviour.   " An organism," says Bartlett, " has
somehow to acquire the capacity to turn round upon its own
' schemata.' . . . It is where and why consciousness comes in ;
it is what gives consciousness its most important function." [1]
We have seen that the present-day view is that man turns
round upon his behaviour by means of symbols, and more
effectively by verbal than by pictorial symbols.

7.

Freud's elucidation of this process is that as mental activity
emerges from the unconscious through the pre-conscious to the
conscious, in the earlier stages it is symbolized by pictures and
then increasingly by means of words, so that fully conscious
thinking is predominantly verbal rather than pictorial. "Thinking in pictures is only a very incomplete form of becoming
conscious.   In some way, too, it approximates more closely
to unconscious processes than does thinking in words, and is
unquestionably older than the latter both ontogenetically and
phylogenetically." [2]

In support of this generalization the Psycho-analysts can
bring a great deal of evidence : the symbols of dreams and
the symbols used by the waking mind when it attempts to
become aware of the sub-conscious or to explore the deeper
levels of the unconscious.   Jung tells us of these deeper levels
that "their language is archaic, symbolic, pre-logical—a picture
language whose meaning can only be discovered through
special methods of interpretation." [3]

In all this there is a strange echo of a remark by Bentham,
who, in the course of his long-continued pondering over the
relation between language and thought, perceived many things
for which we are only to-day obtaining concrete evidence.

[1] Bartlett R 206
[2] Rickman SF 249
[3] Jacobi PJ 39. Cf. Piaget's view that the thinking of the infant is pre-logical
(p. 30 above)

" Unclothed as yet in words, or stripped of them, thoughts are but dreams ; like the shifting clouds of the sky, they float in the mind one moment and are out of it the next." [1] So long as thoughts lack the symbolic vesture of language they are dreamlike, with many of the characteristics of dreams.

What are these characteristics ? Nothing in Freud is more illuminating than his account of the manner in which dreams transform latent, unconscious thoughts so that they may become accessible and acceptable to consciousness : it is also the manner in which the same transition is made in waking life. If we examine dreams, says Freud, we find three characteristic features : the use of *visual imagery*, *condensation*, and *displacement*.

Dreams, he says, [2] consist almost entirely of visual imagery ; there is a minimum of words. This is partly the cause, partly the result, of the fact that in dreams we make no attempt to deal with abstractions or generalizations ; any thinking latent in the dream is given as concrete a form as possible. For, as we saw in the quotation from Freud a moment ago, thinking in pictures approximates more closely to unconscious processes than does thinking in words. We may add that pictures are also better adapted than words to enable us to disguise feelings and desires so that we may admit these to consciousness. Putting them into words makes them too definite, and inconveniently draws too much attention to them.

The second characteristic of dreams is condensation. Dreams are, so to speak, composite pictures of many latent thoughts, desires, and feelings already conglomerated into complexes, and of these complexes only certain elements are allowed to pass over into the manifest content of the dream. Allowed, we say ; for there is a constant " censorship " exercised by the mind : complexes are allowed to pass over in such forms as will not conflict too violently with conscious thoughts, feelings, and desires.

The third means by which the disguise and the transition are effected is displacement. A latent element may be replaced by something more remote from the true centre of the complex,

[1] Ogden BF lxxi   [2] Freud IL 144–6

something in the nature of an *allusion*, so that again consciousness is put off its guard. Or again, the centre of the dream is shifted by removing the accent, the emphasis, from what is really important to something less important, but nevertheless closely associated with it.

Throughout Freud's treatment of dreams it is evident that dreams owe their characteristic pictorialism, condensation, and displacement to the manner in which the mind allows itself to symbolize their latent contents. So long as these contents are unsymbolized, the mind is unconscious of them. And even when they are symbolized, the mind tends to use pictures for them rather than words, and pictorial rather than abstract words. For pictorial imagery and pictorial language lend themselves to the condensation and displacement that the mind demands if it is to entertain the latent contents of the dream at all.

8

We have now reached the point at which we can complete our statement of the current conception of mind. By mind we mean this : the conative direction of behaviour towards the cognition of environment, cognition that may be " practical " or " theoretical," and that may involve affective responses to the environment. The essential characteristic of this mental behaviour is that it uses symbols, both verbal and pictorial. At any moment a man may be conscious of some of his mental behaviour, less immediately of other parts of it, and unconscious of much more. Conscious mind tends to use verbal symbols ; subconscious and unconscious mind, as they emerge into consciousness, tend to be symbolized in pictures or in pictorial transformations of language.

In every man there are constant complexes of thoughts, feelings, and desires, which strongly influence his overt behaviour but of which he tends to remain unconscious, and which he admits to his consciousness only in disguised pictorial forms. All mental behaviour, then, uses symbols of one kind or another ;

the symbols vary with the nature of the mental activity—whether it is predominantly cognitive, affective, or conative—and with the extent to which it is open to consciousness.

In the words of Angyal, who has recently attempted a formulation of the fundamental principles of psychology : " psychological activity may be called the symbolizing function of the organism." [1] In terms more readily helpful to us in our consideration of group mind we shall say : Mind is behaviour mediated by symbolization.

What, then, is group mind ?

[1] Angyal SP 58

CHAPTER 5

LANGUAGE AND GROUP BEHAVIOUR

I

MIND is behaviour mediated by symbols. Group mind is group behaviour mediated by group symbols. In the present chapter we shall consider what this means.

We are driven to take up this question not by the desire to re-open an ancient controversy and discuss once more, as a metaphysical problem, whether there is any such thing as group mind. It is from our concern with the functions of language in society that it becomes necessary to recognize that human group behaviour is at once given a special character wherever group symbolization—that is, communication —enters into it ; and that behaviour of this kind, involving symbolization, has the same functions for the group as mental activity has for the individual. Group remembering, group planning, group feeling, and willing—all these are modified by the existence of some form of symbolical communication within the group. It is symbolical communication that makes it possible for the group to attend to its own behaviour ; and language which enables the group to do this with greater precision. Language makes it possible for the group to symbolize its own group mind, and so gives group mind the power of becoming conscious group mind.

The recognition of all this is so important for our understanding of the functions of language in modern societies that we must give ourselves room here to set out the argument step by step. The nature of group mind is unintelligible unless we see it in relation to group behaviour in general, unless we recognize that group mind is only a special form of group behaviour. Just as psychology to-day sees individual mind as an essential part of the total behaviour of the individual, so we must see group mind as the chief means by which the group engages in its group activities.

In the present chapter we shall therefore begin with group behaviour in general and move from this to the consideration of group mind in relation to language. We shall begin by recalling that group behaviour is distinct from individual behaviour ; that the activities carried out by people in groups have different patterns from any behaviour carried out by individuals in isolation. Then we shall show that human group behaviour—as we know it to-day—is usually, if not always, mediated by symbolical communication, this being the means by which the group is able to organize the rest of its behaviour, by postponing it and directing it, often in the light of its recollection of the past. In other words, symbolical communication becomes the means by which the group is enabled to " turn back upon " its own behaviour ; the means by which a group develops a group mind. If this is true it will follow that there may be a higher development of group mind in some groups than in others, in accordance with the extent and complexity of symbolical communication ; and also that a group may at times engage in group behaviour about which there is no symbolical communication within the group. This will be unconscious group behaviour, behaviour of which the group *as a group* is unaware, even though individuals within the group may be aware of this behaviour. In accordance with the extent and degree of group symbolization of group behaviour, so there will be differences of the extension and the gradation of group awareness of group behaviour.

Finally, we shall show that among the various kinds of symbolical communication, language has a unique place, in that it is the means by which group mind becomes conscious group mind. Group behaviour might therefore be of three grades : without group symbols, with non-verbal group symbols and with language. We shall see, however, that in fact human group behaviour is rarely if ever of the first kind ; in other words, human group behaviour is always in some measure informed by group mind, however rudimentary and however little conscious. Where language is present to a high degree group mind may be fully conscious.

From this it follows that the Linguistic Revolution—the increasing intervention of language in group life—must have important effects upon group mind. These will be discussed in the chapters that follow.

2

Is there such a thing as group behaviour? Has the behaviour of men working in groups any specific characteristics not to be found in the behaviour of individuals working in isolation? Here we take up a definite stand with the assertion that the answer to both these questions is affirmative.

It is clear, first of all, that a great many forms of behaviour are only possible in groups. The smallest group is the group of two; there are certainly a multitude of activities carried out in pairs which cannot be performed by either of the pair in isolation. In talking about pairs, the most obvious instance, sexual behaviour, at once comes to mind; but equally cogent examples are duels and duets—or any game, transaction, or conversation carried on between two. Neither of the pair can do alone what they do together; the patterns of individual action in isolation are different from the patterns of joint action.

What is true of pairs is obviously as true of larger groups. A committee is different from a discussion between two, still more different from private thinking. A rugger match, a battle, a lynching, team-work in a factory, an orchestra—these are forms of action that no individual can carry out on his own. In all these instances the behaviour of each co-operating member is different in many ways from anything he does in isolation; the patterns of group action, precisely because this is the joint behaviour of a number of people working together, are always different from the patterns of individual action.

At the same time, together with these differences, the patterns of human group behaviour run parallel to those of individual behaviour in isolation. The group, like the individual, exists in virtue of the extent to which it is able to impose itself upon its environment. The behaviour of the group is directed upon its environment, both human and non-human, with the intention of maintaining both its internal equilibrium and its external stability in the face of disintegrating forces. The individuals constituting the group will engage in joint behaviour with these ends in view. In the course of this there will obviously be individual mental behaviour, both cognitive and orectic ; as, in their joint action, men explore and exploit the environment of the group, they will obviously think, feel, and will as individuals. The crucial question is, Will there also be *group mental behaviour* ; cognitive and orectic behaviour of the group as a group ?

3

This at once brings us to the question, What part is played in group behaviour by symbolical communication, particularly language ? Here our main concern is with the complex societies of our contemporary civilization, but it will enable us to obtain a clearer view of our own behaviour if we remove ourselves some distance from it and first attempt to obtain a picture of the place of communication in more primitive societies.

As a hypothesis it is possible to conceive of group behaviour quite unmediated by symbolical communication—group behaviour in the development of which symbolical communication has played no part and from the functioning of which it is absent also. It may be that the group behaviour of animals other than man—the hymenoptera, for instance—is of this kind ; we do not know. But respecting human group activities, the more closely we observe, the clearer does it become that some kind of symbolical communication has played a part, either in the course of its development or in its actual functioning. Sapir, one of the few ethnologists who have given due attention to the functions of language—as distinct from its forms—in primitive societies, concludes : " Every cultural

97

pattern and every single act of social behaviour involves communication in either an explicit or an implicit sense." [1]

At first sight this might hardly appear to be true. There would seem to be important forms of group behaviour which appear to function automatically, " intuitively," without gesture, signal, or speech. Take, for instance, hunting. A band of men on the trail work together in a highly co-operative fashion, smoothly, silently, as though they were guided by intuition. It is a typical enough case ; there is plenty of evidence from ethnology that group behaviour of this kind is common in primitive societies—group behaviour carried on in the absence of words.

Three questions about behaviour of this sort might be asked : Is it group behaviour ? Is it " intuitive " ? Has communication any place in its development or functioning ?

As to the first question, it is evident enough that group hunting, for instance, is truly group behaviour. The actions of a hunter who is one of a party are different from those when he is hunting on his own ; they are determined by and obtain their meaning from his membership of this working party. And within the group there is a pattern of action, weaving from one man to another, which is correctly termed group behaviour because it occurs only in the behaviour of a group.

As to intuition, it is clear that this group behaviour functions so smoothly because it is the result of a long process of group training, and that the exigencies of the situation, so long as they are relatively familiar, call out a complexity of actions that have become habitual through this training. And it is clear that in the process of training, some form of communication—whether by gesture, signal, or language—will have played its part.

Where, now, in the actual group act of hunting, is language likely to enter, and with it group thinking and group awareness of group behaviour ? The answer is, as in the case of individual behaviour, when habitual modes of action are inadequate to deal with the unfamiliar. Even in a primitive hunting party,

[1] art. " Communication," *Ency. Soc. Sci.* (1931)

when an unfamiliar circumstance intervenes and the customary modes of behaviour are brought to a halt, there is likely to be some sort of communication. This may be no more than a pause while one member of the party gives gestural indications of what should be the next step—and then the hunt goes on. In other words, there is symbolical communication even though this is still at the pictorial level ; and if the group thinking is rudimentary it is nevertheless group thinking.

We call it " group " thinking because it is thinking carried out jointly by the members of a group. One man makes a sign, others respond ; there are further responses to their responses. In individual thinking both the sign and its responses are within the behaviour of one and the same person ; but here, in this group behaviour, the course of the thinking moves from member to member ; the thinking of each individual is in part determined by and obtains its meaning from the thinking of other members of the group. Group thinking differs from individual thinking in the same way as group hunting differs from individual hunting.

Group thinking conducted by means of gestures and other pictorial signs is, as we have said, only rudimentary thinking ; it becomes more fully developed and more complex where language enters. Even in a primitive hunting party there may be what we—in the terms of our linguistic civilization— would regard as a conference. And now the characteristic differences between group and individual thinking will show themselves more clearly. The process of the thinking, as it moves and grows, forms a pattern that arises from the successive contributions of the several members of the party. One man makes a suggestion ; this is followed up or objected to by another ; this gives rise to a further remark ; and so the group thinking takes its course. It has the movement, the short-cuts, the internal conflicts, the compromises, the halts, the repetitions, that characterize individual thinking ; the difference is that its successive stages arise not within the behaviour of a single individual, but in the joint behaviour of a number of contributory members of a group.

We must also notice that the similarities between group and individual thinking are not simply due to the fact that a group consists of individuals who have already learnt to think separately and now learn to think together. It is evident that the forms of individual thinking are just as likely to be moulded by group thinking as *vice versa*. If, as Plato says, individual thinking is internal conversation, then it is equally true that group thinking is external conversation; and as every person has some experience of thinking in concert with others, his own private thinking will bear the marks of this social experience.

Hypothetically, then, communication is likely to enter into an important group activity in these four ways: it will be a means of recalling past experience; a means of becoming aware of the immediate present environment; a means of anticipating and planning—that is, of directing future activity; and an instrument in the actual conduct of immediate activity. In psychological terms, communication will be a means of group remembering; of group awareness of environment; of group planning—group thinking of the more " theoretical " sort; and of group thinking of the more immediately " practical " sort. And throughout all this, communication will be a means of arousing and maintaining group orexis.

4

When we turn to the ethnographers for actual evidence to test a hypothetical picture of this kind, we find this: that broadly speaking our picture is correct in outline, but that in two respects primitive group communication is in more marked contrast with our own than we had suggested. First, cognitive behaviour is likely to be even more strongly orectic in nature than with us; and secondly, language is likely to play a less important part than non-verbal, pictorial forms of symbolization.

Of the four functions of group communication that we have named in the last section—remembering, spatial awareness, planning, immediate direction—it is the first that is the most obvious in a typical primitive group. For this, at any rate, there is plenty of evidence. Rites, customs, ornaments, all in their diverse ways serve to symbolize the experience of the forbears of the group and to combine with legends and traditional recitals to make it possible for the group, as a group, to remember the past of the group. The processes of recall—as such writers as Halbwachs and Bartlett have made us aware—are highly complex. Halbwachs reminds us that all memory—even in the individual—tends to be shaped by the interchange with others of information about the past ; while Bartlett has studied, both by observation and experiment, the factors that are likely to modify any linguistic communication in the course of its tradition, its passage through time.[1]

What we must recognize here is that behaviour of this kind, the tradition of a narrative of past events, is truly group behaviour, group remembering. When a man narrates events to a group, the auditors as well as the speaker play their part in shaping the narrative that emerges and is again passed on. As Bartlett says, " Any story, or any series of incidents, recalled in the presence, and for the hearing, of other members of the same group will tend to display certain characteristics. . . . There is social control from the auditors to the narrator. . . . What is beyond dispute is that remembering in a group is influenced, as to its manner, directly by the preferred persistent tendencies of that group." [2]

Closely allied to this function of remembering in a group is the narration that enables the group to explore its remoter environment ; to keep in touch with what is happening around it and yet is not within its immediate experience. Here again our evidence is from Bartlett. He describes a custom of the Swazis, a group of the Bantus : " News travels among the native population with great rapidity. There is no native system of signals for its transmission ; but whenever two wanderers on a pathway meet, they make a clean breast one to another of all that they have lately done, seen, or learned." [3]

[1] Halbwachs CM ; Bartlett R   [2] Bartlett R 266–7   [3] the same 265

In this way, by custom, and almost certainly without any clear awareness of the value of this, the group is keeping itself in touch with its remoter environment, and so storing up information that may in due course have an important bearing on group behaviour.

When communication is used in these two ways, as a means of recording and recalling the past, the remote in time ; and as a means of exploring what is spatially remote in the present, it is in fact acting as a " distance-receptor " for the group. It becomes the primary means by which the group can remember and by which it can make itself aware of what is around it. And it is group remembering and rudimentary group thinking in this : that in each case a picture is built up by the co-operation and interaction of the members of a group. The transmission of tradition or of present news involves the influence of the auditor upon the speaker ; and what is received and carried further is modified by the characteristic modes of thought and feeling in the group.

We must not forget orexis ; for in a primitive group—even more than in a modern society—the recall of the past and the exploration of the present are highly charged with emotion and will. Group remembering, no less than individual remembering, is characterized by repressions, distortions, wish-fulfilment. And in the primitive communication of news, as Malinowski points out, the main actual function may not be the information explicitly conveyed ; when one man recites the news to another the major effect may be the establishment of rapport : affective, " phatic," communion rather than cognitive communication.[1]

5

For the third function of communication in a primitive society—as a means of anticipating the future and planning action—we have also some evidence from the ethnographers. Malinowski, again, in describing the " Kula " of the Trobriand Islanders—the intricate system of barter among the archipela-

[1] Malinowski *in* Ogden MM 315 ; also page 25 above

goes of eastern New Guinea—tells us that it is usually preceded by protracted discussions. These are partly in the nature of reminiscences of past expeditions, partly anticipations of the expedition about to be made. " As is usual in such cases, months before the approximate date of sailing, plans and forecasts were made, stories of previous voyages were recounted, old men dwelt on their own reminiscences, and reported what they had been told by their elders. . . . And so, as it always happens when future events are talked over round village fires, imagination outran all bounds of probability ; and hopes and anticipations grew bigger and bigger." [1]

Once more it is clear that this group anticipation of the future is not so much a means of cognitive deliberation as a means of arousing and sustaining group orexis. While there is some actual planning, some group thinking, this tends to play a smaller part in the discussions of the islanders than the emotive recall of the past and the imaginative anticipation of the future. For the actual details of a Kula expedition are determined not so much by those who take part in it as by tradition ; and this, as Malinowski insists, is stronger than economic incentive or even than the force of the present leader's authority. " The real force which binds all the people and ties them down in their tasks is obedience to custom, to tradition." [2]

The function of the preliminary conference is therefore not planning so much as the heightening of emotion and desire in the group, by the revival of the past and the imaginative anticipation of the future. In this anticipative behaviour the group thinking, such as it is, is largely orectic in nature ; another instance of the dominance of feeling and will in the group communication of primitive societies.

6

This is also true of the fourth main function of group communication in primitive societies : communication brought to bear upon behaviour in which the group is actually engaged.

[1] Malinowski AP 148   [2] the same 158

Vital activities of primitive groups are as a rule accompanied by rites, ceremonies, and dances which have the effect of heightening affect and conation in the group ; and language, to the extent that it is used at all, will often also have this effect. Layard, for instance, describes a battle among the natives of Malekula in the New Hebrides. The battle array and the procedures of the warfare are determined by custom ; where language is used it has for the most part another function. " For more than an hour representatives of either side alternately stepped out slightly in advance of their respective parties to harangue the enemy, moving their bodies violently to and fro as they hurled insults at one another, combined with a recitation of present grievances and a repetition of the intricate minutiae of generation-long ancestral disputes. Meanwhile, the opposing sides would send off an occasional volley of stones. . . . At times the harangues were so enthralling that the parties would cease even these hostile acts and would advance to listen spellbound, till some new taunt would set them shouting counter accusations, and the stone-throwing would be resumed." [1]

Here language certainly plays an important part in the group behaviour, but its main function is not cognitive, the direction and organization of behaviour ; its function once more is largely orectic, serving for the expression and arousal of feeling and desire. As orectic responses are aroused in the participants there occurs what can only be regarded as group orexis, for the patterns of feeling and desire take their forms from inter-action and mutual response within the group. The members of the group not only experience emotion and desire but express them. What each man feels and wills is in some measure determined by the feeling and will of those around him ; the patterns of orexis that ripple through the group bear the same relation to the feeling and will of an individual in isolation, as group thinking to individual thinking.

Facts of this kind are now a commonplace of the psychology of crowds ; what we have to emphasize here is that they are facts of *group* psychology. Thus Miller and Dollard, in their

[1] Layard SM 597

close analysis of crowd behaviour, are impelled to invent a term to denote the stimuli to which the members of a crowd are subject, but which they do not experience when alone : " crowd stimuli . . . the provocative strength of the stimuli given off by other persons in the crowd." [1] Each member of the crowd, in responding to these stimuli, is himself the source of stimuli for others ; so there develops an interweaving pattern of stimulus and response which occurs only in groups and never within the individual himself, in isolation. Of course, in such cases of group orexis there may be—as McDougall and others have suggested—some " mass induction " of emotion without the use of symbols, or even some telepathy. [2] But in the main it is clear that normally—in primitive as well as in modern societies—symbols, especially language, play a large part in arousing and maintaining group orectic behaviour.

These orectic functions of language are not confined to the ceremonial aspects of group behaviour. They are at least as important in the practical behaviour of primitive groups ; their group techniques. And as we shall be closely concerned with the functions of language in the practical group techniques of our own societies, it will repay us to consider in detail its functions in the group techniques of primitive groups.

7

We need an instance of practical group activity, behaviour in which the members of a group participate so as to produce some practical result of vital importance to them, and where, therefore, we may expect to witness a full demand on the resources of its participants, including the use of symbolical communication in the operation of skilled group techniques. An example that satisfies these requirements is Malinowski's careful record of the building and launching of a canoe by the

---

[1] Miller SL 220

[2] McDougall OP 156 suggests that in animals other than man, and even in man, the expression of orexis and the response to it are instinctive. " The yap which the dog utters, when he starts a rabbit or other prey, was designed by Nature to bring his fellows to his aid." For telepathy, Carrington T

Trobriand Islanders, a community primitive in social organization, devoid of a written language, and limited in economic life, but with a complex system of maritime barter, the "Kula" mentioned earlier. For them the building and launching of a canoe is obviously a group enterprise of the deepest practical and emotional significance.

Malinowski's description of this group task, from the moment when the tree is felled, to the day when the craft glides out upon the open water, shows that the work is carried forward by two disparate kinds of activity. There are the highly skilled technical operations of constructing, fitting, launching, and decorating the canoe ; but every stage of these is preceded by a magical rite, the essential feature of which is the utterance of spells. Here therefore we have language intervening in a skilled group technique, but once more its functions are mainly orectic. It is hardly used as a means of formulating, organizing, and directing the task in hand.

The craft is constructed by a group of men under the direction of an expert canoe-builder in a series of highly skilled techniques, traditional down to the last detail. There is little or no verbal direction as the men go about their business. It is a group activity exactly comparable with the work of a skilled individual craftsman who has no longer any need to formulate or symbolize to himself what he is doing. To this extent the work is without linguistic guidance. To the casual observer, the men's activities would appear to be almost intuitive ; everyone goes about his business as though he knows what he has to do, without instruction. No doubt this is something of an illusion. It is true that there is little or no instruction at the moment ; people learn by "joining in" with the others. But it is evident that while the expert canoe-builder was learning his craft, even though he acquired his skill mostly through a practical apprenticeship, yet verbal instruction must have played some part in his training. Again, before the building is taken in hand, there are probably discussions between the builder and the owner. Malinowski describes the elaborate and prolonged discussions that precede a Kula expedition [1] ; it would seem likely that similar discussions precede canoe-building.

But even if we allow that language probably played some part in the setting-up of the practical group techniques that constitute the task, important differences between such primitive group behaviour and our own group techniques remain. Our group tasks, both in preliminary training and actual conduct, are much more fully permeated by language. Further, we have detailed formulations of our techniques—specifications, blue-prints, instructions—which thereby become available for the awareness of the whole group engaged in the task, and even in the whole of the society.

These differences are emphasized by that one use of language which is no longer common in our societies : magic. And this, Malinowski insists—and it is a point of great importance for us here—is essentially a matter of uttered spells, the use of words. There are some accompanying rites, but these in fact are only the means by which the power of the magical words is directed upon and transferred to the canoe itself. " The spell is by far the most important constituent of magic. . . . It is the part of the magic which is kept secret and known only to the esoteric circle of practitioners. . . . The mind, *nanola*, by which term intelligence, power of discrimination, capacity for learning magical formulæ, and all forms of non-manual skill are described . . . resides somewhere in the larynx." [2] Evidently the Trobrianders are Behaviourists.

The natives, Malinowski tells us, understand well enough the respective functions of the skilled practical techniques and of the magic that accompanies them. " Both are considered indispensable, but both are understood to act independently. That is, the natives well understand that magic, however efficient, will not make up for bad workmanship. Each of these two has its own province : the builder by his skill and knowledge makes the canoe stable and swift, and magic gives it an additional stability and swiftness." [3] What, then, is the relation of the spell to the task in hand ?

[1] Malinowski AP 148   [2] the same 403, 408   [3] the same 115

The magic is a form of power. It is not, Malinowski tells us, an act of worship or a means of propitiating supernatural powers. The magical rite is for the most part conducted in a straightforward, non-ceremonial fashion ; to the onlooker it appears to be as much a part of the technical process as the carving of the prow or the caulking of the seams. Most of it "is carried out in a matter-of-fact businesslike manner, and nothing in the behaviour of the magician and those casually grouped round him would indicate that anything specially interesting in the routine work is happening." [1] The magician may perform a few simple rites, but the function of these is, as we have said, to convey the power of the spell and direct it upon the canoe and all the varied activities of which it will be the centre.

The magic thus resides in the spell ; it is by means of the spell that man draws upon a hidden source of power. This power is not one that man has captured from the supernatural, or discovered from among the secrets of Nature ; it is rather that in the remote past the mythical ancestor who first taught men to build canoes also taught them the spells. The magical words now spoken recapitulate the historic past of the clan, linking it with the present, and at the same time anticipate the future in expressing the desire of all the participants that their task may prosper, the canoe be stable, strong, and swift, and all its voyages fortunate. [2] The magic is thus an orectic utterance, recalling the past and anticipating the future. It is an expression of feeling and desire, but something more than mere expression, for it has the power of helping to bring about what is desired.

Our interpretation of Malinowski's facts is corroborated by his further observation that the spell is not a means of group *communication* : it is not a medium by which something is said by one person to another. The words are uttered in a low voice, and are unknown and unintelligible to all but the magician. Their orectic power lies in the fact that they are known to be magic. What the participants in the rite are aware of is the

[1] Malinowski AP 142   [2] the same 400-1

symbolic act by which the spell is conveyed to its object. The magician, for instance, speaks the spell into a banana leaf tied round the blade of the adze, so that his voice may be conveyed directly to the very substance of the tool and thus make it more efficient. All the participants know this, and while they are ignorant of the spells themselves, they see the symbolical rites that accompany them. These are not a verbal but a pictorial symbolization, which has the orectic function of making the group as a group conscious of its own feelings and desires, and so of heightening these and directing them upon the wished-for end.

We must notice therefore that in this most important practical activity of a primitive community, a skilled group technique, language has little or no cognitive group function ; it does not serve as a means by which the group as a group are made aware of what they do or of directing their behaviour in doing it. The routine of the group technique is traditional. To stimulate the participants, to arouse and heighten their incentives, there is constant mass-suggestion, chiefly by means of gestural and pictorial, non-verbal symbolism. It is at this point that language enters, in the form of magic ; it is an additional means of arousing and maintaining group orexis, by its appeal to tradition and its hopeful anticipation of the future.

8

The same absence of the cognitive functions of language is also seen in the wider aspects of primitive group behaviour, the general social and political organization of the group. Where a modern society is ruled by minute codification, the customs of a primitive society, rigid though they may be, are rarely codified. There is no formulation, in general terms, of a system of customs ; it is the customs themselves which are handed down. Malinowski tells us that among the Trobriand Islanders the customs and institutions of tribal life " are no-where formulated. There is no written or explicitly expressed code of laws, and their whole tribal tradition, the whole structure of their society, are embodied in the most elusive of all materials : the human being. But not even in human mind or memory are these laws to be found definitely formulated. . . . The regularities in native institutions are an automatic result of the interaction of the mental forces of tradition and of the material conditions of environment." [1]

This, of course, is not to say that the organization of such a primitive society will be loose and casual. On the contrary, it may be very complex ; but it will be held together by the orectic forces of tradition. One of the chief characteristics of primitive societies, as described by the ethnographers, is the remarkable success of their techniques for achieving the integration and direction of group orexis. Dances, ceremonies, rites, images—all, it is to be noted, pictorial rather than verbal symbols—serve to induce a very high level of integration of group orexis and to direct this into the customary channels of group behaviour.

But side by side with this high level of orectic integration there is, in contrast with our own societies, a remarkable absence of the formulation of group *motives*. Malinowski is emphatic on this point. The motives of the Trobrianders may become evident enough to an inquiring ethnographer ; they may possibly be envisaged by particular members of the group, the medicine-men, the magicians, or the chiefs ; but they are not symbolized in group linguistic communication. " Every man knows what is expected of him, in virtue of his position, and he does it ; whether it means the obtaining of a privilege, the performance of a task, or the acquiescence in a *status quo*." [2]

9

The intention of this survey of the behaviour of some primitive groups has not been to attempt to draw conclusions about primitive behaviour in general, but rather, by contrast, to focus attention on the facts of corresponding behaviour in our own societies. It is clear that in primitive society such as

[1] Malinowski AP 11   [2] the same 158–9

that of the Trobrianders the cognitive functions of language are much less fully developed than with us. This primitive group makes little or no use of language as a means of " turning back " upon its own behaviour. We can say that the group engages in group remembering and group imagining, permeated always with group feeling and desiring ; but that it hardly at all engages in group thinking. In the recall of the past, the exploration of the present, the planning of the future, and in actual, immediate, present activity, there is a marked absence of group verbal formulation—and therefore of group thinking—in comparison with our contemporary societies.

This means that although there may be a great deal of group mental behaviour in a primitive society, the society—as compared with our own societies—has much smaller provision for becoming aware of these aspects of its behaviour. Although much of the behaviour of the group may be mediated by symbols, these are comparatively rarely exact verbal symbols. Thus the behaviour of the group largely lies beyond the consciousness of the group *as a group*. There is, in effect, much subconscious or even unconscious group behaviour.

This further step in our analysis is obviously of such importance that we must consider it in some detail.

CHAPTER 6

LANGUAGE AND GROUP CONSCIOUSNESS

I

THE contrasts between primitive and modern societies, in group consciousness of group behaviour, emerge very clearly in each of the four fields that we have indicated in the last chapter : the recall of the past, the exploration of the spatially remote, the anticipation of the future, and the direction and conduct of actual practical activity.

In the recall of its past a primitive society differs from a modern " civilized " society in two important respects, both closely related to the nature of the existing linguistic communication ; group memory is limited and it is distorted. A society that possesses no written language has a limited field of awareness of its own past. G. and M. Wilson, from their observations in Central Africa, conclude that for the primitive communities there the period of historical continuity " is limited by the absence of traditions going back more than ten or twelve generations." [1] And even such history as is possessed by a primitive community tends of course to be distorted : there is myth instead of history. This does not mean that in a primitive society there is little group memory ; on the contrary, its past certainly operates most powerfully upon its present behaviour, but the past is taken up into the present in the form of traditionally determined custom. The past operates upon the present by way of the habits of the group rather than as a formulated group memory.

We have here in fact the exact parallel to the distinction made by Bergson in individual memory, the difference between " pure " and " habit " memory. In habit memory the past experiences of an individual are embodied in his present habits ; only in so far as he is conscious of these past experiences can

[1] Wilson SC 27

he be said to remember them, to have " pure " memory of them ; in our terms, only in so far as he is able to symbolize this past. In its customs, rites, ceremonial, and traditional techniques a primitive society has habits certainly determined by its past. It also has some remembering of its past ; but if this remembering is symbolized only by carvings, drawings, and other monuments—and if by language at all, only in highly pictorial spoken language—then group remembering will be both limited and distorted. The spoken language will operate in this way because the oral transmission of traditions tends inevitably to be pictorial and—as Bartlett has shown—to bring into high relief those features that are in accord with the predominant orectic tendencies of the society.

Group memory in a primitive society is likely therefore to be unconscious and subconscious, and only to a limited extent conscious. The group has unconscious memory of its past when, although its present behaviour is determined by its past, it has no symbolical formulation of this past. A group is subconscious of its past when it recalls this in a distorted and veiled fashion, in pictorial symbols, but where, nevertheless, the recall could be clarified and made more precise by verbal formulation. Only where a group—by examining and interpreting its monuments, myths, and traditions—achieves the formulation of its own history can it be said to have a conscious group memory.

In every group, therefore, the extent of consciousness of its own past is directly in proportion to the nature of the linguistic communication at its disposal. Where the language of recall is predominantly pictorial there can be little more than myth ; more abstract language—including the means of analysis and synthesis—extends the possibility of exact recall ; only a written language, however, provides the conditions for both an exact and an extended group consciousness of the past.

In all this we must distinguish clearly between individual and group memory of the past of the group. In any society a single individual, or a sub-group, may well be aware of the past of the society without there being, however, any formulation of this history for the society as a whole, and without there being, therefore, any conscious group memory of this past in the society as a whole. This in fact is often the case in a primitive society. Certain chosen men—the medicine men, the magicians, and to a lesser extent those skilled in the conduct of group techniques—are able to make some verbal formulation of portions of the history of the society. They are to that extent aware of the past, while the rest of the society have only an unconscious or subconscious memory of it.

In brief, "collective memory" in a group will be of the nature of habit memory so long as the behaviour of the group is confined to traditional routines. It begins to be true remembering when to this is added some pictorial symbolization of the past in the form of rite, monument, and myth. True remembering develops with greater clarity where there is analysis and synthesis of the past in the form of verbalized history ; its fuller and more exact development depends on the possibility of accurate and detailed written history.

2

In each of the other fields of group symbolization mentioned in the last chapter—the exploration of the spatially remote, the anticipation of the future, and the direction of present activity—the nature of the linguistic instrument is likewise reflected in the extent and exactness of group consciousness.

We have seen how, for instance, among the Swazis the symbolization of the spatially remote is carried out by means of the oral transmission of " news." Such a group—as compared with another lacking this institution—would have a relatively sharp formulation of its remoter environment, and to that extent a fairly precise consciousness of this. But if on the other hand we compare such a group with our own Western societies, it is evident that in the absence of written language, group awareness of environment would remain limited and fleeting and liable to pictorial distortion. As an extreme case, one can imagine a society whose awareness of its remoter environment is mediated only by non-verbal symbols. There is, for instance, little doubt that the transmission of "news" by the drum or the tom-tom in some primitive communities, while a powerful means of arousing feeling and putting the group in a state of readiness, conveys little or no precise information. A society possessing no other means of symbolizing its distant environment could have little or no *group* awareness of this. In brief, group unconsciousness, subconsciousness, or consciousness of spatial environment is in close relation with the nature of the instrument available for group communication symbolizing this environment.

Again, in the third, the anticipatory function of group communication, similar limitations in group cognition must result from the absence of written language and the predominance of pictorial symbolization in the spoken language. For as we have seen in the instance of the Trobrianders, where the details of a group technique are determined by custom, while there will be fairly precise formulation of familiar circumstances, there can be little scope for anticipatory planning to meet unfamiliar contingencies. The conference preliminary to an important enterprise will be a recall of what is well known from past experience, together with a full and highly developed orectic preparation for the enterprise. In contrast with this, in a modern society, planning for an important enterprise, while again often strongly orectic, would also aim at an analysis and synthesis of possible contingencies ; there would thus be an attempt at group cognition of the future.

Finally, and indeed as a result of all this, the limitations of group communication in the course of a group activity are likely to correspond to limitations of consciousness in the group in respect of its own group techniques. We have seen indications of this in the instance of warfare among the men of Malekula ; in that of an economic enterprise—canoe-building—among the Trobrianders ; and in that of the general political and social organization of the latter society. In these cases, where military, economic, and political techniques are determined in detail by custom, the group will tend to be unconscious, as a group, of the organization, direction, and conduct of its own group techniques, or at best subconscious of them. At the same time it will tend to be unaware of some of the orectic aspects of its behaviour, particularly of the true incentives that lie behind this.

All these well-attested characteristics of primitive communities throw into sharper relief the corresponding facts of our own modern societies. Here we find that there is a constant tendency to bring group consciousness to bear upon all group behaviour, and upon both its cognitive and its orectic aspects. We shall go on to show that the effects of these developments of group consciousness in modern society are, however, uneven. There is an increasing integration of the society in respect of the conduct of group techniques—economic, military, political. But in respect of group orexis, the immediate effect of increased group consciousness has been an increase of disintegration in the society and a greater potentiality of conflict. To show the fuller implications of these statements we shall now consider, in some detail, instances of group techniques and group orexis.

3

Group techniques in primitive societies are, as we have seen, typically carried on without immediate direction through group communication. To see the relation between this absence of communication and awareness by the group of its own techniques, let us look at another example.

Rivers describes how in the Solomon Islands a group of men will manage a boat, co-ordinating their actions perfectly without the aid of speech. "Whenever we were going ashore, five of the crew would row us in the whale-boat, four rowing and the fifth taking the steer-oar. As soon as we had announced our intention to go ashore, five of the crew would at once separate from the rest and man the boat ; one would go to the steer-oar and the others to the four thwarts. Never once was there any sign of disagreement or doubts which of the ship's company should man the boat, nor was there any hesitation who should take the steer-oar. . . . It is possible that there was some understanding by which the members of the crew arranged who should undertake the different kinds of work, but we could discover no evidence whatever of any such arrangement." [1]

How are we to explain this, and is there anything like it in our own modern societies? Rivers himself suggests an explanation and a parallel : " A speculative Melanesian who watched the traffic in the streets of a great English town would be greatly struck by the passage of the people on the pavements, in which the rarity of the jostling is to be explained by an immediate intuition of the movements of others." [2]

Rivers would appear to mean that in behaviour of this kind there is such delicacy of social adjustment that each member of the group is intuitively aware of the intentions of the rest, so that all act harmoniously together. And in the case of the Melanesians, at any rate, he thinks that the intuitive adjustment is the manifestation of an instinct, " using this much-misused word in the strict sense "—that is, as McDougall uses it : behaviour innately determined. Rivers is, in fact, prepared to maintain that even in so sophisticated a task as manning a boat the teamwork may be due to a group instinct.

But if we take the parallel case that he himself has suggested —the behaviour of townsmen in a street—this, so far from being instinctive, is one of the most obvious examples of habitual behaviour, the result of long training. It is a skilled group habit, exactly similar to a skilled habit in an individual. As we have seen, a man acquiring a skilled habit comes to depend less and less upon verbal symbols as aids in recalling and making the various constituent movements ; so that at last the habit works perfectly well without the need for any mediation of language at all. Habitual group behaviour shows an exactly similar course of development. Townsmen adjust their movements in a crowded street so skilfully, simply because as children they learned from a very early age to thread their way through jostling crowds. It has become a complex group habit in which each member acts unerringly without having to talk about it and without the need of intructions—that is, without group communication. Communication has certainly played its part while the habit was being formed ; the habit, once established, works perfectly well without any communication.

Need we suppose that things happen very differently in Melanesia ? No doubt the small Solomon Islanders soon begin to join in boating expeditions and learn the routine of all the necessary group behaviour. Who shall man the boat and who shall take the steering-oar becomes very much a matter of routine. But it is difficult to believe that the whole process of training can be entirely wordless.

The important point, then, is not that the languageless behaviour of the Solomon Islanders is instinctive while ours is due to training ; in both cases the routine of the group technique is the result of training. But there are noteworthy differences. We have so much less of languageless behaviour than they have ; in the process of training our techniques owe more to language than theirs ; once ours are established they are more likely to undergo the irruption of language. Take again Rivers' own example. Traffic in the street, as soon as it becomes crowded and complicated, demands the aid of communication ; symbols of all kinds, including words, become necessary. With motor cars on the road, so remote is the possibility of a purely intuitive co-operation of pedestrian, cyclist, and motorist that we devise an intricate system of lights, signs, and road markings—and policemen. The pedestrian or driver who relied upon his intuition and the delicacy of intuitive social adjustment, taking no heed of lights or signals, would soon be beyond the reach of either.

It is evident that in a modern society, language is intimately interwoven into every form of group behaviour. We have, it is true, forms of behaviour in which language plays only a minimal part, but it is to be noticed that these are usually the highly trained and closely organized behaviour of small groups only. Even in these cases, where language is relatively absent, other means of symbolization abound. A game of football, for instance, would appear to be like Rivers' instance of the whale-boat—a highly organized and intricate form of group behaviour, with a close harmony of co-operative action and delicate social adjustment. And it may be played relatively silently, without much formal communication. But notice the shouts of the players and the interjections of the referees, the deliberations of each team before the game and at half-time, and by way of non-linguistic symbols the markings on the ground and the corner flags.

All the instances in our societies of group action with the minimum of language tend to be of this kind : the highly organized co-operation of a small group, highly trained and performing a specific task. As soon as we get beyond these comparatively limited group skills, skills carried out by smaller specific groups within the larger society, as soon as we approach social behaviour concerned with the conduct and welfare of the society as a whole, the differences between modern and primitive societies become more pronounced. Our techniques of government are essentially deliberative, and proceed by the explicit formulation of decisions ; in primitive societies, we are told, the " deliberative " councils may largely dispense with explicit formulation of this kind. We have committees, councils, a Parliament—a body whose name hardly suggests silence, whose chief officer is a Speaker, and whose " acts " are words rather than deeds. But, Rivers tells us, " In the Councils [of the Islanders] there is no voting or other means of taking the opinion of the body. . . . When after a time the English observer has found that the people were discussing some wholly different topic, and has inquired when they were going to decide the question in which he was interested, he has been told that it had already been decided, and that they had passed to other business. . . . The members of the council have become aware at a certain point that they are in agreement, and it was not necessary to bring the agreement explicitly to notice." [1] Thus, even the decisions of a primitive group, following upon a

---

[1] Rivers IU 95

" discussion," need not be put into the form of a linguistic statement.

These differences between primitive societies and our own obviously mean important differences of group consciousness. Communication within a group concerning its group techniques means that its members are " thinking together " about these techniques. In a modern society the increase of linguistic communication is the increase of group planning and control of group tasks, leading to a higher level of technical integration.

3

But when we come to the group consciousness of group orexis the case is rather different. Certainly a modern society is much more aware than a primitive society of the processes of arousing and maintaining orexis. A modern society formulates its " motives " to itself. Yet, as we shall show, the higher degree of awareness of group orexis does not lead to a higher degree of orectic integration ; but rather to an increase of disintegration and conflict. It is the primitive, not the modern society, that is well integrated in orexis.

To bring out this contrast let us look first at the nature of group orexis. As we have already pointed out,[1] the integration of feeling in a group is not limited to the arousal of the " same " feeling in its members, as would appear to be suggested by the hypotheses of " primitive passive sympathy " or " telepathy." The plain fact is that we are not in a position to say whether the expression, for instance, of anger does or does not arouse the " same " feeling in others. What, however, is clear is this. When symbols arouse, maintain, and direct the orectic behaviour of a group so that a fuller integration is reached, this occurs not by the induction or the arousal of the same feeling in each of its members, but rather by the interaction of their orectic responses to the symbols and to each other. Just as group cognition moves and develops within a group by opposition and agreement, so

[1] page 105 above

in group orexis there are interaction and mutual responses. The symbols, and the responses to them, become what Miller and Dollard have called " crowd stimuli." [1] Further, we must always remember that orexis and cognition are no more than two aspects of the same mental behaviour. The mutual inter-weaving of response and stimulus includes both orexis and cognition.

Now, in a primitive group, where the language that arouses orexis is largely pictorial, and there is little or no formulation of the orectic behaviour, two results tend to follow. First, the power of arousing orexis is felt to lie in the words themselves ; and second, attention is withdrawn from the true incentives that impel the group in their behaviour.

To illustrate the first point : among the Trobrianders, " the belief in the efficacy of a formula resides in various peculiarities of the language in which it is couched, both as regards meaning and sound. The native is deeply convinced of this mysterious, intrinsic power of certain words ; words which are believed to have their value in their own right, so to speak ; having come into existence from primeval times and exercising their influence directly." [2] The group is moved more by the sounds and forms of the words than by any clear meaning these may convey. Malinowski describes a group of natives awaiting the visit of men from another island, who chant their magic as their canoes approach the shore. " The Dobuans know that powerful forces are at work upon them. They must feel the wave of magical influence slowly advancing, spreading over their villages. . . . They can guess the murmur of the many voices. . . . They know what is expected of them, and they rise to the occasion. On the part of the approaching party this magic, the chant of the many voices, blended with the conch-shell, expresses their hopes and desires and their rising excitement." [3]

The natives will, of course, realize that their feelings have been aroused by the words they have heard and uttered. But if one of them is asked how this comes about, he will probably

[1] page 105 above   [2] Malinowski AP 451   [3] the same 345

reply that it is because the words have a magical power. And, in effect, this is true ; the " magical " words become efficacious in a society that believes them to be magically efficacious. In addition, there is a strong reinforcement of this belief by social heredity : the magical power of certain words has been impressed upon every individual growing up in the society. As Malinowski tells us, the spell brings magic to bear upon an intended act by recalling the ancient origin of the magical power of the spell ; in this way, he says, magic " acts as a link between the mythical and actual realities." [1] The magical words have orectic power because they link the present group with its mythical past. When, engaging in some enterprise, the group feel themselves weak and insecure in the face of the unknown, perhaps hostile forces of their environment, magic brings a sense of security bequeathed by the superhuman knowledge and skill of ancestors in the heroic past.

This means also that the attention of the group is turned away from the deeper orectic sources of its behaviour ; there is an absence of group consciousness of group motives. The primary incentive is the weight of tradition and custom. Thus, if an outsider—the ethnographer, for instance—inquires within the group why these things are done, there is no answer beyond this, that these are the things that have always been done. " The natives obey the forces and commands of the tribal code, but they do not comprehend them ; exactly as they obey their instincts, but could not lay down a single law of psychology. . . . The native can neither get outside his tribal atmosphere and see it objectively, nor if he could, would he have intellectual and linguistic means sufficient to express it." [2] It is the ethnographer who, by reflection on the observations he has made from outside, " brings to light phenomena of human nature which, in their entirety, had remained hidden even from those in whom they happened." [3] In other words, the group behaviour of the society is moved by incentives that are certainly group incentives in that they are the result of stimulation and interaction within the group ; but these incentives are not

[1] Malinowski AP 328   [2] the same 12, 454   [3] the same 397

122

formulated in group communication, so that there is little or no group consciousness of group motives.

When we turn from a primitive society such as this to our modern civilized societies, no contrast could be more striking. In a modern society, attention is constantly being drawn to the nature of communication, and hence to the relation between language and its effects upon group orexis. There is constant analysis and discussion of the power of the radio and the press ; the group, as a group, is made aware of the working of its own group symbols. Side by side with this, and in part arising from it, there is a constant discussion, and so a growing awareness, of group motives. But it is important to recognize that this is usually far from being a total awareness. The spotlight of group consciousness plays upon group motives in such a way that only some, and again only parts of these, are made available for the group. It is this partial consciousness, together with a growing consciousness of the relation between group symbols and group orexis, that tends to foster orectic disintegration in modern societies.

In the chapters that follow we shall consider the effects of increasing linguistic communication, and therefore group consciousness, upon group techniques and group orexis in the economic, military, political, and social tasks of our modern societies.

PART THREE

LANGUAGE IN MODERN SOCIETIES

CHAPTER 7

LANGUAGE IN INDUSTRY AND WARFARE

I

ONE of the chief characteristics of modern societies is the development of group skills. Lewis Mumford in *Technics and Civilization* has shown that the advent of the machine to replace the individual means a parallel change in group behaviour— the transformation of the loosely organized group into the more rigid machine-group. Instead of the craftsman at the forge, the loom, or the bench, working maybe in co-operation with other craftsmen, there is a group of men and machines interacting to carry out a specific task. And these machine-groups tend to become larger and larger, so that even a single specific task may involve a wide and intricate co-ordination of effort in which even a vast factory is only a single unit.

This kind of group action is characteristic not only of modern industry but also of the two other major pre-occupations of a society : warfare and politics. In each of these three fields—economic, military, political—group techniques are devised and developed for the purpose of the group action necessary for the welfare of the society.

Mumford's analysis of industrial group techniques is close and detailed, but there is one point that he—in common with many other sociologists—does not sufficiently emphasize : among all the group techniques language occupies a special place ; language is the technique that stands behind all the other techniques. Group language is the essential condition of group action. If the growth of linguistic communication owes much to machines, it is certainly true that machines owe everything to the growth of communication. The " machine-groups " constituted by men working with machines can function only in virtue of the linguistic communication that links its members. Our task here is to notice the relation between this technique of communication and the other group techniques.

In any group technique there are three possible ways in which the group may be organized for its behaviour : the division and specialization of labour, the automatization of function, and the direction of the group technique by group awareness. These three forms of functioning may be seen with particular clearness in the history of industry, where they appear as three successive phases of group organization. The general pattern of change is this : first, the division of labour as a means of securing a higher degree of efficiency through specialization ; secondly, the consequent automatization of techniques ; and finally, the ebbing of this automatization in favour of growing awareness in the group of its own techniques.

At each of these three phases linguistic communication is a primary means by which group techniques, at that phase, are made possible. At the first stage it is largely through language that the division of labour can be planned and each constituent member of the group instructed in his specific function in the group task. Each worker may also have some awareness of the group task as a whole, although usually this will hardly be necessary for the efficient performance of his own specific work. Corresponding to this simple structure of group organization, the pattern of group communication will be correspondingly simple. The spoken word alone may suffice ; or, where the group task is more intricate, some degree of literacy in the written word may become necessary; although for most of the workers even this need not extend beyond the rudiments of reading, writing, and reckoning.

When the second stage supervenes, and with the advent of machines the group itself becomes something of a machine, the awareness of the individual worker is withdrawn from the details of his own task—which the machine now performs for him—and from the group task as a whole. There are corresponding changes in the functions of linguistic communication. On the one hand, the task of the individual worker becomes relatively languageless, while at the same time the group task becomes too extensive and too intricate for him to be able to formulate it in words and so reach clear awareness of its complexity. The machine-minder will need to use language in his work much less than his skilled forbear in the first phase of the division of labour. On the other hand, with growing automatization, the need for supervision will increase ; for as the worker's task becomes automatic he loses the power of adaptation to the unusual circumstance. The responsibility for initiative and change passes to the overseers. Thus the automatization of techniques among the many brings ultimately the need for a full consciousness of techniques by a few. The operative " hands " carry out their tasks without much need of awareness, while the " heads " do little but supervise and co-ordinate their work. The hands toil without thinking and the heads think without toiling.

At this second stage, then, the function of communication takes a new direction. A high degree of literate education becomes essential for the managing élite, while the majority of the toiling masses need only that minimum which will enable them to obey instructions. There will be an increase in the size of the élite and a raising of the standards of literacy for them. In a society in which some of this élite are allowed to emerge from the ranks of the workers, this may tend to ensure that general literacy is kept at an acceptable level.

Finally, as group techniques become larger, more elaborate, and more complex, the necessity of a more delicate adjustment and co-ordination of the group technique tends to bring about the advent of the third stage, where even many of the toilers are called upon to think about their joint task as one whole. This means that for the mass of the people a higher degree of literacy becomes necessary : a growing number are expected to acquire some technical knowledge of a much wider field of the group technique than their own personal tasks. With this, some of the supervisory function now flows from the centres of direction to the "hands" performing the work. In other words, communication is extended and developed throughout the working group, so that in the group there is an increase of formulation of the work of the group.

Thus, throughout the changes in the extent and development of group communication we see concomitant changes in the extent and development of group awareness. In the first stage each member of the group is aware of his specific task, so that he may co-operate with the rest ; there may also be some individual awareness of the group technique as a whole. With the growing complexity of the group task and its automatization in the second phase, consciousness is withdrawn from the individual members of the group to a few centres of direction—the overseers and the managers ; so that in extreme cases some of the workers may cease to exercise any conscious guidance even of their specific tasks. In the third phase consciousness once more tends to flow out into all the constituent members of the group, demanding from each some awareness of the group technique. Only rarely will there be a group awareness of the whole of the group technique in all its complexity ; there is more likely to be some specialization in the function of thinking, with only an imperfect integration of the thinking of the sub-groups into the thinking of the complete group. Nevertheless, with the development of this third stage there begins to dawn the possibility of group awareness of a complex group technique.

So far we have described the three-phase pattern of change in very general terms. We shall now go on to observe the three phases as they actually occur in modern industry and in modern warfare.

2

At the beginning of the Industrial Revolution it was Adam Smith who coined the phrase " the division of labour " to describe the organization of a group technique to replace traditional individual techniques. More fully and accurately, this should be described as the specialization and integration of labour within a group. Both of these are, of course, inevitable wherever there is the development of any group technique, however rudimentary ; for instance, there is some specialization and integration of tasks in Rivers' instance of the five islanders manning their whale-boat. But the division of labour characteristic of the Industrial Revolution is not only an increase in the intricacy and extent of specialization, but the introduction of machines to replace the individual ; and this is the crucial change.

Adam Smith's own classical example brings out with great clearness all these three features of the division of labour : specialization, integration, and the use of machines. In times past a single craftsman at his bench would laboriously fashion a pin. Now " one man draws out the wire, another straights it, a third cuts it, a fourth points it, a fifth grinds it at the top for receiving the head ; to make the head requires two or three distinct operations ; to put it on is a peculiar business, to whiten the pins is another ; it is even a trade by itself to put them into the paper ; and the important business of making a pin, is, in this manner, divided into about eighteen distinct operations." [1]

Certainly here is the division and specialization of labour, but this alone does not make the group technique. Without the integration of all the specialized tasks into a unified task the whole process would not be worth a pin. Further, as Adam Smith emphasizes, an inevitable result of this specialization is the invention of machines to replace many of the particular specialized tasks ; in other words, the beginning of automatization.

What is the relation of communication to this organization of a group technique ? As an extreme case, it is conceivable that a craftsman might learn to make a pin by imitation alone, without a word being spoken. But in the working of a group

[1] Smith WN bk. i ch. i

technique by the division of labour some language is essential. Because each specialized task is incomplete, and has therefore less meaning than a complete craft, the individual worker must be instructed ; the overseers must be able to give instructions and the workers able to understand them.

Thus the first phase in the development of industrial group techniques—the phase of the " division of labour "—brings with it the necessity of a slight but marked increase of literacy ; this may be only a literacy of the spoken word or it may extend to reading and writing. Instead of acquiring a craft by long-continued day-by-day participation in the routine of the field, the forge or the home, the worker now must learn his specialized task through the aid of words heard and spoken, perhaps read and written.

At this stage the worker is still a craftsman ; the machines he uses are instruments to aid him in his craft ; his task is still skilled and far from being fully automatized. Some power of formulating his own task may be valuable in that it may enable him to modify his procedure within the limits of the specialized function assigned to him in the division of labour.

With the development of machines, industry moves into its second phase : automatization, both of individual and of group technique. Half a century after the publication of *The Wealth of Nations* Andrew Ure, the ingenuous apologist of the factory system, was pointing out that the division of labour had given place to the " equalization " of labour ; that is, specialization of function was moving towards automatization. The great object of the factory system now was to train " human beings to renounce their desultory habits of work, and to identify themselves with the unvarying regularity of the complex automaton. . . . When Adam Smith wrote his immortal elements of economics, automatic machinery being hardly known, he was properly led to regard the division of labour as the grand principle of manufacturing improvement. . . . But what was in Dr. Smith's time a topic of useful illustration cannot now be used without risk of misleading the public mind as to the right principle of manufacturing industry. In fact the division, or rather adaptation, of labour to the different talents of men is little thought of in factory employment. On the contrary, wherever a process requires peculiar dexterity and steadiness of hand, it is withdrawn as soon as possible from the *cunning* workman, who is prone to irregularities of many kinds, and it is placed in charge of a peculiar mechanism so self-regulating that a child may superintend it." [1]

To replace the craftsman by a machine, so that the group technique becomes a mechanized technique and the group a machine-group, working with the smooth precision of an automaton—this, says Ure, has become the ideal of the factory system. Now it became apparent that a major impediment in the smooth running of the machine-group was the presence of the intelligent craftsman, the worker with insight into his own task and the initiative to attempt to modify it. "By the infirmity of human nature it happens," says Ure, "that the more skilful the workman, the more self-willed and intractable he is apt to become, and, of course, the less fit a component of a mechanical system, in which by occasional irregularities he may do great damage to the whole. The grand object of the modern manufacturer is, through the union of capital and science, to reduce the task of his work people to the exercise of vigilance and dexterity." [2]

The less skilful the better the workman. Certainly at this stage of industrial development there is no sense in increasing the literacy of the working classes. If anything, it might be diminished, now that the " grand object of the modern manufacturer " is to turn the craftsman into an automaton—were it not for another factor inherent in the development of this second phase : the increase in size and complexity of the working unit. Just as in the first phase the single worker had been replaced by many, so now the single workshop was replaced by many workshops, the single factory by many factories, all working together to produce a single commodity. A group technique might now cover a vast and intricate system. In-

[1] Ure PM 15, 19   [2] the same 21

stead of a single centre of direction, a multiplicity of centres ; instead of one overseer, a system of overseers. As the task of the individual worker grew simpler and more automatic, the group task as a whole grew more complex, and a greater degree of insight was demanded of those who directed it. More and more the individual worker became a machine-minding machine ; no longer creative himself, his task was limited to ensuring that nothing should impede the creative work of the machine. With this was reached the utmost limit of the withdrawal of individual consciousness from the performance of work ; the minder had become unconscious of the process of the work, for this process had now been transferred to another body—the body of the machine.

But while the worker has less need of language for the performance of his individual task, he has a somewhat greater need of it in order to understand and obey the instructions of the overseer. The worker must be rather more ready to understand and respond to the spoken word. And as he takes his place in an economy whose greater complexity demands an increase in the use of the written word, he needs a minimum, at any rate, of written literacy. Finally, there is a greater demand for overseeing minds, for whom a correspondingly higher degree of literacy must be provided. This means an extension of the field from which they can be drawn.

So we come to the period of universal " elementary " education, together with highly selective " secondary " education. It becomes necessary to give the population as a whole a literacy deep enough to provide the possibility of selecting an élite of about ten per cent. ; the number of " special places " being stringently kept within these bounds by carefully devised tests. In Britain, for instance, in the first two or three decades of this century, the sieve was adjusted so as to retain for secondary education about half a million children out of a total school population of about ten times that number.

To-day, however, we find a slow but marked movement in the direction of a third phase. There is a growing demand for an extension of technical education for everyone engaged in industry, the demand that each worker, however limited and automatic the task he performs, shall command literacy over a field wider than this task alone. It is seen now that the full integration of a group technique in industry demands some awareness in the group of the task of the group. There must be a technique of communication throughout the group commensurate in range and complexity with the industrial techniques of the group.

In Britain this realization has taken the form of a demand for "secondary education for all," a demand that began to make itself heard almost as soon as the special place system had been set on its feet. It was not, however, until the Act of 1944 that any attempt was made to give a practical reply to this demand. The special place system was formally abolished and every child given the right to a secondary education suited to his "age, aptitude, and ability."

It is important to notice that this extension of literacy is not only an effect of the third phase of industrial technique, but also a necessary condition of its development. The extension and integration of an industry do not depend on economic conditions alone ; linguistic communication of adequate complexity is also necessary. Mumford points out that before the advent of the telephone, productive units certainly grew in size, but their efficiency did not keep pace with their growth. On the contrary, they were "afflicted with giantism ; they increased in size and agglomerated together without attempting to scale size to efficiency. In part this grew out of the defective system of communication which antedated the telephone ; this confined efficient administration to a single manufacturing plant and made it difficult to disperse the several units." [1] In brief, efficient communication is the prime condition of efficient development of a group technique. And it is only in the presence of a highly developed system of communication throughout a society that it becomes possible to achieve a sensitive and effective integration of industrial techniques in the society.

[1] Mumford TC 224

3

To-day, therefore, in those societies in which there is a new development of industrial organization, group communication is at once seen to be the one indispensable technique. The Linguistic Revolution becomes part of an industrial revolution. The first step in the development of industry must be the extension of literacy. In Africa, for instance, the attempt is being made at this moment to initiate and foster co-operative techniques in agriculture. The first step is seen to be the promotion of reading and writing. The Advisory Committee of the Colonial Office on Mass Education in Africa (1943) says : " So far, in the British Colonies, we have acted on the assumption that people would eventually adopt improved methods of agriculture . . . without learning to read and write." But all the evidence, they continue, shows the futility of this assumption. Universal adult literacy is the first essential in the organization of a community for the improvement of techniques of living, and all literacy must be specifically directed towards these techniques. " The content of the material used in teaching reading and writing should be related to the people's needs and interests, and it should assist in stimulating their desire to improve and control the conditions in which they live." [1]

This is true at all levels of complexity throughout all industry. No community to-day can be organized to make full use of its economic resources except on the basis of universal literacy ; and with the development of the means of spoken communication, this literacy must include not only reading and writing, but also listening and speaking.

It is the U.S.S.R. that at this moment is giving us the fullest and most detailed picture of a realization of all this and its immediate practical application. Here we have an enormous acceleration of industrialization at a time when the Linguistic Revolution has already begun to provide the means

[1] *Report* pp. 14, 17

of intricate and extensive communication. The three phases of industrial organization have been accelerated and foreshortened into a single phase. Communities that before the Revolution were still working with the minimum of the division and specialization of labour have, in one bound, been called upon to operate group techniques with full group awareness of them.

In *The Russian Peasant* (1942), Maynard describes the linguistic changes that have accompanied the industrialization of agriculture. Once it has been brought home to the people that literacy is the first condition of success in modern co-operative agriculture, in the multitude of isolated villages throughout the wide farmlands of the Union, peasants old and young have been avid to master the written word. Meanwhile automatization of farming has been growing through the introduction of the tractor. But—a striking fact—the Machine Tractor Stations are not only centres of mechanization, they are increasingly centres of education. As the workers learn how to use machines they learn how to live in the modern world. They are being given the means of exercising supervision over their own work : in each group there is a growing awareness of the technique of the group. In the words of Epstein, an official exponent of the aims of Soviet education : the intention is to produce " men who have completely mastered the technique of their labour . . . and so bring the Soviet State nearer that remarkable period when the borderline between mental and physical labour will have been finally eradicated." [1]

In this way the three phases of development have been concentrated into a co-ordinated advance on a single front : the division of labour, the automatization of the task and the inception of group awareness are taking place side by side, so that the literacy necessary for the first phase has been the foundation of the fuller literacy necessary for the third.

And this literacy is a literacy of the spoken as well as of the written word. Over the wide spaces of the steppe, where travel

[1] *Year Book of Education* (London) 1937, 786

is difficult, meetings of the overseers of the collective farms take the form of radio and telephone discussions. Mrs. Seema Allan describes in *Comrades and Citizens* (1938) a " meeting " of farm chairmen : " I found Natashin [the Political Director at Plavsk] sitting before the microphone in the little broadcasting room at the telephone exchange. He was interviewing the farm chairmen—but they were all sitting snugly at their telephones in villages scattered miles out over the frozen steppe. It was a wired broadcast using radio equipment and the telephone network. Each listener could talk with Plavsk, and each could hear what the others said." [1]

Here, then, in the U.S.S.R. the development of group techniques in agriculture and industry has advanced most rapidly precisely because the leaders have been quick to realize the necessity of providing these group techniques with an adequate system of group communication.

It is evident that linguistic communication and economic techniques are interdependent. In the modern world, the elaboration of spoken and written literacy has come about not only because of the existence of the physical means—the schools, the press, the radio—but no less because of the indispensability of developed forms of linguistic communication for the working of modern economic techniques. Group language develops within these techniques because they are highly integrated. At the same time, it is because of the development of group language that the techniques are themselves highly integrated, and that they operate with an increasing measure of group consciousness.

It cannot be too strongly emphasized that this group consciousness is inseparably wedded to language. Just as in the individual, consciousness works in and through symbols, verbal and other, so group consciousness works in and through group symbols. In the group the physical means of communication provides the network in and through which symbolic communication operates. The physical network makes possible group symbols which in turn give birth to group mind.

[1] Allan CC 173

4

The history of warfare shows the same three phases in the development of group techniques as the history of industry : the specialization of function, followed by automatization, from which there finally emerges group awareness of the group technique. Of course, there are differences. Group technique in industry is a modern invention. But fighting is man's oldest profession, so that wherever we encounter warfare, even in primitive communities, we find it already fashioned into group techniques, if only of the most rudimentary kind. Men go out in bands to attack and plunder, and unite to defend their homes.

Where, then, is the beginning of the specialization of technique in fighting? In industry, as Ure pointed out, there may be some *division* of labour wherever there are tools, but *specialization* develops only with the advent of the machine. How, then, does a tool differ from a machine? A tool is a means by which a man may perform an act more powerful, or of wider range and of greater precision, than with his unaided arm ; a tool becomes a machine when it begins to be self-operating. In using a tool a man supplies both the power and the direction, so that a tool, as Samuel Butler said, is only a means of lengthening one's arm. But in a machine the motive force is engendered within the body of the instrument itself, and the operations may even be directed from within this body once the machine is set in motion. Moreover, the more precise and powerful the machine, the narrower the task of the man who minds it ; specialization follows the machine.

Warfare provides an exact parallel. Tools in warfare are those weapons by which man is enabled to engage in destruction more powerful, of wider range, and of greater precision than with his unaided arm. A sling is a better tool than a hand-flung stone, a bow better than a sling. The machines of war are its self-operating weapons. The simplest machine of war is the gun ; and all the machines of war—from the crudest cannon firing stones up to the atomic bomb—are guns.

In warfare, as in industry, specialization follows the machine. In this country, for example, the beginning of specialization in warfare occurred, we are told, in the thirteenth century. Fighters became specialists, and an army—for the first time since the Roman Empire—an organized body of varied arms. But what is not often noticed is that this was the moment of the invention of the first machine of war. The earliest known representation of a gun in this country is said to be dated 1326. It fired arrows.

The bow had been a military tool—a tool of great power and precision, but still a tool, in that the motive force of the propulsion lay in the strong arm of the archer. But the arrow-firing gun was a machine, with the force of propulsion engendered within its own body by the explosion of the charge. The invention of the gun is thus the true beginning of the mechanization of warfare ; that is, of the automatization of military group techniques. The transformation of the loosely-organized band of fighters into the military machine began, therefore, much earlier than the mechanization of industry. Perhaps even, as Mumford suggests, it was warfare that furnished industry with the model of the division, specialization, and mechanization of labour. The first machines, he points out, were the machines of war ; and it was warfare that showed the possibility of a body of drilled men acting together to achieve a co-ordinated task.[1]

On the other hand, the automatization of military techniques, because of the sporadic and intermittent nature of warfare, developed slowly. Six centuries have elapsed from the first use of the gun in this country, but it is only to-day that we see the dawning of the third phase in our military techniques. During these six centuries of growing automatization there are two moments of critical change : the development of machine-like precision in drill in the seventeenth century and the invention of new complex machines of war in the nineteenth.

Cromwell's New Model Army, often taken to be the turning-point in the development of warfare in this country, marks a

[1] Mumford TC 89

great advance in the organization of group technique in warfare, and the perfection of the military unit as a machine. "The New Model," says Sheppard, "was in every way the finest military machine of its day. . . . It seems that Cromwell's military reputation would be more surely founded on his predominant share in the fashioning of this terrible instrument of war than on his methods of conducting a campaign or a battle." [1]

Apparently it comes quite naturally to the historian of warfare to call an army a machine. In warfare, as in industry, the continued use of machines thus brought into being the machine-group. Drill and discipline, implicit obedience. Part of the machine-group, the soldier himself was to be a machine that, once set in motion by the word of command, would move unerringly to its goal or perish. Theirs not to reason why, theirs but to do and die ; the official poet of mid-nineteenth-century England paid tribute to the military automaton in words that were to become its epitaph. For in the very year of Tennyson's poem, 1856, Armstrong produced the first of his inventions that were to transform the gun and with it modern warfare ; it was the beginning of the final stage of full automatization. It is significant that almost at the same moment the first Staff College was instituted : 1858.

Armstrong's inventions were the beginning of complete mechanization ; the Staff College was the recognition of the need to provide training for the directors of the growing complexity of the military machine. As in industry, so in warfare. With the growth of mechanization there is the need for a minimum of literacy in each member of the fighting unit —the private soldier ; while at the same time there is the necessity for a higher degree of literacy in those who lead, who have the control of the complex task and who have therefore to be able to formulate its processes and issue instructions. Colleges for officers become imperative. Thus the second phase develops and takes on its characteristic pattern of organization.

[1] Sheppard SH 16

And again, as in industry, the second phase carries within it both the germs of its own decay and the seeds of the phase that must supersede it. The automatization of warfare makes possible larger fighting units—larger armies and navies dispersed over wider fields of campaign. To make these efficient, new means of communication are sought. These again make possible a further increase in the size and complexity of the fighting unit. But there comes a moment, as in industry, when the organization outgrows its system of communication. The organization is too large for its brain. The only hope of survival is through the further development of a brain and nervous system large enough and intricate enough to serve the needs of the gigantic and complex organism. In other words, there comes a moment when it is indispensable to institute a higher degree of group awareness throughout the fighting group. The third phase is in sight.

Perhaps the extreme limit of automatization, coupled with inadequate means of communication, was reached in the First World War. At sea the immobility of the fleets, on land the inane yet bloody attrition of trench warfare—these were symptoms that the group technique had, from its size and complexity, stultified itself. This is the theme of a series of essays by Holland Rose on the " indecisiveness of modern war." " It is not too much to say," he tells us, " that by the year 1914 scientific discoveries had outpaced the ability of man either to gauge their efficacy or to work them all with full confidence. Man has become more and more the victim of the mechanism he has created. He is in the grip of his own mechanical monster, for his powers have not developed *pari passu*. Rather have they been dwarfed by the feeling of his own impotence. Also, commanders-in-chief are apt to be oppressed by a sense of overwhelming responsibility when wielding the vast and complex mechanism of modern war ; and to this fundamental cause may be ascribed the reason why campaigns, in proportion to the masses employed, have become singularly barren of decisive results." [1] Warfare had become

[1] Rose IW 5

afflicted with the same disease, giantism, that Mumford has diagnosed as the cause of the inanition of industry in the corresponding phase of economic development.

The automatized war machine, the final stage of which had begun with the work of Armstrong in the middle of the previous century, had to develop a more elaborate nervous system or perish. In Britain, as elsewhere, the techniques of warfare therefore entered upon the third phase—group awareness. As the army becomes more mechanized, it becomes more necessary for the individual soldier to understand something of the intricate machines he tends, something of the nature and direction of the technique in the group of which he is one, something of the progress of the battle, something even of the nature and direction of the war. It is the beginning of group awareness in warfare, the pervasion of consciousness throughout a technique whose central ideal for so long had been drill ; the negation of individual and group awareness, and the highest degree of mechanical precision for the majority of its participants.

5

In warfare as in industry, communication takes on a characteristic form and has specific functions at each phase of development. Since the soldier is traditionally illiterate it may at first sight seem absurd to emphasize the functions of literacy in warfare, and a paradox to suggest that each phase in the development of military group technique demands a higher degree of literacy than the corresponding phase in industry. But this is undoubtedly true if we remember that there are degrees of spoken as well as of written literacy. Group techniques in warfare constantly demand an all-pervasive use of the spoken word, because of the frightful penalty for allowing the techniques to become so automatized that they are unable to meet the unforeseen contingency.

Comparing warfare with industry, phase by phase, it is clear that while specialization of function in industry cannot be set up without some use of the spoken word, uttered and understood, once the worker has been trained in his specialized task he may go on from day to day with little or no need for communication. He knows what he has to do ; there may be a good deal of talk in the workshop, but it need have nothing to do with the work. In warfare, however, not only does the training of the soldier call for a vast expenditure of language, as any sergeant-major will testify ; all the time that the soldier is actually at work, in the heat of the battle, he must be given his orders from moment to moment.

The history of warfare shows that it must never be allowed to become as completely automatized as industry. As armies became organized they accumulated a rich store of technical terms. Indeed, the earliest technical terms employed in any group technique were those of the soldier, not of the worker. Long before the factory had its few " terms of art," warfare had acquired a rich vocabulary of technical terms and idioms. In 1598, for instance—a generation or so before the birth of the New Model Army—Barret, in his *Theorike and Praktike of Moderne Warres*, gives a list of more than two hundred military words and phrases then in current use.[1] Long before industry had its rudimentary means of communication, every battlefield had a complicated apparatus of signallers and dispatch-riders. And if the organisms of modern industry are kept alive, as we have seen, by an increasing circulation of paper through their arteries, certainly instantaneous and world-wide communication is the life-blood of modern warfare.

The traditional illiteracy of the common soldier, up to the beginning of the third phase in the history of military techniques, was an illiteracy of the written word only. During the Napoleonic Wars, for instance, probably two-thirds of the British army was illiterate, as compared with one-third of the general population.[2] And as late as 1900 H. G. Wells could say that the army cherished the tradition that its privates were illiterate.[3] But we must notice that even in Wellington's

---

[1] *Journ. Soc. Army Hist. Res.* (1932) 149
[2] Fortescue HB xi 16 ; Young VE 59   [3] Wells A 96

time this could only have been true of literacy in reading and writing : in a highly drilled army the literacy of the common soldier is a spoken literacy. He does not need the art of writing, and as for the art of reading, this might be dangerous—he might begin to reason and so perhaps be less ready to do and die. On the other hand, he is specifically and highly trained to respond to the spoken word ; no other work demands so ready and so precise a response to language.

Further automatization, however, with the increased size of the fighting unit and devolution of command, demands an elaboration of written literacy among the officers. Tactics and strategy ; these cannot exist without a close and constant interchange of written orders, maps, diagrams, reports, dispatches. One of the main functions of a Staff College is to provide the direction of warfare with these linguistic instruments. So much attention, indeed, may be given to perfecting them that they become an end in themselves. Here a characteristic weakness of automatized group techniques shows itself. The direction and control of the technique may become too centralized. The functioning of the central brain may become too rigid, too much the victim of habit. The theory of warfare may be too much the subject of rule ; the planning of a campaign too detailed ; the central control, in fact, too highly systematized for its task of directing and co-ordinating what should be a flexible group technique. As Tolstoy is never tired of repeating in *War and Peace*, what is planned at headquarters may entirely fail to operate in the heat and turmoil of the battle, where the unexpected always happens.

In a word, the techniques of warfare tend to be permeated by communication incomparably more than industrial techniques. As a result, warfare is a highly literate occupation, relying upon spoken literacy in its early phases, and later demanding a high degree of written literacy, at any rate among those in command. And when, as to-day, warfare passes into its third phase, that of group awareness, this means that even written literacy becomes a universal necessity for all those engaged in it. The enormous increase in the use of the spoken and the written word in warfare to-day is in itself one of the main currents in the Linguistic Revolution.

Thus already very early in the Second World War it became impossible to tolerate any illiteracy at all in the British Army. As we have seen, the two per cent. or so who were completely illiterate were sent back to school to acquire at any rate the rudiments of reading and writing. As soon, in fact, as the literacy of the written word becomes a necessary instrument of general communication in military group technique, there can be no exceptions. Every soldier must be able to read and write, and a professional army may have to become more literate than the general population.

As for the spoken word, nowhere in industrial or political group techniques has this taken over such important functions as in modern warfare. Contrast, for instance, the " theirs not to reason why " of the Crimean War with a rapidly developing innovation of our contemporary war, instruction of the troops in the progress of the fighting. Communication on the field of battle is now more than a primary instrument of an auto-matized technique, the means of giving orders. To-day, com-munication, principally in the form of radio, is indispensable as a means of maintaining group awareness of the conditions and purposes of the group technique. Perhaps the most striking instance—because it marks so profound a change in age-long habits and attitudes—is the novel practice of broadcasting throughout a ship, in the thick of a naval engagement, con-tinued information of the progress of the battle. Admiral Kirk, Commander of the U.S.A. task force in the Sicilian operations in 1944, believing that " our soldiers and sailors are better for knowing the score," had on his flagship a broadcaster entrusted with the task of keeping the men informed of what was going on.[1]

All this means that with the complete mechanization of warfare and the gigantic growth in size of the fighting unit and of the field of operations, the group techniques are possible only if there is linguistic communication throughout the whole group ; this means group awareness. The individual fighter

[1] London *Observer* May 28, 1944

is no longer a unit. As a fighter what he does ceases to have meaning except in relation to the acts of a group, which may be as small as a gun-crew or air-crew or as large as an army. There is little scope for initiative except as a means of making his fighting *unit* more effective—that is, more secure and more destructive. Throughout all this, group communication is the indispensable instrument in giving the acts of the individual fighter meaning. In the absence of communication, the acts of the individual soldier, sailor, or airman lose some of the attributes of vision and sanity. He acts, but can hardly discern the effects of what he does ; and since he is trained to act as one of a group, when he tries to carry out his accustomed actions in isolation from his group, his behaviour may have little or no meaning in relation to what is going on around him. To move forward or backward, to fire or refrain from firing, to take cover to come out into the open—any of these acts may bring destruction on himself or his fellows. He can hardly tell. Vision and coherence come to him only when he is aware of the part he plays in relation to the behaviour of others ; and this awareness is only possible when he is in communication with them.

This, we must notice, is real communication, not merely silent obedience. The fighter not only listens and obeys, he replies. There is group thinking. The soldier at an isolated post has his radio-telephone—his talkie-box, as the Americans called it ; every ship at sea is in constant " touch " with a whole network of others ; the airman keeping a course hundreds of miles from his base is still in unbroken " touch " with it. And at the same time he keeps in touch with his fellow-airmen in the same machine by no other means than linguistic communication ; mutually invisible while they fly, each knows the other only as a voice heard over the " inter-comm."

Everywhere in warfare to-day it is only inter-communication that gives coherence to the task of the group. It is only by virtue of inter-communication that the unit—the division, the fleet, the bomber formation, or the air-crew—is a fighting unit. It is true that the very progress of communication means that the spoken or written word is in part replaced by other kinds of symbols : a point on a dial or a pattern on a screen. But as long as these are used as means of communication between men, they are language in that they are systems of symbols determining behaviour. We can still say, therefore, that it is only by the interchange of language that the unit gains awareness of itself as a group ; only by means of language do these units cohere together and work together as a single co-ordinated armament. Ultimately, then, it is only by the permeation of group awareness throughout the whole of the vast military machine that tactics and strategy are made possible in modern warfare.

More than this : in warfare to-day group awareness must extend beyond the limits of the fighting machine. Modern warfare is total warfare ; it brings into operation not only the soldier, the sailor, and the airman, but every member of the society at war. Daily command and exhortation to maintain an unbroken front against the enemy ; to keep silence about what is going on, lest the enemy may overhear ; to ignore or resist the flood of words daily pouring from the enemy camp ; this co-ordination and integration of a whole society through words and in the face of words is itself a major part of the Linguistic Revolution. Further still, the radio and the airborne leaflet are linguistic projectiles of great potency in the task of subduing the enemy, and in gaining and directing the adherence of those within his power. Before the allied invasion of Europe began in 1944, the daily broadcasts from General Eisenhower's headquarters to the partisan forces in occupied countries were a linguistic penetration behind the enemy lines.

These, then, are the indispensable functions of language in a society at war to-day : to be the means of group awareness of group techniques, for centuries ruled by traditions of drill and discipline—the utmost negation of group thinking ; to be a weapon of offence against the enemy, a projectile carried by the ether through every line of defence and into every stronghold ; and to be the means of closing the ranks against the onslaught of the projectiles issuing ceaselessly by day and by night from the enemy camp.

But because modern war is total war, bringing the whole of the society into the front line, we cannot separate the military from the political organization of a modern society. In modern war, the belligerent societies use political as well as military weapons against one another, and defence includes the close organization of political structures within each society. The group techniques of politics, directed towards maintaining the internal equilibrium as well as the external security of a society, are in many respects like military group techniques. This is the theme of our next chapter : the place of linguistic communication in the political group behaviour of modern societies.

CHAPTER 8

LANGUAGE IN POLITICS

I

EVERY society to-day uses political group techniques—that is, techniques directed to the maintenance of the society as a polity. In the present chapter we shall attempt a survey of the place of linguistic communication in the political group techniques of each of the three major forms of polity engaged in the recent war : German Nazism, Soviet socialism, and British democracy.

A crude hypothesis might expect to find a simple contrast in political group techniques between the totalitarian and the democratic states : specialization and automatization of function in Nazi Germany and the U.S.S.R., as contrasted with the development of free and spontaneous group awareness in the British and American democracies. But the mere statement of this hypothesis is enough to reveal its crudity and inadequacy. Every form of political structure in the modern world is a compromise between an ideology and the complex conditions bequeathed by the past and developing to-day ; each form of polity therefore uses a mixture of political group techniques. Even the democracy that aims at individual freedom must resort to some specialization and automatization of function ; and the totalitarian state that puts society above the individual must still attempt to develop group awareness in its members, and secure their willing participation in the political techniques of the society.

For the ultimate aim of every state, in its political structure and functioning, is to secure the union of all its members, in thought, feeling, and action, towards the maintenance of the society as a characteristic polity —that is, the achievement of equilibrium within the state and the conservation and assertion of its identity in the face of other states, its potential enemies or friends. What marks off one state from another is the organization of its group behaviour to bring about this internal union and group feeling—that is, group mind.

In the years preceding the Second World War and during the war itself there could be clearly seen in each of the three forms of polity the emergence of a rudimentary group mind with its own specific characteristics ; but certain political group techniques were common to all, and in all alike there was a rapid development of the use of linguistic communication in the service of these group techniques. The logic of events forces upon every state—and its leaders—the necessity of inspiring the citizen with a desire to foster the purposes of the state and of training him how to perform his political functions. To-day this means that as many as possible of the people must be brought within the politically active society ; that they must all, therefore, be given some training in the political group techniques suited to the maintenance of the characteristic polity ; that there must be put before them some goal as the purpose of the state ; and that they must be incited to desire to achieve this goal. It is evident that all these phases of political group behaviour involve both group cognition and group orexis.

In the present chapter we shall consider the cognitive, in the following chapter the orectic, aspects. We shall observe how, in each of the three forms of polity, the possibility of developing political behaviour rests upon the presence of adequate linguistic communication. We shall therefore have to attempt a brief survey of the general intention and organization of each form of polity, notice the use of group techniques in accordance with these, and the use of communication as an instrument of the techniques.

2

It is hardly possible to give even an outline picture of the political techniques used in Germany before and during the Second World War, partly because of the difficulty anyone not a Nazi has in understanding Nazi mentality, more because of the real disparity between what the Nazis told one another and what they told the outside world. One thing, however, is quite clear, that even in Nazi Germany an autocratic régime could not, in the circumstances of the present day, function only by virtue of autocratic group techniques. The theory of the state was simple : a hierarchy of leaders and led. The straightforward application of this in group techniques would imply the specialization of functions and the attempt to make the specialized functions automatic. The individual German need learn only to obey the leader set immediately above him. But in practice much more than this automatic obedience was necessary. The Nazi leaders, while aiming at a high degree of specialization and automatization for all members of the Nazi state, still had to come to terms with the necessity of group awareness throughout the state. For the conditions of linguistic communication in our day make it inevitable that wherever there is a society there will be some group awareness, which can only be ignored at the risk of danger to the stability of the society, and which every state must therefore harness in the service of its purposes.

The Nazi state in theory was a hierarchy, of which the apex was the fixed point from which all else must depend. The Nazi leaders set themselves to foster group thought, orexis, and action in consonance with this idea : group conception of the hierarchical structure, a desire to achieve it, and action directed towards its development and conservation. In effect, they sought to bring about the emergence of a hierarchical group mind : the subordination of the thought, feeling, will, and action of each individual to the leader set above him—always a leader chosen by Providence. One of Hitler's chief problems, then, was to use linguistic communication, the power of the word, to the end of establishing, maintaining, and keeping at work a group mind in the pattern of a dynamic hierarchy.

Before the Linguistic Revolution a hierarchy of this kind might perhaps have been kept in being by the mere strength of custom reinforced maybe by crude physical action. Physical force could be used to compel obedience. But once and for all, the permeation of all social behaviour by communication brings group mind into every political group technique. Communication as it has developed in our day is never simply command and obedience. The individual is called upon not only to hear and obey ; inevitably he will also listen, understand, and reply. By communication and interchange among its members the group will become aware of its own behaviour as a group. Communication thus becomes an instrument of group awareness of political group behaviour. How, then, to reconcile this with the Nazi conception of a total hierarchy, where each man is committed to total and unquestioning obedience to the voice of the leader above him—even the Leader obeying the voice of his Intuition ?

The need to come to terms with this all-pervading force of linguistic communication was inescapable. The Nazi leaders at once recognized the overwhelming importance of propaganda —the use of symbols, particularly language, as the primary means of arousing and directing thought, feeling, and action. A few months after Hitler came to power—in October 1933— the Reich Chamber of Culture was set up under Goebbels. Throughout its seven divisions—Literature, Press, Radio, Art, Music, Theatre, Films—there was a single intention : that " all creative forces in all spheres must be assembled under Reich leadership with a view to the uniform moulding of the will." [1]

" Creative forces . . . and the uniform moulding of the will " : how can these be reconciled ? The dilemma did not unduly perturb Nazi metaphysics. In the statute constituting the Chamber of Culture it was explicitly set forth that " creative effort is to be individual and unrestricted." In other words, the principle of leadership (*Führerprinzip*) did not demand the negation of individual initiative. On the contrary each member of the state must *actively* seek the subordination of his will to his leader ; he must exercise personal will in

[1] Roberts HB 242

fullest strength in order to bring about subordination of his will. Thus in the attempt to achieve the psychological conquest of the individual, a paradoxical theory was invoked, closely reflecting the dilemma of totalitarianism in a world of universal communication.

Given the thousand years that Hitler postulated for the duration of his Reich, Nazi psychology might have produced the Nazi man. But history has rarely granted the reformer the millennium that he needs. Within two years of the founding of the Chamber of Culture, Goebbels had to complain that the artist and the intellectual were too intractable and self-willed,[1] thus unwittingly echoing the words of Andrew Ure exactly a century earlier, that the better the workman the less fitted to become an automaton.[2]

Hitler himself had foreseen this difficulty of dealing with those who could not whole-heartedly devote themselves to self-subordination in the service to the state. In *Mein Kampf* he had found it necessary to distinguish between those who submit only in thought and feeling and those who carry their submission as far as will and action. " The follower [*Anhänger*] of a movement is he who understands and accepts its aims, the member [*Mitglied*] is he who fights for them." [3]

The problem of the Nazis was the transformation of the followers of a Party into members of a State : the translation of thought and feeling into will and action. And this, they constantly realized, was always as much a problem of persuasion as of coercion ; so that at no time could they abandon the hope of securing domination over will and action through the psychological conquest of thought and feeling. " The art of propaganda," the Leader had said, " lies precisely in this, that having aroused the imagination of the great mass of the people by appealing to their feelings, it adopts the most effective psychological form with which to find the way to their attention and their hearts." [4] The whip, the machine gun and the concentration camp may secure power ; propaganda is the uneasy tribute that power pays to psychology.

[1] Roberts HB 242   [2] page 130 above   [3] Hitler MK 651   [4] the same 198

It is unnecessary to emphasize the consequent care given by the Nazi leaders to every detail of both non-linguistic and linguistic symbols. The swastika ; the ritual of march, music, and song ; the salute and greeting " *Heil Hitler* "— these are varied forms of symbolic communication which express ·and at the same time direct thought, feeling, and action. More important still was the need to use the two dominant forms of linguistic communication in a modern society—the press and the radio, the chief physical instruments of the Linguistic Revolution. With the press Goebbels was perhaps successful. But it is a measure of the power of the spoken word in the modern world that even Goebbels failed to bring the radio entirely under control. Radio waves ignore national boundaries, and foreign languages are foreign to fewer and fewer men. To confiscate all private radio receivers throughout the Reich would have been a simple means of keeping the thought and feeling of the German people unsullied by the barbarian beyond ; but to confiscate all radio receivers would also have been to deprive the Leader of his most potent instrument. As a result, before the war at any rate, news from without constantly penetrated into the Reich in spite of the most repressive regulations.[1]

This is only one instance of the constant dilemma of political group techniques to-day, that while the Linguistic Revolution provides the means of fuller integration within a society, at the same time it lays the society open to disintegrating influences from without. To take a still wider view, this is in fact a constant condition of every step in man's development of linguistic communication from the beginning of time. As man learns to speak with his neighbour, the possibilities of social action are immeasurably increased, and with them the security of each member of the speaking group in a hostile world ; but the development of language also increases the danger that an enemy may, himself unseen, over-hear the discussion of proposed action, or again by this very instrument of speech lure a man from his allegiance to his group.

[1] Roberts HB 254

Yet within the limits afforded by this over-riding potency of the communicated word the Nazi leaders appear to have reached a high level of success in their political task, the organization of a Nazi group mind : the co-ordination of thought and action throughout a large area of the people ; the stability of the group structure and the efficiency of its functioning being assured by an intricate and refined system of linguistic communication. Each individual politically active within the state was made aware of those political purposes that it was fitting for him to know and trained in the appropriate group techniques. Group awareness, envisaging group purposes and directing group action, was thus developed throughout a major part of the society ; formulated by communication both within the society and to the world beyond, it enhanced the consciousness of identity. To this extent there was a Nazi group mind.

In itself the hierarchical form of political structure might be highly stable. Each man has his place in the hierarchy ; and as the group constantly symbolizes the pattern of its structure by every kind of symbolic communication, there develops in the group, thought, feeling, and action directed towards the maintenance and functioning of the group structure.

If, then, there was a weakness in the Nazi polity, it lay neither in the ideal pattern of the political structure nor in the group techniques employed to maintain this. The weakness was in the inevitable confinement of group awareness to what the leaders wished the society to know ; in particular the deflection of group awareness from attention to certain group incentives. This latter limitation of group awareness is particularly dangerous to political stability. As we have already suggested, the direction of group awareness upon group techniques, while it brings greater efficiency into the functioning of these techniques, may at the same time tend to withdraw awareness from group motives. The very efficiency of communication, in making possible a clearer cognition and direction of group conduct, may result in leaving in greater obscurity the important orectic aspects of this conduct. This is made all the more likely by every increase in the power of linguistic communication. The more that group consciousness is mediated by language, so that the group becomes accustomed to attend to that part of its behaviour that is symbolized in words, the greater the likelihood that behaviour not so symbolized will be left beyond full consciousness.

This was the case in Nazi Germany. Group communication did not extend throughout the whole field of group thought, feeling, and action. Much that was thought, felt, desired, and done by the leaders of the state—often in its name— was not given public formulation and remained therefore concealed from the full awareness of the society as a whole. But in this present age of highly developed linguistic communication, such concealment can hardly ever be complete. Knowledge about itself is reflected back upon every society by the world outside. Thus in Germany there was constant movement below the surface, movement of which the polity, as a group, kept itself unaware, movement repressed below the level of group consciousness. To the nature of this kind of underground movement in a society, and its relation to language, we shall revert in the following chapter.

3

The pattern of the Soviet polity is also hierarchical. But while the Nazi pyramid depends downwards from its apex, the Soviet pyramid stands solidly on its base. The Germans must obey Hitler because he is appointed by Providence; the Russians Stalin because they have appointed him themselves. The essence of the Soviet system is that it is a system of soviets, that is, of people's committees; it is these that constitute the base and the constituent units of the whole structure.

The political group techniques of the Union are devised so as to maintain this structure. By the Constitution of 1936 (the " Stalin Constitution ") the first step in the election of all deputies—from the two Chambers of the Supreme Soviet of the Union down to local Soviets of Toilers' Deputies—is the

nomination of candidates by the people's electoral circles.
The right to nominate is confined to these circles, which must
be recognized groups such as organizations of the Communist
Party, trade unions, co-operatives, youth organizations, and
cultural societies. It is in the discussions concerning nomination in these electoral circles that the work of electing deputies
is actually done, for in the formal ballot that follows, only
one candidate is named on the voting paper, so that the
initiative of the citizen is limited to the approval or disapproval
of the candidate already nominated by the electoral circle.

It is well understood by the leaders of the Union that
nomination discussions of this kind constitute a process of
political education through which the citizen may be made
aware of political problems and become familiar with possible
measures for their solution. He is called on to fit himself
to be an active member of a group ; by playing his part in
this he is fulfilling his primary duty to the state. For his
circle—itself a soviet—nominates deputies who in turn form
soviets again electing further soviets. The Union is thus a
hierarchy of soviets, so that political education must be social
education, the education of the individual in and through a
group of which he is a member. He functions politically not as
an individual but as a member of a group. The smallest active
political unit is really the local soviet. This is the practical
application of the primary Marxist principle quoted with
approval by Bukharin when he was a close associate of Stalin :
" It is not the consciousness of men that determines their
being, but on the contrary, their social being that determines
their consciousness." [1]

This social education is in fact the chief instrument of Soviet
organization of group political action. Maynard, attempting
to explain what may seem to the foreigner somewhat strange
features of Soviet internal politics, continually reiterates that
the Russian people is at school, is being educated by the
Communist Party.[2] It is the same threefold education as is
now necessary in any society politically alive : the people must

[1] Bukharin HM 207   [2] Maynard RP 450, 453 ; also Barker RG 325

be made aware of the purposes of the Union, inspired to desire their achievement, and practised in the necessary techniques.

As to the purposes, since it is an inherent characteristic of the Soviet State that it is always on the march, constantly adapting itself to changing circumstances, its ideology too must be in constant process of change. It is recognized, therefore, that special provision must be made to re-formulate ideology as it changes ; in other words, to make sure the society is kept in touch with its own purposes. For it is always possible for a society ás a whole to be unaware of the purposes determined for it by its leaders. In the Soviet specialization of labour, there must be someone with the specific task of watching the trend of movement and interpreting the acts of the society to itself, thus making the group conscious of its own behaviour. In the words once more of Bukharin, " the ideological processes may be considered as a special form of labour within the general labour system." [1]

Awareness of purposes is, of course, not enough ; there must be the desire to achieve them. Soviet philosophy is well aware that this is the central problem of political education : the substitution of new goals for those already established by nature or tradition ; in place of the stimulus of private profit, the incentive of the welfare of the society. It is reconditioning— exactly in the spirit of Pavlov's work ; a new stimulus, the welfare of society, is made to take the place of the existing stimulus of private welfare. It is therefore not as surprising as is sometimes suggested that Pavlov, anti-revolutionary though he was, should have been accepted and acclaimed by the Revolution and the resources of a gigantic institute of research put at his disposal. He represented for the leaders of the Revolution the research technologist of human psychology seeking to reveal the scientific bases of the techniques they would have to employ.

Pavlov himself was quite explicit that men could be reconditioned to accept new purposes as incentives to social action. As early as 1916, at the dawn of the Revolution, he

[1] Bukharin HM 217

urged his fellow countrymen to recognize the importance of the "reflex of purpose," a reflex that could be established, he said, as firmly as any other conditioned reflex. He exhorted them to cast off the shackles of their chief national characteristic, inconstancy of purpose, a characteristic no more ineradicable than any other habit and just as susceptible to reconditioning.

"When the negative features of the Russian character—laziness, lack of enterprise, and even a slovenly attitude to every vital work—provoke a melancholy mood, I say to myself, No, these are not our real qualities ; they are only a veneer, the damning inheritance of slavery. . . . The reflex of purpose which has been suppressed during Russia's history can be restored. If every one of us will cherish within himself this reflex as the most precious part of his being, if parents and instructors of all ranks make their chief problem the strengthening and developing of this reflex in the masses, if our society and state will provide a full opportunity for the exercise of this reflex, then we shall become that which we should and can be." [1]

This belief in the necessity and possibility of reconditioning men, of establishing new reflexes in them by means of training, is in effect the central doctrine of Soviet political education. By means of the school, the press, and the radio the mass of the people must be brought to understand the purposes of the State and conditioned to direct both feeling and action towards achieving them. Illiteracy must be liquidated throughout the Union ; and in order that the newspaper and the radio may function as organs of discussion, it is explicitly laid down in the 1936 Constitution (Article 125) that there shall be freedom of the press and freedom of speech.

This is another of the points at which a foreigner, trying to understand Soviet political practice, finds himself at a loss. For this freedom of discussion as guaranteed by the Constitution is certainly not freedom as conceived in Western democracies. The Constitution in making its guarantee adds the

[1] Pavlov CR (i) 280

important qualification that this is granted "in order to strengthen the socialist system." Thus the citizen is guaranteed freedom in the sense of personal initiative ; freedom to seek an understanding of the purposes of the State, freedom to apply his powers to the achievement of these purposes, but not freedom to work against them. It is freedom to work within the limits of a pre-determined social pattern ; and, as Maynard points out, it is freedom not of the individual as an individual but as a member of a group, only those groups being allowed to exist which promote the welfare of the State. There is no freedom to establish a political party in opposition to the Communist Party ; no freedom to utter or propagate opinions at variance with the doctrines of the Party ; only freedom for each man to do what he can to make his contribution to the work of the State by understanding its purposes and directing his energies towards their achievement.

There is thus, as Maynard suggests, a clear opposition between the Soviet State and the Western democracies in the functions of the individual, in political as contrasted with industrial group techniques. In Britain and the U.S.A. there is a wide range within which the individual is free to utter and propagate political doctrine, but in industry his freedom is limited to the promotion of the industrial system in which he finds himself. In the U.S.S.R. there is, in the sphere of industry, a wide range within which the citizen is free to utter and propagate opinion, but in politics he has freedom only to promote the political system of the State.

The political function of the citizen of the U.S.S.R. is thus clearly defined : to be an active member of the local soviet or other electoral circle, so that the candidate nominated shall be the best man available to represent its wishes. The citizen should train himself to play this part with efficiency. But he is not called on to cultivate personal opinions on the major policies of the Union. His political activity is in effect limited to the part he takes in the discussions in his electoral circle, and to the vote he is afterwards free to cast in support of the nominated candidate.

4

This technique was seen in operation in the elections of 1937, which followed immediately on the promulgation of the new constitution. Ninety-six per cent. of ninety-four million enfranchised citizens voted, but only for or against the one candidate on the voting paper. Discussions and choice had already taken place in the nomination of candidates by the electoral circles ; the election itself was little more than an occasion for the people to acclaim the candidates of their choice.

To call the development of a technique of this kind a free political education might seem a travesty to the theorist of Western democracy, but for Russia it is certainly something new in political education, a revolutionary attempt to make every citizen an active worker in the political group techniques of the state.

The task of the leaders of the U.S.S.R. is to bring the arts of communication into the service of this political education. It becomes more important to develop a technique of discussion at the lowest level than to develop in the individual a critical attitude towards the central policies of the state. Provision, it is true, is made for the humblest citizen of the Union to reach the ear of Stalin himself, but the difficulties and uncertainties of such direct access are obvious. For the most part, reliance is placed on the functioning of the hierarchical structure, from the lowest level upwards. The working political unit is the electoral group, not the individual citizen.

As always, this political group technique is a compromise between doctrine and circumstance. In the U.S.S.R. there is no doubt as to the intentions of the leaders, as evinced by the practical measures they have taken. They have set themselves to educate the people—that is, to provide them with the spoken and written literacy necessary for the efficient working of group discussion. Every form of symbolical communication, using every art and all the mechanical media of our time—the press, the cinema, the radio—is to be used in making the people aware of their needs and duties.

The central principle of Soviet political technique to-day, if we may judge by what we know of its practice, is this : every man must be literate, using speech and writing, listening and reading effectively ; for only by these means can he be an active and efficient member of a group. The aim of discussion in each group is to be the unification of thought, feeling, and action ; these minor groups being organized to form the basis of the hierarchical group mind of the whole Union. In a society so constituted there is no need for formal disfranchisement of the illiterate ; by the nature of things he is cut off from active participation in political life. Literacy is the necessary condition of enfranchisement.

It is evident that this pattern of political functioning is well adapted to the needs of the Union. Based upon the traditional local communism of the village,[1] it brings compactness and integration to this huge population. By developing and systematizing the means of communication it achieves—as the War has shown—an extraordinary degree of integration within the hierarchical state. But, like the Nazi polity, the Soviet political organization has limitations inherent in its form and functioning. Once again the very efficiency and complexity of communication have made it possible to canalize group awareness. In the U.S.S.R. the resulting limitations are to be detected at two points : the attention of the local soviet or electoral circle is directed towards its own immediate purposes rather than to those of the Union ; and even within the group no voice is given to thought or feeling that is not in consonance with Soviet socialization, as far as it is understood at that level.

This confinement of the attention of the group to its own concerns is an immediate consequence of the hierarchical structure in which the group is the unit. The group performs its functions adequately when it elects a representative who, in the opinion of the group, will most efficiently foster the socialist purposes of the group. Discussion within the group tends therefore to be taken up with its own purposes, and only these receive clear group formulation. The group does

[1] Maynard RP 448

not allow itself to give full expression to thought and feeling that are not in conformity with Soviet socialism. Thus for the most part they remain beyond the consciousness of the group. Again, feeling concerning the major purposes of the Union as a whole, and the motives underlying these purposes, also escape group formulation. Thus, the unit of the hierarchy is not called on to be actively concerned with the purposes or motives of the hierarchy as a whole.

In these ways the development of communication, by leading to greater efficiency in the techniques of political group behaviour, may serve to diminish integration in other aspects of this behaviour. The more fully some aspects of thought and feeling are mediated by language, the more certainly other aspects not so well mediated by language will be kept below the level of group awareness. Yet all the time, all around the Soviet citizen, the compass of group communication is increasing until it may embrace the whole world, and becoming so insistent that few can wholly escape it. The individual citizen, as he becomes more literate, is correspondingly subject to incessant bombardment by symbols of thought and feeling that still lie beyond the awareness of his group as a group. Here, then, are the potentialities of conflict and disintegration in the thought, feeling, and behaviour of the society.

5

The central intention and the corresponding group techniques of Democracy are as well defined, in its political theory, as those of Nazism or Soviet socialization. The ultimate goal is freedom for the individual to develop his personality ; the technique by which this is to be achieved is parliamentary party government resting on free discussion. It is from the clash of individual differences of opinion that final agreement is fashioned. In theory, at any rate, it is held that the integration of thought, feeling, and action can only be achieved where there is full scope for opposing views to make themselves heard. The technical problem of a democracy then, is this : to provide the means of discussion out of which there may come the basis of group action.

Discussion is group thinking ; the indispensable instrument of this is communication. Already at the beginning of the formulation of modern democratic political theory, a century ago, we find a preoccupation with this question of communication. The traditional individualism of the Englishman was being rationalized and systematized into an ideal of free expression and interchange of individual opinion within the structure of an organized society. Rousseau's theory of a Social Contract came under the lash of Bentham's satire because it took no account of communication. " Rousseau . . . invented his fiction of a Social Contract—a contract according to which any number of millions, without having communicated with each other, agree to govern one another in conformity to certain ends, without anything said about either means or ends." [1]

Communication with each other : in the development of democratic political theory this comes to mean the free participation of individuals in group thought, feeling, and action. For Bentham the ultimate political unit is the individual, not the group. " The community is a fictitious body, composed of the individual persons who are considered as constituting as it were its members. The interest of the community then is what ?—the sum of the interests of the several members who compose it." [2] At the same time it is a fundamental tenet of his utilitarian philosophy that government should be directed by the interests of the majority of the members of the community—the greatest happiness of the greatest number.

By the time we reach Bentham's disciple John Stuart Mill this has become the central dogma of democratic doctrine : the right of the individual to freedom of speech for the sake of the welfare of society—which is the welfare of the majority of the individuals that compose it. In the terms of Mill's classical statement of the nature of democratic liberty, " If any opinion is compelled to silence, that opinion may, for aught we can certainly know, be true." [3] With this goes so extreme a

[1] Bentham OF xxvii   [2] the same 4   [3] Mill OL 63

valuation of individual expression as must seem entirely per-
verted to Nazi or Soviet theory : " If all mankind minus one
were of one opinion, and only one person were of the contrary
opinion, mankind would be no more justified in silencing that
one person than he, if he had the power, would be justified in
silencing mankind." [1] The sanction of this individual freedom
of speech is the welfare of society ; it is only through freedom
of speech that the welfare of society can be secured.

These still remain the fundamentals of the theory of
Democracy. Discussion is still held to be its indispensable
means. In the words of one who may be regarded as a representative modern exponent of its theory : " Free discussion
among individuals was the source and origin of this system :
free discussion among individuals continues to be its method
and its essence. . . . Its process is discussion—discussion of competing ideas, leading to a compromise in which all ideas are
reconciled and which can be accepted by all because it bears
the imprint of all." [2]

Closely bound up with this is the democratic view of the
relation between the individual and the group, in clear contrast
with Soviet doctrine. Both recognize that the mind of the
individual is shaped by the various groups to which he belongs.
Soviet doctrine takes this to mean that in a group the individual
learns to conform ; in the words of Bukharin that we have
quoted before, it is the social being of men that determines their
consciousness.[3] Against this, democratic doctrine asserts that
a man can realize his individuality only through discussion—
its strife, its discordance, and its clashes as well as its harmonies.
Thus, as Ernest Barker puts it, democracy assumed that society
is " constituted and actuated by its members," and that in the
end the democratic state exists for the sake of the personal
liberty of each of its members.[4] As to the consequent development of each person as an individual, a typical statement is
that of the psychologist McDougall in his study of group mind.
Speaking at about the same moment as Bukharin, he says :
" The individual's consciousness of self is developed chiefly

[1] Mill OL 19   [2] Barker RG 12, 36   [3] page 155 above   [4] Barker RG 167, 10

by intercourse with other individuals—by imitation, by conflict, by compulsion and by co-operation. Without such intercourse it must remain rudimentary." [1]

Democratic political group technique conceives of the value of free discussion in this way ; not that men, as in Soviet doctrine, may grow more alike, but that individuality may be fostered ; then, in the marriage of diversities of opinion, not conformity but agreement may be born. The ultimate co-operation of individuals within a society must spring from diversity as well as similarity, so that provision must be made at every stage of the process of government for the expression of diverse opinion. It is the institution of government by a progressive dialectic. It is through discussion that parliamentary candidates are to be nominated, and by further discussion the members elected. The legislature should be constituted of varieties of opinion ; but the theory of party government is that the range of diversity should be reduced to a dialectic of simple opposition. As Mr. Churchill pointed out to the House of Commons, the arrangement of the chamber fosters the division of the House into those who support His Majesty's Government and the Opposition. Finally, the institution of two Houses marks the last stage of the parliamentary dialectic.

Throughout this long process of discussion it is not conformity that is sought, but the agreement of those who differ. So that when at last assent is given to a legislative measure it is an assertion, not that there is an identity of opinion throughout the society, but only that men of different opinions have agreed to act in accordance with the views of the majority.

The group mind of a democracy is therefore not hierarchical but dialectical in structure, a constant dynamic of opposing forces ; opposition in thinking and opposition in feeling, issuing in action that expresses the highest common factor of agreement. To serve the purposes of such a group mind there are needed highly complex and highly flexible group techniques, with instruments much more refined than are demanded by the techniques of a hierarchical structure. In

[1] McDougall GM 165

particular there must be complex and flexible means of linguistic communication. There must not only be freedom of discussion—this is only the beginning. Freedom of speech, if it is to be more than empty sound uttered by the blind, must rest upon other freedoms. Those who are free only to speak are, in Milton's scaring phrase, blind mouths. Freedom of speech is no more than a voice unless it carries with it the freedom, and the *means*, of acquiring the knowledge necessary for judgment, as well as the freedom of leisure to arrive at judgment. Freedom of speech is blind unless it is guided by an awareness of the purposes of the society. It is anarchic unless it is moved by a desire to achieve the welfare of the society. Here lies the potential weakness of the democratic state : the failure of the instrument of communication to keep pace with the demands of free discussion.

Since the beginning of the nineteenth century we have seen sporadic and repeated attempts at education, both voluntary and state-controlled, to supply the general literacy necessary for the efficient working of the democratic group techniques. But a wide gap has always remained. To-day, as the democratic societies change more rapidly with the more rapid movement of circumstances, there is constant improvisation of their political group techniques to meet their new needs. But the gap between the efficiency of the technique and the complexity of the task grows wider.

The mere fact that the democratic polity has grown up throughout many decades instead of being planned as a whole, at one moment, as in Nazi Germany or the U.S.S.R., is itself a source of inertia. There is lacking the stimulus that comes from a recent formulation of purposes, as in *Mein Kampf* or the Stalin Constitution. In the democracies the members of the society, leaders and led, also lack the day-to-day guidance that emerges from the constant attention given in the newer polities to their political techniques. In the democracies it is as though it were taken for granted that every citizen is aware of his particular part in the political group task and is moved to carry it out ; in other words, that there is specialization of function as the result of tradition, and without the necessity of group formulation and direction.

As a result, the ordinary citizen in the democracies has long tended to remain politically inert. Only with difficulty is he induced to act, and he is therefore prone to remain inactive where it is nobody's business to stir him and where indeed it may be somebody's business to ensure that he remains inactive. Add to this that the instruments of communication—particularly the press—that might be the means of giving him knowledge and rousing him to action, may perhaps be under the control of those to whom his knowledge and activity might be dangerous or, at the least, unpalatable.

The democratic polity suffers also from two difficulties arising from the special conditions of our day—difficulties rather more readily overcome in the hierarchical state. The first is the complexity of the modern polity, the second its size.

6

The complexity of the modern polity lies in the increasing number of the activities that government takes over from the individual and thus brings within the field of politics. The welfare of the young and old, the sick and the hale, in every aspect of their physical and mental well-being—all this becomes progressively and in larger measure the concern of the state. Much of this complexity of function is feasible only in the presence of widespread and intricate means of linguistic communication. More and more the vitality of the state depends on a healthy circulation of paper. To extend the term by which Mumford characterizes the modern city, the state to-day is a Paper State.[1]

This means that if the citizen of a democratic society is to play his part in its political group techniques, he must be put within reach of information, acquire the power of understanding its significance, and be practised in the performance of his consequent tasks. There must be a technique within the society

[1] Mumford CC 255

directed to the acquisition of information, a development of the means of communicating this information, and education in its use. In hierarchical polities the concern of the citizen need extend only to a limited range of function—in the Nazi polity to the obedience of his immediate leader ; in the Soviet polity to the functions of the immediate group of which he is a member. · But the dialectic technique of a democracy demands, in theory at any rate, that the concern of the citizen shall extend to all the functions of the entire polity—that there shall be full group awareness of the whole range of its purposes and techniques.

This is a heroic task for any society to undertake ; some may think an impossible one. But so far from recognizing the magnitude of the task, the democracies have, as societies, hitherto hardly shown any awareness of it at all.

First, the acquisition of information. Lippmann has pointed out that in the U.S.A. even the members of the legislature are ignorant of the facts of many of the questions they are called on to discuss. The most that can be expected of the average congressman is some knowledge of the affairs of his own State.[1] So too in the British Parliament there must be many matters on which the ordinary back-bencher cannot be sufficiently well-informed. What likelihood is there then of well-informed opinion among his ordinary constituents ?

Ignorance of this kind is inevitable as long as there is no adequate technique for the transformation of brute facts into systematic knowledge, organized so as to form the basis of action. The Second World War made only too apparent the need for the preparation and publication of social and political statistics, but only in the fifth year was there the rudimentary stirrings of a demand for an " economic general staff " and " the better training of civil servants in statistical method." [2]

Side by side with a technique for the acquisition and organization of information is needed a technique for its dissemination. This can never mean that in a democracy every man and woman will have sufficient information to come to an independent opinion concerning even the major purposes

[1] Lippmann PO 290   [2] *Manchester Guardian* June 16, 1944

and acts of the state. As Ernest Barker points out, there must be a specialization and " division of labour " in political no less than in industrial group techniques.[1] The information presented to the ordinary citizen, though accurate, can only be given in broad outline. But recent tendencies in adult education, the press, and the radio suggest that it is possible to achieve a much wider broadcasting of the knowledge basic to the discussion of social and political questions than has hitherto seemed feasible.

These are group habits that are developing in response to half-conscious group demands. Can a technique for the dissemination of political information be provided and directed by the society ? The complexity of political issues could, we have suggested, be simplified without the loss of fundamental accuracy. But we are still left with the problem of size. The modern polity, no less than modern industry and modern warfare, is " afflicted with giantism." Can all the citizens of a modern democracy be brought within the range of the state provision of information ? Or are the British Commonwealth and the United States huge organisms blundering into self-destruction because their brains are too small for their bodies ?

But one of the chief causes of political giantism is also the chief means of its alleviation. A primary condition of the growth of vast polities—whether democratic or totalitarian—is the existence of a single common language ; but this is also in turn the chief instrument of the development of common thought, feeling, and action throughout the polity ; the only means, in fact, by which a huge democracy can hope to achieve a group mind commensurate with the size of its body politic. Hence the importance of a common language in the United States, and the significance of the adoption in 1944 of Basic English as an auxiliary language by the British Government. Mr. Churchill, in his statement to Parliament on this occasion, made it clear that it was the intention of the Government to promote the use of Basic English not only as a medium of communication between the Commonwealth and other states,

[1] Barker RG 38

but also as a single common language for all the peoples of the Commonwealth.[1]

A single common language, although the first necessity of a democratic society, is still only the condition, not the fulfilment, of an efficient technique. Every polity, democratic or other, needs a single common language. But the democratic way of life demands also that the common language shall be made the means of common education, in the democratic sense. Communication must be used to disseminate the knowledge from which alone can spring valid individual opinion ; it must provide each citizen with the opportunity of taking part in discussion and must train him to achieve the skill that will make discussion fruitful. Of all this there is in the Western democracies still no more than the promise. In the U.S.A. the average citizen is said to be strikingly ignorant of the purposes and problems of the Union. We are sometimes told that the British citizen is rather better informed, but this can hardly mean very much.

The first stage—but only the first—in the process of democratic political education is obviously the school ; and certainly both the Western democracies are now fully alive to the importance of providing every citizen with something more than " elementary " education. Lewis Mumford, himself a product of both democracies, in making a progressive list of the institutions that have successively dominated the typical city since the Middle Ages, names them in this order : the fortress, the church, the palace, the shop, the factory ; to-day the school.[2] In Britain, the Education Act of 1944 has the intention of ensuring that ultimately every citizen shall remain wholly or partly at school until the threshold of adult life. But even this is not enough. It is increasingly evident that the indispensable need in a democracy is adult education in the fullest sense of this term.

Adult education in political technique must consist, as we have said, of the dissemination of the knowledge that forms the basis of discussion as well as training in discussion itself. And of neither of these can one see more than the merest rudi-

[1] page 61 above   [2] Mumford CC 472

ments of our democracies. In Britain the daily provision by the B.B.C. of straight news such as is rarely to be found in the more popular newspaper is perhaps a step in the right direction. Another step is the enormous circulation during the War of such government publications as the White Papers on education, a national health service, and social security.[1] And —what would have seemed specially significant to any of the Radicals of a century ago—the demand for the continuous broadcasting of the proceedings of Parliament, the publication of extracts in " Penguins," and finally the formation of a Hansard Society with the object of the dissemination of knowledge about Parliament.[2]

For the technique of discussion the radio provides the obvious medium and instrument of training. This is an aspect of social education in which the U.S.A. has certainly anticipated Britain. During the War the " Blue Network " was giving every citizen the opportunity of taking part in a telephone and radio discussion—" America's Town Meeting of the Air "— a broadcast of uncensored debate in a public gathering, the members of which freely intervene.[3] At this time there was no corresponding service by the B.B.C.

There remains what is perhaps the most difficult problem in the development of political group consciousness by means of linguistic communication : the integration of group orexis and the group awareness of group motives. It is a problem whose importance can hardly be over-rated, for the behaviour of a society is far more powerfully determined by what is felt and desired than by what is known. What, then, are the conditions of group orexis and of group consciousness of motives ? This is the subject of the following chapter.

7

As a preliminary,· let us summarize the facts of group political behaviour in the three forms of polity that we have

---

[1] A quarter of a million copies of the Beveridge Report were sold.—*Observer* June 6, 1943
[2] *Manchester Guardian* September 26, 1944   [3] *Observer* May 28, 1944

reviewed. In spite of wide differences in political intention and corresponding differences in political techniques, there are nevertheless marked similarities. All three forms of polity alike recognize the necessity of the psychological integration of their members : the integration of thought, feeling, and action in the pursuit of the political purposes of the group. And whether the integration be sought within the pattern of a hierarchical or within that of a dialectical structure, it is recognized that its indispensable instrument is communication, chiefly linguistic.

In the Nazi hierarchical polity the integration is of command and obedience, clarified by some group awareness of some of the purposes of the state, under the stress of a constant incitement—by many and diverse forms of appeal—to pursue these purposes. All these three techniques—command and obedience in action, cognition of purpose, and orectic incitement—make the fullest use of group communication, linguistic and other. The weaknesses of these techniques are that the presence of the very means that make them possible also renders the Nazi citizen susceptible to communication from fields beyond the leaders' control. While these attempt to secure the limitation of political knowledge and the repression of unapproved tendencies in group orexis, the group is constantly assailed by cognitive and orectic stimuli from beyond the borders of the society as well as from subversive " movements " within. These are conditions conducive to disintegration and conflict.

In the Soviet hierarchical state, integration is sought by limiting the political action of the individual to his membership of a local soviet or discussion group. The great majority of Soviet citizens are gathered into such groups, which form the base of a hierarchy of soviets. In place, therefore, of the Nazi technique of command and obedience, is the Soviet technique of group discussion : the citizen is incited to take part in this, is given the literacy—written and spoken—necessary for fruitful participation in it, and is constantly practised in it. The technique is well planned, and is an effective means of securing integration in a huge and diverse population.

It has, however, potential weaknesses parallel to those of

the Nazi techniques. The group awareness of the local soviet is limited to its own purposes ; group feelings not in accord with approved orexis are denied group discussion. And all the time, like everyone else in the modern world, the Soviet citizen is subject to the bombardment of unapproved cognitive and orectic stimuli from both without and within the society. There is this to be said, however, by way of contrast with Nazism : the freedom of the Soviet citizen to discuss ways and means, and even, to some extent, purposes, probably has the effect that the integration of the society is not threatened to the same degree as that of the Nazi state.

In the democratic dialectical polities both the degree of integration secured, and the possibilities of disintegration and conflict, are probably less than in the hierarchical polities. Parliamentary party government has, in neither of the Western democracies, constructed a machine capable of achieving the clarity of group knowledge or the integration of group motive and action that characterizes the Nazi or the Soviet regime. But the greater freedom of discussion means a smaller potentiality of conflict, a smaller susceptibility to the assailment of group cognition and orexis from without and within.

On the other hand, in comparison with the totalitarian techniques, the democratic techniques also betray characteristic weaknesses. The democracies have not yet succeeded in adapting their technique of discussion—that is, of free group thinking and feeling—to their size and complexity. They have not achieved the systematic division of labour that the theory of democratic government demands, or constructed machinery for the systematization and dissemination of the knowledge essential for enlightened and effective discussion, or provided training in the art of this discussion. Nor have they succeeded in providing the means of communication necessary for the integration of group orexis and the group awareness of motives. It is to this last question that we now turn : the relations between communication, orexis, and motives.

CHAPTER 9

LANGUAGE AND SOCIAL INTEGRATION

I

A MODERN society constantly asks Why about itself. This increase of self-questioning is both a cause and an effect of increased linguistic communication. A society's growing awareness of itself means a greater demand for talk and writing about itself : books on its history, geography, economics ; statistics, reports, newspapers ; novels, plays—the flood continues and grows. In its turn all this self-questioning obviously leads to further self-awareness. But talk and writing not immediately about the society's own affairs may also lead in the same direction. As a society gains knowledge of other societies, including the metamorphoses of its own past, it learns to " turn back upon " itself, to become aware of itself.

The growth of self-awareness may, as we have seen, contribute to the integration of techniques. Does it tend towards the integration of orexis ? Certainly it is a characteristic of modern societies to achieve a high degree of technical integration, coupled with considerable conflict and disintegration in the field of emotions and incentives. We shall now endeavour to show that this conflict and disintegration are in fact closely related to the contemporary state of linguistic communication. The Linguistic Revolution works in two directions at the same time. It constantly provides the conditions for affective and conative integration, but at the same time increases the possibilities of affective and conative conflict. In the present chapter we shall consider the conditions making for orectic integration, in the following chapter those leading to orectic conflict.

In dealing with orexis in society, the parallel in individual psychology is at once illuminating. The most commonplace fact of everyday life is the conflict in the ordinary man between his conduct and his ideals. Freud has added to our understanding of this conflict by reminding us that the true incentives of a man's conduct are for the most part hidden from him. When a man cognizes his incentives by putting them into words or other symbols he tends to " rationalize " them ; that is, to effect some sort of reconciliation between them and the more or less organized system of his beliefs and ideals. In a man's conduct there are, then, to so speak, three levels of motivation : his primary incentives, the " motives " which he declares to himself, and his ideals. In Freudian terms these levels correspond to the id, the ego, and the super-ego. The id is the source of the primary incentives ; the ego admits these—mostly in disguised forms—as declared motives ; the super-ego is the realm of ideals. A man looking at his own conduct presents his motives to himself in forms adapted to the ideals that he accepts : these declared motives both revealing and hiding incentives of which he himself is hardly or not at all aware. The incentives thus enter his awareness—in his dreams or in his waking life—in the guise of accepted motives, which, because they are transformations of what would otherwise be unconscious, will be expressed by pictorial imagery, characterized by displacement and condensation.[1] For where they are in conflict with ideals, it is often impossible to give incentives the close verbal formulation that would reveal them in their nakedness. There is resistance by the man's conscious self (his ego) to the full recognition of those incentives (emerging from the id) which conflict with his ideals (his super-ego).

Thus one function of language and other symbols in the individual is to enable him to " come to terms " with his own incentives, and to this extent to enable him to resolve conflicts between competing incentives and again between these and incompatible ideals. But this very same symbolization of incentives also tends to increase conflict. As a man extends his awareness of himself, that is, as he expresses more and more of his behaviour in words or other symbols, he is likely to become more aware of the inconsistencies of his behaviour. To this extent the civilized man may be more neurotic than the uncivilized, because he is more literate. The man who is

[1] page 91 above

unconscious of the roots of his behaviour is so much the less subject to conflict.

Our question now is the parallel state of affairs in a society. There are societies, as Malinowski has shown us, with little or no group-awareness of group incentives ; they have few, or no, formulated ideals of conduct, and they do not attempt to bring their group incentives into the light of day in the guise of accepted motives. Their problems of group behaviour are problems of *how* and not *why*. They learn how to behave in this or that contingency ; and if ever they ask why—and they rarely ask this unless some Malinowski asks them—the answer is, This is how we have always behaved. The society is unified and integrated by the sharp clarity of its techniques coupled with the complete obscurity of its motives.

But when a group begins to ask itself why about its behaviour as a group, the possibility of internal conflict at once increases. Ideals of conduct are formulated, and where these are inconsistent with actual behaviour—determined as this is by cruder incentives—the need arises for acceptable motives to bridge the gap between the ideals and the incentives. So in a civilized society we find three levels of motivation parallel to the three levels in an individual. There are the *ideals* formulated for the society and accepted by its members ; *incentives* which strongly move the society but which—even though they may be recognized by individuals or sub-groups—are not formulated to itself by the society as a whole ; and, finally, accepted *motives*, publicly formulated, but in such a way as to disguise and obscure the points of conflict.

A society, for instance, has as one of its constantly formulated ideals, the principles of humanity to the vanquished—in conscious opposition maybe to the *Vae victis* of another civilization. War brings victory, and at once individuals or subgroups, less susceptible of the influence of this ideal of humanity, suggest severe and even ruthless treatment of the defeated enemy. This severity and ruthlessness express incentives that the group as a whole does not nakedly reveal to itself ; mere revenge, the satisfaction of primitive anger, even downright xenophobia—fear of the foreigner and the wish to destroy him. If allowed to appear in their nakedness these impulses would conflict with the humanitarian ideal ; the need for reconciling the actual incentives and the valued ideals becomes vital for the preservation of social stability. Acceptable " motives " are consequently formulated by those who speak within the society—the writers, the " publicists," the debaters ; punishment, for instance, is justified as retribution for the atrocities committed by the enemy during the war. Thus the cruder incentives of anger, revenge, and fear are given the protective colouring of retributive justice, and so are allowed to emerge as acceptable group motives.

A mechanism of this kind is, however, in the presence of the highly developed linguistic communication of our day, no more than partially successful. The need for the declaration of motives has grown because the group as a whole has become more accustomed to keep an eye on the conduct of group affairs ; to inquire into and talk about, that is, to verbalize, its incentives. But individuals or sub-groups within the society will continue to emphasize—that is, to express in words or other symbols—ideals incompatible with declared motives ; in the instance just mentioned they would emphasize the humanitarian ideal. Others, on the other hand, may venture to bring into the light of group awareness the actual incentives, although statements of these are likely to be less " popular " and may even be " censored " by those who act for or lead the society. Instead, therefore, of the integration that characterizes the more primitive, less literate society, we have the characteristic disintegration and conflict of the modern society. The literate society asks itself questions, and this should make for self-awareness ; but the answers it gives are only partially true, emphasizing some of its motives and leaving others obscured but none the less powerful. Instead of the society acting as a single group, we have sub-groups in conflict with each other within the society. The behaviour of the society as a whole is marked by inconsistencies and uncertainties reflecting the incoherence of its motivations.

Something of this was said by Pareto thirty years ago. His terminology is far from exact or consistent ; but, broadly speaking, he presents a picture of " unknown " incentives, " residues " (declared motives) and " derivations " (accepted ideals). Men, he tells us, constantly feel the need to justify their actions to themselves in a logical way. Unwilling to recognize their true incentives, which therefore remain " unknown " to them, they adopt " pseudo-logical " residues and derivations. Thus a partial reconciliation is achieved.

But one of the main weaknesses of his treatment is his inadequate recognition of the part played in these social processes by language and other symbols. He pays tribute, it is true, to the effects of mere repetition : if a derivation is simple enough and repeated often enough it will frequently gain a strong motive power of itself, whatever its validity.[1] The echo of this in Hitler's *Mein Kampf* comes to mind ; but then Lewis Carroll had already credited this discovery to his Marxist [2] Bellman in *The Hunting of the Snark* : " What I tell you three times is true."

But of the close relation of the machinery of residues and derivations to group communication, Pareto says little or nothing. It is perhaps a measure of the growth of our attention to communication, in the thirty years since he wrote, that his neglect of it now strikes us so forcibly. To us it is clear that motives are expressed in a society chiefly in answer to questions asked within the society. In all ages such questions have been asked by a few—the " thinkers " ; to-day, because communication covers an increasingly larger area of society, the questions are asked by larger and larger groups within the society, sometimes by the society as a whole. The development of communication means that every society tends to give more attention to—and so to symbolize in words—the roots of its group conduct, thus admitting some of these to group awareness in the form of acceptable " motives."

We go on to consider instances of the relation between communication and the integration of motives in a modern

[1] Pareto MS, sect. 973, 1737, 1749, 1426   [2] the Brothers, not Karl

society, just as in the two preceding chapters we have considered the relation between communication and the integration of techniques.

2

We begin this time with war ; for when the safety of a
society is at stake, not only are feeling and desire enormously
intensified, but it becomes indispensable that any conflict
within the society shall be reconciled in the interests of the
general security. In a society at war we see the conflicts—
and the means adopted to reconcile them—more sharply, in a
shorter period, and at a higher degree of concentration, than
we can observe them in the more diluted form and in the slower
tempo of its normal economic or social life.

A modern society at war constantly asks itself why. The
Linguistic Revolution means that a society talks more about
itself, turns the searchlight of awareness upon its behaviour
and so upon its motives. At the same time, since in modern
war the whole society must be enlisted in the group techniques
of warfare, it becomes necessary to give the whole society
incentives that will mobilize its energies to a high point of
efficiency. The soldier at the front and the worker behind the
lines are not only encouraged to ask why about the techniques
of their tasks, they demand the right and are even allowed
to ask why about the motives of their society in making war
at all.

Every society finds its own justification for taking part
in a war. No doubt in every war there have been some critical
spirits who questioned the motives of the leaders. But while
in the past the communication of motives could be confined,
and therefore could be questioned only by a few, to-day the
motives must be expressed in a form that can be communicated
to all and can in some measure meet the questions of many.
It is no longer possible that only a few shall know why, while
the rest are merely told how. There must be group motives
that the whole society can understand and accept.

To see the relation of such motives to national ideals and to the real incentives is not easy in our own contemporary wars, where our feelings are so immediately engaged. Let us begin, therefore, with a case whose remoteness gives us the necessary distance and perspective—the Napoleonic War. The actual incentives that led to the outbreak of war in 1792 between revolutionary France and Austria and Prussia are now clear enough : the desire of the revolutionaries to stabilize and extend their dominion and the fear of the monarchs that this would happen—very simple fundamental incentives of aggression and self-preservation. A long way above these were the ideals on either side : on the one hand justice for the downtrodden masses throughout Europe, on the other the divine right of kings and their duty to protect their peoples against bloodthirsty assassins greedy for spoil.

What of the declared motives ? These the historian, with the disengaged impartiality lent by distance, may call " pretexts." Thus H. A. L. Fisher—perhaps the leading authority in our language on the Napoleonic War—says, " Pretexts for a war were not lacking. Leopold of Austria could complain of French encouragement given to a revolution in Belgium, of German princes dispossessed of feudal rights in Alsace, of Avignon snatched from the Pope and annexed to France, of the novel and disquieting principle that the people of a country have the right to determine their own allegiance, and yet more important than these other occasions of friction, of the dangerous position of the Queen of France." [1] These declared motives, we must notice, do not directly appeal to ideals, for ideals are not only too remote from the everyday life of the ordinary man, but they lay themselves open too readily to question and dispute ; declared motives, however, pretend to be concerned with " facts." The declared motives stand between the incentives and the ideals, attempting a reconciliation, or at any rate a compromise. Symbolizing, for group awareness, the true incentives, they give this underlying orexis an acceptable and relatively coherent form ; which—like its counterpart in

[1] Fisher HE 809

individual psychology—is likely to be characterized by displacement, pictorial imagery, and condensation.

Displacement : as understood by Freud, this is the shifting of emphasis from what had better be concealed to what is more readily acceptable—narrowing the searchlight of consciousness to a spotlight that picks out some of the features of the actual incentives while leaving others in shadow. In Leopold's pretexts, displacement keeps his own self-interest discreetly in the obscure background. What is brought forward into the full light of day is much more publicly acceptable : the welfare of others—Belgium, Germany, the Pope, Marie Antoinette—or the abstract principle of a people's allegiance to their traditional rulers.

There is also condensation and pictorial imagery. A phrase such as " Avignon snatched from the Pope " is typical of the form in which a war motive is expressed. It is a condensed and pictorial symbol standing for a whole series of events ; it reduces the unintelligible vast and confused processes of politics and war to a simple picture of theft, much more readily comprehensible to group awareness than the welter of day-to-day incidents.

" Avignon snatched from the Pope " is exactly the kind of phrase that is seized upon by the political cartoonist. This is not just a happy accident : a cartoon is a pictorial medium for the expression of group feeling. In modern times cartoons have become one of the chief means of communicating within a group what does not readily receive public verbal expression. They express the orectic side of political life more effectively than words, for with their pictorial, condensed, allusive features they are fitted to symbolize the actual incentives of group life in the same way as dreams and day-dreams those of individual life. In fact, it is because cartoons are directed to appeal to the half-spoken desires and feelings of those to whom they are addressed that they take on their special pictorial, condensed, and allusive characteristics.

3

Look at any of Gillray's caricatures of the Napoleonic War ; at the one, for instance, of George III and Napoleon at the time of the anticipated invasion of 1803 (reproduced facing page 192 of this book). This is pictorial symbolization that, because of its function in expressing group affect, is strongly characterized by condensation and displacement.

Let us notice first that it is a " composite picture "—the phrase used by Freud in describing dreams.[1] There is con-- densation, the laying of a series of images one upon another, so that less approved ideas may be presented in the form of approved symbols. The latent idea of the contrast between the might of England and the contemptible littleness of France. combines with the overt contrast of George and Napoleon, and again with that between the King and the tiny Grildrig.

With this condensation there goes a characteristic displace- ment of accent. The emphasis is put heavily upon the supposed comparative might of the protagonists ; nothing being said, for instance, of opposing ideals or of relative military efficiency. And there is also what Freud finds a common feature of dis- placement in dreams : the use of *allusion* where, as he says, apparently remote ideas are brought in to reinforce and enrich the pictorial expression of the central latent thoughts and feelings. In Gillray's cartoon the allusion—as often in cari- cature and cartoon—is twofold : allusion to current events, known and taken for granted within the group to whom the caricature is addressed, and allusion to some image familiar to the group, embodying an event real or imaginary. By the end of the eighteenth century *Gulliver's Travels* was part of the common experience of the majority of Englishmen ; Wright tells us in his *History of Caricature* that in broadsides of the period Napoleon was commonly referred to as the Lilliputian, or the contemptible puny Grildrig opposing the Brobding- nagian might of Britain.[2] A caricature takes for granted a common tradition such as this. As a result, to anyone not within

[1] page 91 above   [2] Wright CH 596

the common tradition—to anyone, that is, not within the community of allusion—a caricature tends to be devoid of meaning, just as dreams may be " meaningless " divorced from their context in the life of the dreamer.

We must notice also the long quotation issuing from the mouth of George, the explanation in words which was felt to be necessary in the caricatures of Gillray's time, and which has become progressively of smaller importance in the more allusive, more fully pictorial cartoons of our day ; for, as we shall see, the cartoonist of to-day is able to assume a much richer background of common reference in the group to which he addresses himself.

It is evident from an example such as this that the function of a political cartoon is not simply to symbolize briefly a particular event or series of events ; much more than this it gathers up, symbolizes, and arouses group affect. Gillray's cartoon has a meaning and force for his society because it arouses a responsive chord in the society. It is shaped as much by latent thoughts and feelings present in the society as by Gillray himself. His genius lies as much in the insight by which he catches the prevailing mood as in the vigour by which he pictures it. A caricature such as this symbolizes what is more or less obscurely felt by many, but does not receive explicit verbal formulation. It is expressive of orexis ; of affect and conation not yet made fully public. For the group, it symbolizes feelings and desires of which as a group it has not yet made itself fully aware. They may be clearly recognized and even symbolized by individuals or sub-groups, but have not yet been given currency in group communication for the society.

Indeed, if the " latent elements "—as Freud terms the unconscious meanings beneath the symbolizations of dreams—were publicly verbalized, their subjectiveness, absurdity, even fear, might become too apparent. The British people—John Bull, another condensed symbol—would *like* Napoleon to be contemptible and puny, would like to feel that he is small and insignificant. This is how they would " like to picture " him. The caricature is wish-fulfilment ; the unspoken fear is pictured as a wish, a wish that can only hope to pass the censor if it is translated into an allusive caricature. Sometimes, of course, a caricature is too " candid " or too " subversive " to pass the censor. Note that a symbol can be subversive only by virtue of its dangerous potentiality of evoking feelings already there, feelings that might jeopardize public morale if they were too explicitly expressed.

In brief, a caricature has the function of symbolizing unconscious and subconscious group-mind—thoughts, feelings, and desires not verbalized for the group. For the purpose of symbolizing orexis it is much better fitted than words. Its fluidity, its imagery, the possibilities it allows for condensation, displacement, allusion—all these characteristics render it fitter than words to symbolize the fluid and ill-ordered affect and conation that the group needs to keep from its common awareness. At times of stress in a society a caricature may therefore act as a safety-valve, helping to reconcile the cruder emotions and incentives of a group with its ideal valuations of itself and its ideals of conduct. But complete reconciliation is not achieved. The existence of the caricature, the fact that it has " point," means that the gap between the inadmissible reality and the unattainable ideal remains.

Perhaps in Napoleonic times, when communication on political issues was still confined to individuals and sub-groups —islands of political awareness within the society—the possibilities of conflict were correspondingly limited. Perhaps it was only the few, the politically educated, who took sides for or against the war with France ; probably the mass of the people were at first indifferent, later uncompromisingly anti-Boney. But in our own time, when both verbal and pictorial means of communication extend throughout the whole society, the possibilities of conflict are greater. For while words and pictures to-day combine to reinforce each other in public symbols of great potency for the expression of approved group motives, they are subjected as never before to public scrutiny. They are laid open to a public analysis that often reveals the underlying group incentives that they are intended to conceal.

4

The one hundred and thirty years that have elapsed since Napoleon's day have seen the birth and progress of the Linguistic Revolution, and the development of powerful means of pictorial communication. Now while, in the stress of war, this may lead to an unparalleled degree of orectic integration in each of the belligerent societies, there is, on the other hand, an increased tendency towards orectic disintegration and conflict in the politics preceding and following wars.

This is because the increase of communication has two major effects upon group orexis, one of which will be in abeyance in time of war. On the one hand, the word and the picture have acquired enormous power in determining, directing, and focusing the attention of the society upon a limited field of its behaviour, to the temporary exclusion of all else. On the other hand, the increase of symbolic communication tends, when the stress of crisis is relaxed, to make a society more aware of its own political behaviour, especially the orectic forces underlying this behaviour. Orexis repressed in time of war is allowed some emergence into group consciousness. The political life of our modern societies in time of " peace " therefore shows two conflicting tendencies : an increased general political education, and at the same time the direction of group awareness upon a narrow field of motive.

The ordinary man of to-day, in every modern society, has throughout his life been subjected to some sort of political education—sporadic and imperfect, no doubt, but unremitting. The popular press, and now the radio, whatever their shortcomings, have at any rate brought home to the ordinary man the chief national and international problems of his time. Above all, they have made him critical if not suspicious of the motives of other societies and of his own. His attention is constantly being beckoned from all sides ; by the words that incessantly stream in from without, and by the words that no less unceasingly well up from within, in the press and on the radio. Little or nothing escapes some publicity. Thus, before the Second War, such concepts as the rights of minorities, collective security; and mutual disarmament—translated into everyday speech—had by 1939 become the commonplace of the bar-room and the railway carriage to an extent unknown even as recently as the previous generation. This means that to-day, when a society is moving towards war, whatever may be the " official " motives, many more than these are expressed and scrutinized by sub-groups or individuals within the society.

Now it is precisely because of this extension of political group-education that it becomes more urgent for those who mean to direct the behaviour of the group, to narrow and focus group awareness. In Napoleon's day the printed word and picture could reach only a small minority ; the mass of the people could be approached only by face-to-face word-of-mouth—a means of communication ideally suited to the propagation of misrepresentation, misunderstanding, and rumour and almost entirely beyond control once set in motion. To-day the planned incitement and direction of feeling are possible to the propagandist through at least four powerful instruments all operating throughout the society with inescapable insistence and repetition—the newspaper, the hoarding, the cinema, the radio. Each of these in its own way can employ both the word and the picture. As a result, what is now publicly said through these instruments speaks with so loud, clear, and unceasing a voice as to overbear the murmur of the individual or even the minority. Those who cannot command one of the instruments of public communication cannot make themselves heard. First-hand experience is replaced by what is received through communication. Symbolic communication makes a further encroachment on behaviour. Instead of the traditional emphasis on " seeing is believing " we have the new potency of the verbal and pictorial symbol. Reading, looking at the screen, listening-in—to-day these are believing.

Thus at all times, and especially at a time of crisis, there are the most powerful of forces driving the awareness of the society into a narrow beam, that while it throws a hard white dazzling light upon a small area, leaves by contrast everything else all the more obscure. Within this obscurity move incentives, powerful but hidden, not yet given full group symbolization in the form of declared motives. Group consciousness is fixed on a range of motive narrower than the full range of actual incentives ; so that even in the presence of extending political education, the group as a group will remain unaware, or at best uneasily half-aware, of the incentives underlying its behaviour as a group.

5

Let us now take an example of each of these three determinants of group motivation—general political education, the word, and the picture—as we find them to-day in our society, Britain.

Political education : an interesting instance of the manner in which extended political education demands a closer limitation of group awareness, is seen in government policy towards public knowledge of national armament. In the present century, in war or peace alike, the state of armament in this country has been kept hidden from our society as a whole. Some persons are, of course, fully aware of the facts ; the society as a whole is unaware of them. This is exactly the position we mean to describe when we speak of the group-unconscious—facts open to the awareness of individuals and sub-groups but hidden from the consciousness of the group as a group.

Now it is precisely the extension of communication that has increased the need for secrecy. The existence of the instrument of communication means that there are people incessantly engaged in finding something to say ; the machine must be fed. There is always someone ready to publish anything. There is always a chiel amang us takin' notes, the enfant terrible of our time. And what is known within the society is simultaneously known beyond it ; modern linguistic communication ignores national barriers. Then, through the increasing political education that follows general literacy, the ordinary man in a society such as ours has been made suspicious of any increase of armament. He has come to believe that this is always in the interests of a few and to the detriment of the many. It is as a result of political education that the conscience of a society becomes more sensitive to the behaviour carried on in its name and for which it will be held responsible.

Before each of the two World Wars the leaders of our society became aware that increased armament was necessary. In both cases they deliberately kept the fact hidden from public awareness. The evidence is irrefutable. With regard to the First World War, H. A. L. Fisher tells us that in the earlier part of 1914 there were careful and extensive preparations : " The country had never been better equipped for war. . . . Of these studied preparations little or nothing was known to the man in the street. . . . The technical preparations of the war machine had no counterpart in the psychological education of the public mind." [1]

It is interesting to notice the language used by this historian, not specially concerned with our theme of communication and group consciousness. He speaks freely of the psychological education of the public mind, a phrase exactly naming what we have called political education through linguistic communication. He is saying that certain important facts about the behaviour of the group were kept from the awareness of the group. An observer from the outside—or a spy in our midst— would have said, Britain is re-arming. Yet we, Britain, were unaware of this. This is exactly the parallel, in group psychology, of a man's unconsciousness of some part of his behaviour.

Before the Second World War the same problem of the secrecy of re-armament arose, but with a somewhat different emphasis. Lord Baldwin has told us that before 1936 the government was acutely aware of the need for re-armament. He himself was strongly of the opinion that armament should be greatly increased, but was afraid to say so, especially before a general election in which the future of his party would be at stake.

[1] Fisher HE 1105

"From 1933, I and my friends were all very worried about what was happening in Europe. You will remember that at that time the Disarmament Conference was sitting in Geneva. You will remember that at that time there was probably a stronger pacifist feeling running through this country than at any time since the War. . . . My position as the leader of a great party was not altogether a comfortable one. . . . Supposing I had gone to the country and said that Germany was re-arming and that we must re-arm, does anybody think that this pacifist democracy would have rallied to that cry at that moment? I cannot think of anything that would have made the loss of the election from my point of view more certain." [1]

In other words, a leader of the society was certain that a particular course of behaviour was necessary for its welfare, and saw the need for securing the integration of group thought, feeling, and will in the society in carrying this out. But he also knew that any open demand for re-armament would evoke a storm of opposition. For at that time the only justification that could be sought for re-armament was self-preservation, an incentive too crude to figure as a declared motive, too violently in conflict with the then widely held and deeply orectic ideal of international peace. He therefore remained silent.

It is true that there was not silence throughout the society. There were incessant internal rumblings ; individuals, sub-groups, were vocal. Some people knew and some spoke. But since there was no formulation of the facts for the society as a whole, the society remained unconscious of this very important act of its own behaviour in external affairs ; and unconscious —or at least subconscious—of the strong incentives determining this behaviour.

Now we can hardly emphasize too strongly that, in a society, this unconsciousness of its own behaviour, including its incentives, is achieved by the simple means of keeping the facts out of the field of linguistic communication. There can

[1] *Hansard* November 12, 1936

be no public censorship of individual thoughts and feelings ; only of the public expression of them. And censorship of this kind, we have suggested, is made much more possible by the increased potency, in our day, of the word and the picture. The public " organs " of communication have become the organs of the group mind, so that whatever is not conveyed through them tends to be lost to group awareness. The group mind is so taken up with what is loudly and clearly emphasized, that by contrast whatever is less loudly said escapes group consciousness.

In this battle between growing political education and the power of censorship and propaganda, the development of symbolic communication thus plays a complex part. On the one hand it is the chief means of growing political education ; on the other hand the chief instrument of the limitation of public awareness.

6

Let us glance now at this increased potency of the word and the picture as symbols of group motives, and at the degree of their success in integrating group orexis.

As our example of a verbal symbol we shall take the word which for six years was the focus of so much feeling : Nazi. The war-cry on one side of the battle, the word of execration on the other ; on both sides a potent instrument of the integration of thought, feeling, and will ; like other symbols of group orexis it is characterized by condensation, displacement, and allusion.

Condensation : the word Nazi itself is condensed, abbreviated, and this is not accidental. It begins, no doubt, as a convenient abbreviation of " National Socialist " ; but its use is soon reinforced from sources deeper and more powerful than mere convenience. On both sides of the battle the abbreviation became better fitted for its psychological functions than the full phrase.

In Germany both terms National and Socialist were potent rallying-cries at the outset of Hitler's campaign. After 1918

the regeneration of German national morale had become a
primary necessity : the re-creation of belief in the destiny of
the German nation, the rebirth of national self-confidence, the
rejuvenation and re-dedication of group thought, feeling, and
will towards the re-establishment of the Fatherland among the
nations. All this was symbolized and focused by the word
National.

But after a time, Nationalism was not enough. Political
education in Germany as elsewhere—in Germany probably
more than elsewhere—had turned the group consciousness
upon the problems of the economic structure and organization
of society. In the complete disillusionment, bewilderment, and
disintegration following the Peace any doctrine that hoped
to win popular support, to become a vivid incentive of group
effort, must put some form of socialism in the forefront of its
programme. " Socialism," therefore, was a necessary term in
the verbal symbol by means of which Hitler and his party set
out to stir up, integrate, and direct the thoughts, feelings, and
motives of the German people.

With their growing success, and as the primary symbol
National Socialism did its work, a change of emphasis became
necessary. Nationalism gave way to the wider aim of the
regeneration and salvation of Europe in the face of the threaten-
ing hordes of Bolshevism. This meant that it was also necessary
to increase the distance between the national socialism of the
original Nazi doctrine and the communism of Russia ; to
forget that Nazism was socialism. The symbol Nazi by its
condensation made possible this obscuration of both the
national and the socialist features of Hitler's original programme, and helped also the displacement of emphasis, the
movement of group attention away from the motives once
kept so much in the foreground of group consciousness. Attention was now withdrawn from nationalism and socialism and
directed by the abbreviated name towards new and now more
acceptable group motives.

On the other hand, here in Britain, the condensation and
displacement of the word Nazi made it an equally powerful

symbol of group orexis directed against Germany ; much more so than the original name National Socialist. It helped us to keep out of mind both the national and the socialist features of Hitler's programme. For both nationalism and socialism were widely accepted in this country. Political education had made people tolerant if not sympathetic towards nationalist aspirations ; German nationalism would of itself hardly have been an incentive sufficient to arouse hostility. Socialism perhaps even less : indeed to have proclaimed that the War was a crusade against socialism would obviously have provoked widespread opposition rather than support. The name Nazi was successful as our symbol for the enemy not least because it helped to keep the nationalism and socialism of Hitlerism removed from the full public awareness of our society.

But it also had positive virtues. The name Nazi was new, unfamiliar, strange, foreign ; it was thus well fitted to arouse the deep-seated incentives of suspicion and hatred of the unknown—xenophobia. The growth of pacifism after the First World War, the constant polemic against the Treaty of Versailles, had made many people in Britain sympathetic towards and tolerant of Germany. What, therefore, we might find it difficult to believe of Germans we could much more readily believe of Nazis. The theatricality, posturing, arrogance, narrow-mindedness, intolerance, cruelty of the Nazis we could learn to credit. It would have been much more difficult to fit all these attributes into the picture, which had been shaping between the two wars, of the easy-going, bewildered, well-meaning German who had been so severely punished because he had been unwise enough to follow the crazy ambitions of the Kaiser. In all these ways the name Nazi was a term well suited to symbolize and canalize group motives, as the time approached for the British people to be unified for the struggle against Hitler's Germany.

But now notice that precisely because the name Nazi was new and strange, it was less well fitted to act as an orectic symbol for the more slowly moving members of our society. The establishment of a new symbol as an effective means of directing group orexis takes time. Here in Britain the time-lag was very obvious. Churchill himself, with his clear and immediate insight into all the techniques of warfare, always used the name Nazi, and it is not without significance that he pronounced the word in such a way as to divorce it from any human language. On his lips it was a " word of fear," of hatred, ridicule, and contempt ; as remote from ordinary everyday life as the Hottentot and Timbuctoo of fiction.

But the popular press, rightly assuming a slower rate of change in its readers, dare not move beyond the names the last war had invested with orectic power—Hun and Boche. In the appeal to the feelings and desires of the less well-informed part of the society, " Hun " was a far more potent symbol than the new-fangled " Nazi."

It is, however, of very great interest to notice that, in spite of the deliberate efforts of the leaders and the propagandists to arouse, canalize, and direct group orexis by means of chosen verbal symbols, there was a strong tendency for our society to adopt and popularize a symbol of its own, closely reflecting a current of orexis somewhat deflected from the main stream of hostility. In the First World War a common name for the enemy had been " Jerry," symbolizing good-humoured contempt rather than fear and hatred. In the Second War this was revived and became popular both at home and in the Forces. It is a word in which the not wholly unintended—and typically Freudian—allusion to an article of domestic use, carries just that note of humorous contempt which seems characteristic of the attitude of the mass of the British people towards their enemies even in war-time. Compare with this, " Kaiser Bill," " Little Willie," and " Boney."

All this illustrates both the complexity of group orexis and the complexity and many-sidedness of its symbolization for the group. While propaganda may attempt to limit and focus public awareness, and may in part succeed, there will be group incentives that, though not fully open to public awareness, will yet find some reflection, distorted perhaps, in public symbols.

A Low cartoon of "The New Order," 1940
By courtesy of Mr David Low and "The Evening Standard"

GEORGE III, AND BONAPARTE

AS

The King of Brobdignag and Gulliver.

A Gillray cartoon at the time of the anticipated
invasion of 1803

The name Nazi shows condensation and displacement. How does it acquire its background of allusion—that is, its power of making us aware of ideas which it does not directly symbolize, but which add to the richness of its content? There is no doubt that every common verbal symbol such as this gains much of its allusive power from the images that grow up around it. In the past, this occurred as the slow accretion of pictorial tradition round a word ; to-day the universal presence of pictures—on the hoarding, the screen, and in the newspaper—accelerates this process and brings within a year what formerly needed a decade or even a generation. How quickly, for instance, did Mickey Mouse or Colonel Blimp become a character clearly pictured by large masses of men— a symbol that can be used in common intercourse throughout a society with something approaching a common content of imagery.

The mention of Blimp reminds us that no man has done more to build up a pictorial background to the word Nazi than Low, the Gillray of our time. For comparison with Gillray's Gulliver cartoon, look at the Low reproduction opposite.

Taking first the obvious characteristics, perhaps the most striking difference is the absence of words in Low's cartoon as compared with the long quotation in Gillray's, typical of the style of his day, when every caricature was adorned with unwieldy balloons of dialogue, to say nothing of elaborate captions. To-day the cartoonist is able to rely immeasurably more on the meaning the picture itself carries. This has in its turn its own background of allusion. The communication and establishment of a common background of this kind to-day is the result of the rapid repetition and wide broadcasting made possible by newspaper, hoarding, and screen, together with the effects of extended political education. The cartoonist to-day can soon take it for granted that masses of men will have seen his pictures, and seen them often, have read pretty much the same news and listened to the same broadcasts.

The picture of the Nazi and the other figures in this cartoon may therefore each take for granted its own background of allusion. But as compared with Gillray the allusion here is implied rather than explicit. Where Gillray leaves us in no doubt, telling us that Gulliver's King and Grildrig are George III and Napoleon, Low takes his allusions for granted : the romantic Wagnerian-Siegfried predilections of Nazism, the Abyssinian-African ambitions of Fascism, the Mikado-imperialistic aspirations of Japan, the delusive simplicity of Stalin, the slyness of Ribbentrop. Each of these figures has been made what it is in the British public mind by constant political education through word and picture. By taking for granted such a background of allusion—including the implications of humour in the Siegfried Hitler, the Hottentot Mussolini, and the Gilbert-and-Sullivan Mikado—the cartoonist is able to put the weight of a rich content behind the keen point of his central thrust—The New Order. This phrase is, of course, itself allusive, with a double-meaning, punning intention that takes it for granted the reader will leap to the comparison between Hitler's New Order and the " orders " conferred as public decorations.

In saying that the economy and pregnant allusiveness of Low's cartoon are made possible by the political knowledge it assumes, we do not mean to exaggerate the depth of this knowledge. Much of it no doubt is superficial enough, but it is sufficient to form a common awareness—a group cognition—upon which a pictorial symbol may operate with power. In their turn the images in a cartoon such as this provide a fuller background of meaning for verbal symbols : Nazi, Hitler, Mussolini, Mikado, Stalin. In our day, with the easy and rapid reproduction of pictures, it is as much through these as through words that the meaning of any public symbol is built up. It would be difficult, if not impossible, to put into words all the shades of meaning suggested by this one drawing of the posturing Hitler. It was by a succession of images of this kind rather than by words that the background of allusion for the word Nazi was built up, in public communication and so in group consciousness.

In our time it is pictures, therefore, that give words much of their orectic content, especially that which is not available for full verbal formulation. What cannot be openly said can nevertheless be suggested. To say in so many words what this caricature suggests about Hitler, for instance, would invite too close a scrutiny, and, in revealing the affective and somewhat irrational elements in this conception of him, provoke perhaps a critical response or even rejection. The verbal proposition, for instance, that " Nazism is a theatrical atavistic revival of romantic paganism," invites critical consideration of its truth, and may arouse the suspicion that the apparently cool rational formulation masks feeling. But because a picture makes no proposition, criticisms and suspicion of what it suggests are lulled.

A picture, again, is able to express our fears without openly stating them. Thus there is little doubt that our ridicule of Hitler, like our ridicule of Napoleon, had more than a tinge of fear. A cartoon such as this can serve to obscure the fear that words might reveal ; it can keep at a subconscious level for the group those incentives, feelings, and wishes that cannot be allowed verbal formulation.

The date of the cartoon is October 1940, when the pact between Nazi Germany, Fascist Italy, and Japan declared a " New Order." In Britain it was feared that in the alliance between Stalin and Hitler the latter was becoming the dominant partner. Thus, under the good-humoured ridicule of the cartoon there is certainly the fear that the increasing dominance of Hitler even in Russia would destroy our last hope of Soviet aid against Germany. As in Gillray's cartoon, fear of the enemy and wish for his destruction are disguised as contempt and ridicule ; the disguise being effected by the condensation, displacement, and allusion of the picture. In the figure of Hitler, for instance, these are all very obvious : the condensation and concentration of a constellation of feelings and attitudes towards him ; the displacement of emphasis from the danger he threatens, to his absurd revival of Germany's pagan past ; and the allusions to a host of ideas that have come to cluster about the image of Hitler since he came to power : *Mein Kampf*, Wagner, the Herrenvolk, Nazi cruelty, and much else. The caricature expresses the contempt and ridicule the British people feel towards him, still more would " like to feel." Like Gillray's, the cartoon is wish-fulfilment ; it is Hitler as we should " like to picture " him.

So, too, Mussolini and the Mikado ; but notice the difference in affect and conation symbolized in the drawing of Stalin. Here there is certainly no contempt ; instead a good-natured tolerance mingled perhaps with alarm lest he should be taken in by the fair words and specious promises of the Axis. It need hardly be pointed out that this, again, symbolizes much of the affect and conation current in this country at the time. Stalin might be toying with the Axis, but his heart was in the right place—at least we hoped so. This was Stalin as we should like to picture him ; but to say this in so many words would have been dangerous, especially through the open medium of the press. It would, for instance, have been too clear an admission that we were concerned about the loss of the U.S.S.R. as an ally, and thus a confession of weakness.

8

Cartoons of this kind—operating day after day through one medium of communication or another—arouse, reinforce, and integrate group attitudes which then are ready as responses to the group verbal symbols. As a result, a name such as Nazi will come to carry latent orectic significance, will symbolize and arouse feeling and incentives without bringing these fully to the awareness of the group mind. Group affect and conation are aroused and developed without being fully formulated, and so without being brought beneath the close scrutiny of the group. Because of this function of symbolizing group orexis, a public verbal symbol will have the characteristics of condensation, displacement, and allusion—of the same kind as are seen in the " declared motives " of the conduct of a group or in the dreams that symbolize and " declare " individual orexis.

To-day, symbols rich in condensation, displacement, and allusion may be adopted and fashioned, and then—through the constant operation of communication through the press, the radio, and other " public organs "—deliberately built up into group symbols. In any conflict the names adopted by the conflicting groups for themselves or each other are likely to be of this kind. Sometimes, as in the case of Nazi, the characteristic of the name lends itself for use by both groups ; in other cases, as in internal politics, the name taken by a group will not be accepted by the other. The Conservatives call the Labour Party Socialists, who in turn call them Tories.

Thus words and pictures work together, each providing a background of allusion for the other. The word gains force from its implied context of images, the picture from its implied context of words. Political education proceeds by means of linguistic communication through all the varied channels open to-day while images are propagated through newspaper cartoons, posters, and the cinema. The images have, if anything, rather more of condensation, displacement, and allusion than the words—they are closer to the orexis they symbolize than any words can be. On the other hand, words are perhaps more readily communicable from man to man within the society, being spoken as well as written, heard as well as seen.

Where, as in time of war, conditions are favourable for the integration of group orexis, this may certainly be fostered by means of words and pictures. The society, under the stress of fear for its safety, will submit to the censorship of any symbolization and communication not in accord with orexis directed towards winning the war. Most of this unapproved orexis will be repressed below the level of group awareness. The control of communication will thus have been used in the service of integrating the society ; and the more elaborate and widespread the means of communication, the more successful this integration will have been.

But when the safety of a society is not threatened from without, the internal orectic conflicts, always latent, emerge. The effects of communication are then by no means wholly in the direction of integration. The growth of communication may even intensify conflict. This is the topic of our next chapter.

CHAPTER 10

LANGUAGE AND SOCIAL CONFLICT

I

In the last chapter we have dealt with the functions of verbal and pictorial symbolization in fostering orectic integration under the favourable conditions of warfare, where there is every incentive within the group to unite in thought, feeling, and action, and to conform to the direction of its leaders. We turn now to the functions of symbolization where there is internal conflict ; the more normal state of affairs, for in every modern society internal war ceases only under the stress of external war. War without, peace within ; peace without, war within—this is the characteristic alternation of society to-day.

We could therefore readily find instances from every aspect of social life. Our examples of the integration of group techniques and group orexis were drawn from industry, war, and politics. To illustrate orectic conflict we shall take an instance that touches all these as well as almost every other aspect of the life of the society in which it occurs : the problem of the " minority." Our instance is the Negro problem in the United States, one example of what is common throughout the world to-day—conflict in a society between the ruling majority and a minority, and conflict therefore within each of the two sub-groups.[1]

The Negro problem in America is certainly very much an

[1] It is tempting to enlarge upon the parallel between the disintegrated group mind and disintegrated individual personality—but I shall content myself with quoting Morton Prince's classical description of the latter : " By a breaking up of the original personality at different moments along different lines of cleavage, there may be formed several different personalities which may take turns with one another. Again, in the break-up, certain conscious states, which are rejected in the synthesis of the new personality, may remain outside the consciousness of the latter, synthesized among themselves, and thus form a second simultaneously acting consciousness. This is called a sub-consciousness " (Prince DP 3). Substituting " society " for " personality," and making one or two consequent verbal changes, we get a close description of a disintegrated society.

199

orectic problem, a conflict in which group orexis determines and shapes group awareness and group formulations, so that the relations between orectic conflict and communication clearly appear. Further, it is a problem that we in Britain can view with a detachment that we cannot achieve in our own internal conflicts, but whose relation to communication we can more readily understand than if the language were different from our own. And not the least important reason for the choice is that the problem has recently been the subject of dispassionate and detailed study by a group of sociologists. Under the guidance of Gunnar Myrdal, *An American Dilemma* (1942) leaves nothing to be desired from the fullness of the evidence it presents and the range of aspects it explores.

Since Myrdal and his associates have no immediate concern with problems of communication, it is all the more valuable to us to find a recurring impact of these problems upon their central theme. Their work constitutes a full ethnographical study of a contemporary social conflict, where the means and effects of communication fall quite naturally into place in the general picture.

Here, as throughout our study of language in society, we shall have to begin with a somewhat detailed account of the facts of the conflict before we pass to a consideration of their relation to communication. The functions of language and other group symbols can only be understood in their relation to the social life in which they arise and operate. First, then, for the facts.

2

Concerning the Negro problem, we have an abundance of evidence that enables us to describe with precision its genesis, development, and present condition. Behind the problem of to-day lies the history of the importation of Negro slaves and the long story of the southern plantations, culminating in the Civil War, which bequeaths its fateful legacy of conflict. Threefold conflict : between Negro and White, again within each of these two groups, and again within many individual members of both groups. For, as Myrdal points out, the Negro problem is a White man's problem—the White Americans are in conflict with each other on the Negro question ; at the same time there is a parallel, though perhaps less powerful, conflict within the Negro community.[1] The debates and conflict of feeling among the Whites as to the place of the Negro in the American Society are exactly paralleled by conflicts of opinion and feeling among the Negroes on this same question ; these conflicts are of course reflected in a certain disintegration and conflict in the minds and hearts of many members of both groups. Here, then, is conflict in the society as a whole, in its two sub-groups and in individuals ; conflict disturbing, abiding, and deep.

The fundamental fact in the problem is the difference of race and colour. It is this which provides the primary incentive in the conflict. Looked at in a purely rational way, the right of Negroes to be fully taken up and absorbed in the American Society is unquestionable. They form one-tenth of the entire population, and they are among the oldest-established settlers in the land. The majority of them could boast an American ancestry reaching back at least one hundred and fifty years : the date of the federal law prohibiting the slave trade is 1808. They have at least as ancient a status in the land as many of the streams of immigrants that during the past two centuries have flowed together to form contemporary American society. As for traditions of culture, here again there is convergence with the rest of the society. As Myrdal clearly shows, nobody is more adherent to the traditional ideals of American life than Negroes. Together with all other Americans, they accept what Myrdal calls the American Creed : the national ideal of national conduct, constituted partly by the rights embodied in the written Constitution and partly by traditional beliefs that come from the Bible, from the revolutionary philosophy that was the background of the birth of the Republic, from history, and from myth. And a fundamental tenet of this American Creed, accepted alike by the Negro and the White, is the equality of all men, irrespective of race and colour.

[1] Myrdal AD 26

It is important to notice that the Negro belief in the American Creed is not merely a rationalizing justification by Negroes of their demand for equality ; it is a belief sustained by strong feeling—what we have called group orexis—even in the face of contrary evidence. " The American Negroes know that they are a subordinated group experiencing, more than anybody else in the nation, the consequences of the fact that the Creed is not lived up to in America. Yet their faith in the Creed is not simply a means of pleading their unfulfilled rights. They, like the Whites, are under the spell of the great national suggestion. With one part of themselves, they actually believe, as do the Whites, that the Creed is ruling America." [1]

The Negroes are in fact potentially a part of the American people, in that they fully participate in the common beliefs and the common culture. There is little or no rational ground for their exclusion. The real incentives are undoubtedly orectic.

3

Group incentives, as we have tried to show, are revealed much less clearly in the form of declared motives than in the customary behaviour of the group. It is this that we have to examine for clues to primary incentives. And here, as everywhere, the external observer sees uniformities of behaviour not so apparent to the society itself. Myrdal is able to draw up a series of " principles " that emerge from the actual relations of the Whites to the Negroes, in the North not so obviously perhaps as in the South, but everywhere in the same order of relative importance. First comes the bar against inter-marriage and inter-racial sexual intercourse, particularly as far as this involves White women ; next, a bar against general social intercourse—for instance, dancing or eating together ; then segregation in the use of public facilities ; political disenfranchisement ; discrimination in the law courts and by the police ; finally, economic discrimination, particularly exclusion from favoured occupations.

[1] Myrdal AD 4

The order of importance of these discriminations reveals the underlying incentives : the deep-seated orectic reactions to the difference of race and colour. Probably the great majority of White people—in America at any rate—would admit to an " instinctive " characteristic attitude towards Negroes : a combination perhaps of tolerance, sympathy, patronage, fear, and dislike, together with a mingled sense of mental and moral superiority and physical inferiority. Negroes for their part would perhaps admit to a combination of admiration, dislike, and fear of the Whites—a mixture of feelings of inferiority in some respects and superiority in others. The existence of this mutual xenophobia cannot be gainsaid, even though it is possible to demonstrate, as Myrdal does, that on both sides it owes so much to tradition, including unconscious tradition, as to make it unlikely that it is in any large measure innate. He goes so far as to maintain that by education, in the widest sense, this mutual xenophobia might be eliminated ; but in the meantime we must certainly accept it as the fundamental fact of the conflict.

It finds its immediate expression in two issues of primary importance to any society and of particular significance in relation to the history of American society : sex, and the onward march of the group. Nothing else in the conflict compares with the depth of the White man's passionate resentment of sexual relations between Negro men and White women, a resentment that, however—in the past at any rate—has been compatible with some condonation of relations between White men and Negro women. Inversely, the Negro resents sexual relations between his women and the White man, while he has tended to condone relations between Negro men and White women. Thus, as Myrdal concludes, on both sides it is fundamentally a *male* attitude ; if so, we may add that it is only one instance of the sexual jealousy of the male, roused at the possibility of sexual competition from males beyond the clan—everywhere a very common feature of racial antagonism between intimately associated groups.

Closely allied to this sexual jealousy is jealousy of anything that may hinder the onward march of the group. Thus the Whites fear that the Negroes, because of what is thought to be inferior in them, may drag down the American people from the heights to which it is destined ; while the Negroes, for their part, resent the discriminations that prevent their progress in American society and in the world.

These two jealousies arise immediately from the primary xenophobia, but there is no doubt, as Myrdal points out, that they draw added strength from the circumstances of American history and tradition.[1] A band of pioneers in a strange land are likely to be fiercely jealous of the possession of their womankind and also sensitive to anything that might impair the integrity of the group or impede its forward progress. These two preoccupations thus reinforce already powerful moral traditions of the original American stock : the traditional Puritan attitude towards sex and the egalitarian ideal of the American Creed, which claims the right of every man to freedom of social progress. It is at this point that the internal conflict begins, for it is also a strongly held tenet of the American Creed that no man should be denied this right on the ground of race.

Secondary only to these primary incentives are economic fear and jealousy. The battle for livelihood in an industrialized society produces the constant incentive to exclude from the field of labour sub-groups within the society—women, or Jews, or Negroes. In this last instance exclusion from favoured occupations produces in its turn twin responses : resentment at the exclusion, mingled with a proud withdrawal to occupations from which White competition is absent. The Negro community provides most of its own pastors and teachers.[2]

Associated with these deeply rooted incentives of sexual, social, and economic forces, and in part arising from them, are important differences of social tradition and customary ways of life—religion, amusements, dress, and general everyday attitudes. These we need not recall in detail. It is clear enough that the Christianity of some members of the Negro

---

[1] Myrdal AD 60   [2] the same 305

community has highly characteristic features, which in the extremer cases impinge even upon beliefs. The heaven of Marc Connelly's *The Green Pastures* has something, but not much, in common with the Protestant heaven in the tradition of *Paradise Lost*.

In general, the ethnographer moving from a predominantly White to a predominantly Negro community would probably have to report less urgent personal ambitions in industry, and more free, easy, and light-hearted ways of filling leisure time. Negro song and dance have their characteristic idioms. Although these differences are no doubt largely the result of the treatment that the Negroes have received since their entry into America, they are felt on both sides to be fundamental.

From these primary and secondary orectic incentives, and from the associated differences in ways of life, the conflicts arise. Here we shall consider the internal conflict in each of the two groups, the same kind of internal conflict as we have already observed in nations at war—conflict between valued ideals and real incentives. The ideals, we have seen, are those held alike by Whites and Negroes and expressed in the American Creed. The incentives, primarily xenophobic, are sexual, social, and economic fears, reinforced by differences of custom and outlook. The conflict: although the American Creed denounces in the most uncompromising terms any discrimination on racial grounds, yet throughout the White community, orectic attitudes and actual group behaviour are permeated by discriminations on this very ground. The Negro community is torn by a parallel conflict between its faith and its circumstances. Of course this is only one instance of the conflicts throughout the modern world arising from the incompatibility of " liberal " egalitarian ideals and the actual discrimination practised against less-favoured minority groups.

How does American White society deal with its internal conflict? What group motive has emerged as a means of reconciling incentives with ideals?

4

The motive declared by White America in justification of anti-Negro discrimination has been " racial purity." Whether this has been compatible with the American Creed or again with other approved social ideals, or whether indeed it has any clear meaning, was not in question. It has been a faith and, like group motives everywhere, a faith that has performed miracles of reconcilement between inconsistent facts and attitudes. Once the faith is accepted, everything falls more or less into place. To prevent miscegenation, there must be no inter-racial sexual intercourse ; and since almost all social relations may open the way to sexual intercourse, social discriminations must be practised. It is even important to make the Negro feel that he could never enter White society on equal terms.

This, then, has always been the declared motive, and it will be seen to have the characteristic features of group declared motives in general. It rationalizes the deep orectic incentive of White anti-Negro xenophobia—the shuddering aversion from admitting him as a sexual and social equal—by raising this to the level of a defence of racial purity. Since mere xenophobia is too irrational to serve as a declared motive—out of keeping with ideals of reason and justice—the declared motive is a publicly acceptable formulation whose function it is to keep the irrational xenophobia obscured from the light of group awareness.

It is worth noticing that even this declared motive does not quite succeed in reconciling all incompatibilities. As we have seen, the admission of Negro men as sexual partners is most passionately resented, while the parallel admission of Negro women is condoned ; yet both practices offend equally against " racial purity." Again, neither the American Creed nor the doctrine of racial purity demands any discrimination against the Negroes so long as they are segregated—" separate but equal "—yet in fact, as Myrdal shows, they have been both segregated and at the same time subject to disabilities.

It is evident that we have here a sharply defined instance of the emergence of a declared motive as a group means of bridging a gap between group incentives and group ideals. The declared motive becomes a doctrine not to be questioned : to question it is to put oneself " outside the pale " ; discussion ceases. So its incompatibilities with the true xenophobic incentives, on the one hand, and the American Creed on the other, are kept from group awareness.

It would be impertinent to offer any ethical judgment on this state of affairs which, in one form or another, in greater or less degree, can be paralleled in almost every modern society, certainly in our own. Indeed, as we shall see, the very sharpness and clarity of this conflict arise from the fact that the American society is more aware of itself—more " honest with itself "—than most other societies. Our concern here is to take the conflict as a fact, and to ask what relation it bears to group symbolization and communication.

5

The traditional means, in every society, of dealing with a conflict of this sort is to forget about the real incentives or distort them, or both. In terms of our discussion of communication, not to symbolize them, or to symbolize them in distorted forms. In terms of social psychology : either to repress them into group unconsciousness, or admit them into group consciousness through the medium of symbols, which will be characterized by condensation, pictorial imagery, allusion, and displacement.

But in the American society neither of these mechanisms—repression or distortion—is any longer fully available. For it is a society with a long tradition of self-awareness and honesty in facing up to its own shortcomings. To go back only as far as 1893, we can quote the unexceptionable evidence of Bryce : " They know, and are content that all the world should know, the worst as well as the best of themselves. They have a boundless faith in free inquiry and full discussion." Myrdal cites this with earlier evidence in the same sense, adding his own tribute to the constant desire of Americans to make themselves aware of their social incentives, beliefs, and behaviour.[1] To these traditions and desires the contemporary development of communication—the Linguistic Revolution—comes as a means by which the American society may reach a high level of self-awareness.

Yet it would be surprising if—even in the presence of this group tradition and group desire to face facts—strong tendencies both to repress and to distort did not remain. First, repression. Although there is little or no deliberate concealment of the facts of the Negro problem—there is, on the contrary, a growth of communication concerning all its aspects—nevertheless there is still a great deal of unacknowledged repression, resulting in misapprehension, misinterpretation, and misinformation, and even sheer ignorance.

This, of course, is truer of the South than of the North. In the South, Myrdal tells us, there is a marked dislike of discussing the problem at all ; to some extent the subject is taboo. Among Southern Whites, he says, it is commonly held that there is "no Negro problem," so that at inter-racial gatherings it has become a sort of etiquette for Negro leaders to declare that race relations present no difficulty.[2] Further, it has become customary to ignore the problem in Southern white schools and the Southern white press. In other words, it is excluded from what we have seen to be the chief agencies in establishing linguistic communication—the initiation of the young and the continued education of the adult. Still more striking is an older social tradition excluding the pictorial symbolization of the Negro : " There was earlier an unwritten rule in the South that a picture of a Negro should never appear in print, and even now it is rare." [3] We have noticed some of the functions of pictures in group communication. In an imperfectly literate community, and in a matter where orexis is so deeply engaged, pictorial symbols may obviously be more important than language.

[1] Myrdal AD 21   [2] the same 31   [3] the same 37

Further, where there is discussion, it often takes on a queer " depersonalized " form, as if the speakers could not bring themselves to accept responsibility for the beliefs they actually voice, but must take refuge in the anonymity of the group. " The Whites practically never discuss the issue in terms of ' I ' or ' we,' but always in terms of ' they,' ' people in this community.' . . . One can go around for weeks talking to White people in all walks of life and constantly hear about the wishes and beliefs of this collective being, yet seldom meeting a person who actually identifies himself with it. But he follows it." [1] This almost casual observation of Myrdal's is a fact of unusual interest to us here. He is not primarily concerned, as we are, with the psychological analysis of group behaviour, so that he does not give further attention to this depersonalization. But here we must recognize that it is a very important fact of group psychology : that where there is strong group orexis towards another group—for instance, racial or national prejudice—individuals experiencing it may feel this as a force beyond their personal control. We must recognize that this sense of individual helplessness and irresponsibility is due precisely to the fact that within the society there is truly group orexis, the integration of orexis in a group by means of symbols communicated within the group.

Closely connected with this depersonalization is the constant allusion to the Negro problem in the form of characteristic Negro jokes. In the South, says Myrdal, the Negro is the standard joke, as much among the Negro community as among the Whites. And, he adds, " The main function of the joke is thus to create a collective surreptitious approbation for something which cannot be approved explicitly because of moral inhibitions." [2] The parallel between this interpretation of the popularity of Negro jokes and what we have noticed about the function of caricature in the last chapter is striking.

As a result of the repression of the discussion of the Negro problem, or of its admission only, so to speak, obliquely, there is extraordinary ignorance among many Whites as to the true

[1] Myrdal AD 37   [2] the same 38

facts about the Negro. One encounters Southern White physicians, says Myrdal, who are totally misinformed concerning the physical characteristics of the Negro ; educators with a totally false conception of his intelligence and educable capacity. And the remarkable fact throughout is the constant assertion by the Southerner that nobody knows the Negro as well as he does.[1] In other words, not only is there group repression of the facts, but also a very marked group unconsciousness of this repression.

To come now to distortion. The ignorance about the Negro does not remain an empty void ; knowledge is replaced by distortions of the reality. Instead of the truth about the Negro there is a series of " stereotypes." These are built up into a more or less coherent and consistent picture of the Negro —a group symbolization of him current among Southern Whites, a group picture that stands in place of the true facts.

This group picture is worth examining in some detail, because it is so typical a case of the powerful combination of verbal and pictorial symbolization. It is permeated by a conception of the Negro's biological inferiority which, as Myrdal points out, is a modern substitute for an older theological conception.[2] The Negro, black—the colour of the Devil and his satellites—was a barbarian and a heathen, probably without a soul. In our contemporary climate of thought such a conception has no longer any cogency ; it is no longer " respectable." The ancient prejudice must be given a new statement : in other words, the abiding group orexis must be provided with a new rationalization. Theology has been superseded by biology : the Negro is now held to be biologically inferior, having innate characteristics that environment can do little to change. Quite simply he is held to be lower than we are in the scale of evolution, so that there is little prospect of his being able to overcome this handicap. Thus as late as 1915 it was possible to gain wide acceptance for such a book as Shufeldt's *America's Greatest Problem*, in which one of the principal

[1] Myrdal AD 41   [2] the same 88

illustrations is a picture of a Negro standing between two monkeys.

On the basis of this conception of the biological inferiority of the Negro, there grows up a picture composed of detailed physical and moral stereotypes. Physically, the Negro is thought to be more powerful than the White—that is, more brutal ; sexually, more vigorous—again an indication of his propinquity to the brutes and of his constant danger to the White woman. He is believed to have a smaller and less complicated brain and correspondingly lower intelligence ; to lack the mechanical aptitude, the persistence, the attention to detail, the initiative, all so necessary for the industrial group techniques of modern life. Ethically, he is thought to be more lax in sexual morals, lazier, and more prone to crime of all kinds ; in general, prone to relapse into the barbarism from which he has so recently emerged. And all these characteristics, it is to be noted, are held to be innate—that is, not only ineradicable, but liable to infect any member of another race who may intermarry with him. Thus it becomes a primary necessity for the welfare of White American society to set up a biological fence round the ideal egalitarian creed. Myrdal points out that it is precisely because of the existence of the American Creed with its condemnation of racial discriminations, that it becomes necessary to invoke belief in hereditary biological distinctions [1] ; although, as he adds quite categorically, every one of the generalizations we have enumerated has been shown to be without scientific foundation.

Further, it is held that because the Negro's hereditary constitution renders him incapable of adaptation to the needs of modern civilization, his personality inevitably becomes warped. In fiction and the drama he appears, therefore, as one or other of several conventional figures, each in its own way lacking something of wholesome manliness : The Contented Slave, The Wretched Freeman, The Comic Negro, The Brute Negro, The Tragic Mulatto, The Local Colour Negro, the Exotic Primitive.[2]

[1] Myrdal AD 89, 106   [2] the same 1196

The Freudian condensation, displacement, and allusion in the resulting common group pictorial symbol of the Negro are clear enough. Once more we have a composite picture in which the numerous stereotypes are laid one on top of the other. The inconsistencies are blurred to an inconspicuous vagueness, while recurrent features—whether true or false—become disproportionately salient. Into this composite picture are condensed all the varied symbols of anti-Negro orexis ; and although the Negro may be credited with characteristics that are mutally incompatible, the inconsistencies are not clearly brought to group awareness because they are not often verbally formulated. To take one instance that Myrdal puts into words for us. It is commonly held that since the Negro has " lower costs of living " than the White, he is therefore fully satisfied to receive low wages ; yet at the same time he is suspected of a lust for possessions which incites him to try to oust the White man from the better-paid occupations.[1]

Displacement, too, is evident enough. In the current group picture unremitting emphasis is brought to bear upon all those differences that mark off the Negro from the White, while neglecting the likenesses—all that would suggest a common Americanism. Thus the big, loose-limbed, thick-lipped, woolly-headed, genial black is the figure that stands as a group symbol of the Negro for so many American Whites, substituting a cruder, but more readily-grasped and more readily-retained, picture for the less highly coloured and more subtle truth.

6

So much for the group picture. Turn now to group verbal symbolism. As so often in group conflict of this kind, there is a derogatory name for the minority ; here, " nigger." Originally—and little more than one hundred and fifty years ago—a name baldly stating the mere fact of colour, to-day it carries so heavy an orectic load that it must be banished from polite vocabulary. Myrdal explicitly refuses to use it.[2]

[1] Myrdal AD 39 [2] It is taboo in Hollywood. Mencken AL 305

The changes that have occurred in both form and meaning reflect its functions in the group conflict. The *Oxford Dictionary* gives the expected etymology, *niger*, the first occurrence in literature being dated 1786. Soon the spelling changes, suggesting that the word has been brought roughly into line with the large class of agent-words ending in -*er*. Stated in a purely rational way, the suffix -*er* denotes an agent or " doer " without any sense of derogation ; but barber, butcher, baker, and candlestick-maker are all names carrying with them a burden of centuries of class-snobbery. To this group other words come to adhere through the working of analogy. For instance, as the word " fellow " comes to have a derogatory meaning it is pronounced " feller." In the same way, Negro —so spelt—is pronounced " nigger." [1]

This is not to say that the analogy is conscious ; on the contrary, unconscious analogy is now a fully accepted principle of linguistics, going back as far as Hermann Paul's *Prinzipien* (1880). And it is precisely where there is some orectic incentive that the analogy is most likely to occur. Here the effect of using the form " nigger " is to transfer the emphasis from the primary meaning of colour ; the name acquires something of the significance of the other -*er* words. There is something of the implication of " doing "—a nigger is felt to be one who behaves in characteristic ways rather than one who is of a certain race and colour. The name is, so to speak, drawn away from the realm of rational, scientific meanings, and in their place acquires a fuller orectic significance. To-day, therefore, when a White—or even a Negro, for that matter— uses the word " nigger," it expresses something of contempt, which may range from humorous, good-natured tolerance to the extreme of dislike. To call a group of men Negroes is to range them—in a rational, unemotional, " respectable " fashion —alongside of other races. To call them " niggers " is to slur

---

[1] " In informal speech, especially in the South, *Negro* is often pronounced as if spelled *Nigger* "—Craigie and Hulbert, *Dict. Amer. Eng.* Webster (*Amer. Dict.* 1828) gives *Neger* for Negro, an indication of the contemporary pronunciation. Mencken AL 385

over the fact that the primary difference is racial. The name " nigger " puts them in a class by themselves, without parallel among the rest of mankind. In other words, the name Negro invites rational consideration of the real difference between the man so named and White men ; the name " nigger " obscures the point of difference, and in the place of rational consideration expresses a complex emotional attitude.

This emotional attitude, if we analyse it, shows very clearly the characteristics of condensation, displacement, and allusion of the group picture to which the word is so closely linked. As a means of condensation, the word helps to gather together many of the stereotypes described by Myrdal ; and at the same time it helps the displacement of emphasis, from those qualities of the Negro that command respect and evoke the consideration of what is due to a fellow-man, to those qualities that are supposed to characterize the nigger. As for allusion, it is evident that the word " nigger " draws along behind it a long tradition of picture, song, and story ; and here it is most interesting to notice once again the presence of a " group myth," with the function of providing a background of allusion to group verbal or pictorial symbols. Our previous example was *Gulliver's Travels* in relation to Gillray's cartoon. In the present instance, much of what is sentimental, pitiful, and pathetic in the figure of the Negro springs from the tradition of *Uncle Tom's Cabin.* Familiar to every American from childhood, few stories can be so widely diffused or form so common a heritage in any civilized society.[1]

If now, after our brief analysis of this verbal symbol for the Negro, we ask what is its function, there can be little doubt about the answer : it is one more instance of an orectic symbol used by one group to name another group ; compare " Nazi." To-day " nigger " is being replaced by " Negro "—and this change is itself significant of a change in the Negro problem. So long as the word " nigger " has been used, it has symbolized the group orexis of American White society towards the Negro,

[1] Among Negroes, we are told, the phrase " to Uncle Tom " means to show subservience to the White man in speech and manner : Cayton BM 67

and again of the Negroes towards themselves. With a body of myth and imagery behind it, on both sides it has been a symbol, serving to express some aspects of group orexis while obscuring others. For the Whites, it has expressed a certain semi-humorous contemptuous familiarity that may verge upon derogatory insult ; at the same time it has obscured the true core of orexis, the emphasis upon colour and race. For the Negroes themselves it has also expressed semi-humorous derogatory familiarity ; but again has removed emphasis from the point of true conflict, for until recently—and still, to some extent, to-day—the Negroes have wished to minimize the difference of race and colour and to find themselves accepted as full members of the American Society. On both sides the word has thus served to obscure the less acceptable elements of group orexis, those features which each group would rather not face up to. The Whites have been enabled to remain unconscious of the xenophobic incentives that might conflict with their group ideal of egalitarian justice—what might well be called the " super-ego " of the group. The Negroes, for their part, have been enabled to keep their attention diverted away from this very troublesome point of racial difference which, if they faced it, would have reminded them of the enormous difficulty of overcoming the xenophobia against them, and at the same time of what should be their own pride of race.

Finally, there can be no doubt as to the relation of this symbol to group action. It has become a current symbol on either side because the group has needed to act in a certain way—and in doing so has needed to reconcile unacceptable incentives with valued formulated ideals. Once established, such a group symbol—the means of group thought and feeling —determines subsequent group action. To this we may bring, although it is hardly necessary, the testimony of a Negro writer, James Weldon Johnson : " What the greater part of White America *thinks* about us is an influential factor in making our actual condition what it is." [1]

[1] Myrdal AD 102

7

What happens now when, under such conditions, communication increases? The answer, disturbing though it may be, is as we have suggested : that the immediate effect of increased communication may well be increased conflict. Communication, left to flourish and proliferate, may be either valuable or harmful. If we mean it to diminish or resolve conflict we must deliberately guide it in that direction.

Where there is a conflict between groups one can see how in general the immediate effect of the Linguistic Revolution is that the conflict becomes more acute. First, and most obviously, we have seen in Chapter 9 that communication may be used by a group to arm itself against another group, an uneasy internal equilibrium being secured by the repression within the society of thoughts and feelings that might weaken its fighting front. There will be an increase of conflict between the groups at the cost of true orectic integration within each group.

The further increase of communication brings with it a greater self-awareness within each group ; that is, each group becomes aware of the inconsistencies of its own behaviour—the incompatibilities subsisting among its true incentives, declared motives, and valued ideals. In fact—in the same way as in individual psychology—it is the absence of symbolization of orexis that is an aid to orectic equilibrium. The group, so long as it is relatively unaware of itself, is so much the less troubled by doubt. But as internal communication—that is, group self-consciousness—grows, the group becomes aware of its internal conflict.

Further, where the groups share a common language and are provided with the machines of inter-group communication —literature, newspapers, the radio, the cinema—both inter-group and internal conflict will become even sharper as each group becomes more readily aware of the other's thoughts, feelings, and actions. Inter-group conflict will increase as each group becomes aware of the hatred shown by the other group, and of the internal weaknesses within that group. At the same time the internal conflict within each group becomes stronger, as each group becomes aware that there is some justification for the behaviour of the other.

The facts of the Negro problem clearly exemplify all these tendencies. First, in both groups there has been a growth of awareness of the attitudes of the group towards the problem. Myrdal's book is itself a testimony of the desire of American society to know as much as it can both of the facts and of the attitudes underlying the conflict. But this book is only one of many. As Myrdal tells us, there is a bibliography of the subject running into several hundred thousand titles.[1] In the Negro community there are at least two powerful special agencies of communication : the National Association for the Advancement of Coloured Peoples, with its membership of 85,000 Negroes and its own organ, *The Crisis*, and the general Negro Press, consisting of some 340 periodicals devoted almost entirely to the theme—in one form or another—of the Negro problem. " The Press defines the Negro group to the Negroes themselves."[2] And this self-awareness runs through most of the community ; for except in the South, attendance at elementary schools is as widespread among Negroes as among Whites and " practically all Negroes who can read are exposed to the influence of the Negro Press at least some of the time."[3]

The first effect of this increase of communication concerning the problem has been to intensify the conflict both between the groups and within each group. Among the White community, books and the press have been, and still are, used to intensify anti-Negro attitudes. In the Negro community, Myrdal tells us, " by expressing the protest, the Press also magnifies it, acting like a huge sounding-board. The Press is also the chief agency of group control. It tells the individual how he should think and feel as an American Negro."[4] And in both groups, as he constantly repeats, there has been a growing sense of the

<hr />

[1] Myrdal AD 27   [2] the same 911   [3] the same 911, 943   [4] the same 911

inconsistencies of the thought, feeling, and behaviour of the community in relation to the problem.

All this has been intensified by the growth of inter-communication between the two groups. Although the Negro Press has little currency beyond its own community, few White Americans can escape some contact with the problem—through the White Press, books, the radio, or the cinema. On the other hand, the White Press has an extensive circulation throughout the Negro society, so that, by virtue of the fact that the two groups speak a common language, each becomes more fully aware of the attitudes of the other to itself, and this may increase conflict.

To bring out the orectic effects of this increase of inter-communication more clearly, we may recall the position of the Jew in the medieval ghetto. Not only did the walls of the ghetto effectively sever communication with those beyond, but in addition, the Jews spoke a language not current in the outside world and also erected a strong barrier of taboo against much of the learning of the Gentiles. Thus, although the Jews were downtrodden, exploited, and periodically massacred in almost every European society, yet there was a sort of equili-brium set up, a certain stability of group psychology both within each group and between the groups. There was no " Jewish problem " until the Jews became emancipated ; until, that is, the walls of the ghetto were broken down and the Jews became a sub-group within each gentile society, with free inter-communication.[1]

In the same way the Negro problem becomes more acute with the growth of free intercourse between Negroes and Whites. Sooner or later both groups are compelled to come to terms with the realities of the problem, and although this may in the end lead to a resolution of the conflict, there is an intervening period of greater intensification. Notice, for

[1] " In a sense it may be said that the same train of ideas which brought about the Jewish emancipation (and the theoretical abolition of anti-semitism) actually promoted the development of the new anti-semitism."—*Ency. Soc. Sciences ; Anti-semitism*

instance, the recent substitution, in both groups, of the word " Negro " for " nigger." [1] " Negro," as we have said, symbolizes the central issue ; and its growing use to-day indicates that in both groups this central issue is increasingly being faced. For the Whites, the adoption of the name shows that they are coming to recognize that the fundamental difference between themselves and Negroes is race, and therefore are being led to ask whether the maintenance of Negro disabilities is in keeping with the American Creed. For the Negroes, its adoption shows that they too are coming to face the issue squarely and to recognize that there is a real conflict between the desire to be absorbed into American Society and pride in their own customs and way of life.

Writing during the Second World War, Myrdal is convinced that although the problem is for the time being quiescent it will probably become one of the more important national issues in America after the War. And as a contributory factor he explicitly mentions the " rising educational level and intensified group consciousness and discontent of the Negro people themselves." [2] Couple this with his constant insistence that most White Americans are aware of the problem, and it is clear that he is telling us that it is the growth of group consciousness of the problem that is leading to its intensification.

In the light of our analysis of this conflict we may now go on to recognize that the same processes are likely to occur more widely. Where there is conflict between groups the development of inter-communication may at first increase rather than diminish the conflict. This is likely to be specially true of sub-groups within a single society, sharing the same language and other forms of symbolization and within reach of the same machines of communication. As communication grows within a society, the incompatibilities of its conduct, incentives, motives, ideals become more apparent to the society ; as a conflict becomes more sharply defined it becomes in fact a

---

[1] On March 7, 1930 the New York *Times* announced that it would thereafter use a capital letter for the word *Negro*.—Mencken AL 299
[2] Myrdal AD 37

sharper conflict. There is a parallel process in individual psychology. As through self-analysis an individual becomes more fully aware of himself—as he brings into consciousness what might otherwise have been sub-conscious and unconscious —the immediate effect may be to increase the conflict within himself. To keep potentially disturbing orexis repressed below the level of awareness is a valuable defence mechanism against conflict. Full self-awareness may rob the self of some of its defences against conflict within itself.

In the same way, as communication develops between societies, the immediate effect may be an increase of conflict between them. When societies share a common language and other forms of symbolization, they become aware of the differences as well as the likenesses in their behaviour, their incentives, their motives, their ideals. Discords as well as harmonies become sharper ; as the conflicts become more sharply defined they become sharper conflicts.

What, then, are the possibilities that the growth of symbolic communication may diminish conflicts within and between societies ? This is our final question.

CHAPTER II

POSSIBILITIES

I

WE shall attempt to answer this question by looking first at the conditions in which the growth of communication may lead to the solution of such a conflict as the Negro problem, and then go on to consider, in the light of this, the wider question of the possibilities of communication as a means of resolving group conflicts in general. What is the relation between communication and the *desire* for the resolution of a conflict ; how far can communication be a *means* of integration within and between groups ? These are our questions.

In the case of the Negro problem there exists the one condition indispensable for the resolution of any conflict : the desire to come to grips with the problem, to face the issues and therefore to increase and extend awareness of the facts and—what is at least as important—of the feelings and attitudes lying at the root of the problem. In the psychological terms we have here used, there is a group desire to foster group consciousness of both the cognitive and the orectic aspects of the problem.

Myrdal insists with some emphasis that throughout American society there is a growing desire " to know the truth and to think straight." [1] Now it is of the first importance to notice that although this desire is certainly a result of the increase of communication it is even more surely a cause of it. The increase of communication does not inevitably breed the desire for understanding ; and even where understanding exists it will not lead to the resolution of conflict unless there is a desire for this. It has often been thought that the growth of understanding between groups must lead to the disappearance of conflict : *tout comprendre c'est tout pardonner.* But the truth is that

[1] Myrdal AD 109

understanding can only exist where there is the desire to understand. It is not so much that misunderstanding gives rise to conflict as that conflict is the cause of misunderstanding. It is the desire to resolve the conflict that is the fundamental condition ; given this, communication becomes the means by which the conflict may be resolved. Once there is strong orexis towards the solving of a conflict, the groups concerned will apply themselves to use communication as a technique whereby this orexis may be translated into action.

For, as we have seen, the mere development of the means of communication may, so far from helping to resolve a conflict, actually intensify and exacerbate it. On the cognitive side, communication may be used to suppress the truth or simply to spread downright false doctrine ; on the orectic side, to arouse and intensify the very attitudes that foster conflict. Communication may serve to suppress the truth, as we have seen throughout the last two chapters ; that is, by turning the attention of the group upon certain aspects of the problem, to the exclusion of others ; for instance, by keeping well in the forefront of group consciousness all those facts about the Negro that emphasize the differences between him and the White Man—in particular, his traditional customs and ways of life. Or communication may be used to spread false doctrine ; as, for instance, that the innate intelligence of the Negro is less than that of the White man. Or again, communication may be used to intensify the attitudes leading to conflict, as, for instance, by the dissemination of stories that the constant desire of the Negro is to mate with White women.

To put this plainly : in the past the need and therefore the desire of White America has been to exclude the Negro from full participation in American society ; and although this desire may rarely, if ever, have been expressed—that is, brought to group consciousness—communication has never-theless been used in its service. The unconscious, or conscious, desire to exclude the Negro has been stronger than the desire to resolve the consequent conflict. It was *as though* the American White people had said to itself, At whatever cost in conflict, the Negro must not be allowed to participate fully in American society. But now the desire to resolve the conflict is gaining ground, and with it the possibility of using communication to this end. The desire to know the truth leads to the communication of the truth.

So much for the growing awareness of the cognitive aspects of the problem. It is clear also that there is growing attention to its orectic aspects. Perhaps the most striking evidence of this is the origin of Myrdal's own book. When the Carnegie Corporation decided to initiate an unsparing and detailed investigation of the Negro problem they showed their recognition of its orectic nature by insisting that its director must be "someone who could approach his task with a fresh mind, uninfluenced by traditional attitudes." [1] This necessity seemed to them to exclude all American scholars, whether White or Negro. Myrdal's own main thesis, constantly reiterated, is that conflict arises not from the "facts" of the case, but from the beliefs that underlie them—particularly the beliefs of the Whites.[2] He therefore emphasizes the need for the fuller study of these beliefs ; in our terms, for a fuller group consciousness of its own orexis.

A striking instance of the manner in which group beliefs determine group attention to facts is seen in this statement of Myrdal's : "It is now becoming difficult for even popular writers to express other views than the ones of racial equalitarianism and still retain intellectual respect." [3] That is to say, the very views that formerly were in the forefront of group consciousness are now being repressed because they have become incompatible with group orexis ; while the views that were formerly repressed are now brought into the full light of group consciousness. In this again there is obvious danger. There can never be full resolution of conflict where there remains some repression of the truth.

Clearly, however, there is hope for the future of the American

---

[1] Myrdal AD vi ; Foreword by President of Carnegie Corporation
[2] Myrdal AD 110
[3] the same 96

Negro problem. Through the darkness and strife of to-day we see the prospect of ultimate resolution of the conflict ; but not simply as the inevitable result of the blind growth of communication. There is hope because there is the desire to resolve the conflict ; and this will bring all the resources of communication into its service. In its turn, the growth of communication—by developing group consciousness of both the orectic and the cognitive bases of the problem—will strengthen the desire to resolve the conflict.

In the light of this analysis of the Negro problem, let us glance finally at the possibilities of communication as a means of resolving conflicts in and between societies to-day.

2

In modern times, the recognition that full communication within a society is requisite to secure full social integration goes back at least as far as the French Revolution. Bentham and Mill, as we have seen,[1] urged that communication is the chief condition of social order. By its use, they saw, conflict could be resolved within a society and equilibrium established and maintained. But they took it for granted that every society would be moved by the desire that its equilibrium should rest upon the true resolution of its internal conflicts.

It is this assumption that has more and more clearly been brought into question by the history of the past century. It is abundantly clear that again and again societies have used the resources of communication in the attempt to establish internal equilibrium, not by the resolution of conflict, but by the repression, away from group consciousness, of knowledge and attitudes that would give rise to conflict. In the same way, societies have resorted to the repression of group cognition and group orexis in the interest of inter-group equilibrium— for instance, the balance of power.

When we say that societies have made these attempts, we mean sometimes through their customs and traditional ways

[1] see above, page 162

of life, sometimes as a result of the deliberate intention of their governors. In both cases these attempts have, in our day, been aided by the new and developing means of communication, which have proved to be techniques of the highest efficiency in promoting the repression of group cognition and group orexis.

But here we are saying that the equilibrium secured by the repression of facts and beliefs is at best an uneasy, precarious equilibrium ; that if the development of communication is to result in the resolution of conflict within and between groups, there must be a desire in these groups towards real integration. Unless there is the strong desire to resolve conflicts, communication will not resolve them. To-day we have the techniques. The machines of language and the group techniques of communication have been brought to a high level of efficiency. What use are we to make of them ?

To-day we have at our disposal the possibility not only of full communication within a society, but of full communication throughout the societies of the world. Already a single language for world communication is within possibility. With that, the last barriers will be down. The spoken word, the written word, and the picture—the three powerful forms of symbolic communication—will be communicable, without limit and without distortion, over the entire globe. Singly, or in combination, they can constitute means of immediate group symbolization within a community as wide as the whole of mankind ; on the cinema and the television screen, the spoken word and the picture ; through the press, the written word and the picture.

As with so many other techniques whose development has been immeasurably accelerated by war, world communication can be either a weapon of conflict or an agent of peace ; as we use it. In 1939 the means available in this country for the gathering of information and for broadcasting news and propaganda abroad were in their infancy ; six years later they had become indispensable techniques of internal and external politics. What use are we to make of them ? Symbolic communication, it has been the object of this book to suggest, is the technique fundamental to all other techniques. Our problem to-day is how to use it in the resolution of conflicts in and between societies.

For this three things are necessary : three forms of group action. We must really desire to use communication in this way ; we must apply ourselves to understand what sort of instrument it is, how it works ; and we must learn how to use it.

3

We must desire to resolve conflicts, and desire to use communication to this end.

No doubt there is a growing desire to achieve orectic integration within and between societies. But something more than this is needed. It is not enough that a few, even the leaders, within each group shall desire it. If the desire is to have life and vigour, it must run throughout the group ; group orexis. To achieve integration within a group there must be group desire towards it, and inter-group orexis to achieve integration between groups.

Now, as we have seen, there may be some group orexis that is not open to the full consciousness of the group ; but if this orexis is to be the efficient guide and servant of group action, it must be known to the group as a group. Group orexis must be made conscious group orexis. In other words, it must be given group symbolization. In practical terms—in terms of group behaviour—it is necessary that symbolic communication shall be used to arouse desire and will both within and between groups, in the direction of resolving conflicts ; and so in the direction of using communication to this end, as the chief technique of group and inter-group action.

Here, then, we have, as so often in human affairs, a circular or rather a spiral process. To resolve orectic conflict within a group we must develop and integrate group desire to achieve this. In the integration of this desire an indispensable instrument is communication. Then one of the objects of this group desire must be to use communication as an instrument in resolving conflict within the group.

Another way of stating this is to say that the problem must be attempted from all sides at the same time. We must use communication as a means of stirring up desire to achieve integration within society, and also the desire to use communication as a means towards this integration.

What we have said about internal group conflict obviously applies, with the necessary changes, to inter-group conflict. We must use communication as a means of arousing in groups the desire to resolve the conflicts between them, and with this the desire to use communication as a means of resolving these conflicts.

Put in this way, nothing could be more reasonable ; nothing could more readily win general acceptance. But we must recognize that at this moment we are far from seeing it put into general effect. There is certainly not free communication either within or between societies. Within societies there are agencies that for one end or another use the techniques of communication in order to hinder communication, and at the same time seek to repress from group awareness what is incompatible with their intended objects. Seen at its height in the totalitarian states before the War, it is also in greater or less degree to be found in every society of our day.

As for free communication between societies, here the obstacles are clearer only because they are the result of deliberate and declared intention. Once again it is the totalitarian society that has most clearly limited and distorted communication between itself and other societies, but no other society of our time is to be wholly acquitted of this intention.

Social communication must be directed. Now that societies have begun the planning and direction of communication, they have for ever abandoned the option of allowing it to grow and flourish at hazard. But to resolve the conflicts of societies it is not enough that communication shall be directed ; it must be rightly directed.

4

To direct the use of communication we have to understand the nature of this instrument. It is a group technique that for the most part has developed without our realizing this. Its origin is with the beginning of human society ; it has grown as societies have grown ; its complexity to-day is part of the complexity of our social life. What the printing press and the speech machines have done is enormously to increase its scope and power and to open up unprecedented and immeasurable possibilities for its use. Because communication is so ancient a group technique, and is so constant a part of our lives, we take it for granted, and so perhaps fail to see how it is changing for us and changing us. What is this instrument : how does it work ?

Although it is so old a group technique we still know very little about it. To-day we are only beginning the study of the functioning of language in society. Our ignorance of this supremely important form of group behaviour is in fact part of our ignorance of the nature of group behaviour in general.

In the past, language has been studied in almost complete divorce from its social context. This is especially true of the positive aspects of linguistics : history—whether the imaginary history of the origin of language or the factual history of grammatical, phonetic, or semantic change ; philology, concerned as it has been with the establishment and clarification of texts ; literary criticism. It is naturally less true of normative studies such as grammar and the principles of artificial languages, but even here attention to the social context of language has been scant enough. All this is readily understood if we recognize that the study of the social functioning of language has only to-day become urgent with the sudden growth of its actual scope and power.

As may be seen in the Appendix, there has been some approach to the study of semantics during the past century, and particularly during the past fifty years. This is the study that must now be developed. We need to know as much as we can about the functioning of language in relation to the behaviour of the individual and of the group.

Some beginning has been made with the study of language and thought in the individual : both the discussion of theoretical principles and the inductive investigation of facts. There have been detailed studies of the growth and operation of language in infancy, childhood, and adult life, including retardation and the pathological impairment of function. On the whole it is true to say that inductive investigation has hardly kept pace with speculation.

This disparity is certainly even greater in the field of social linguistics. There has been much speculation, but little investigation of the facts. For the best empirical work we have to go to ethnographers such as Malinowski, who are, however, concerned with communities whose social structure and behaviour are far removed from those of our own complex societies. There is, as yet, nothing in the field of first-hand investigation of social semantics to compare, for instance, with the elaborate speculative discussions of Cassirer and Urban. But it is inductive investigation of the functioning of language in our own societies that is most needed. Perhaps for the first time we are to-day in a position to make this investigation ; certainly we cannot dispense with it if we are to use communication for the resolution of group conflicts. We need men, and groups of men, who will devote themselves to this new discipline—the social semantics of language.

5

But the desire to use communication to the end of achieving better understanding, and the knowledge of how communication works in society, are nothing unless we know how to use it. In our day the clear-sighted and efficient exploitation of communication by individuals and sub-groups contrasts only too strongly with the fumbling attempts of societies to use it for the common good. But as in all other aspects of social planning, the frustrations and setbacks of the first crude attempts are no criterion of the value or the ultimate success of the task. The story of our epoch is the attempt of one society after another, more or less rapidly and thoroughly, to take over the control of its group techniques—political, military, economic. In doing this every society inevitably moves towards the control of communication.

Yet whatever may be the most desirable structure of any other group technique, there is no such thing as full communication controlled by the few. The control, limitation, direction of communication are its stultification. Symbolic communication is not an instrument to be constructed and operated; it is a pattern of behaviour that must be allowed to grow. The society that seeks the full benefits of full communication must guard, foster, and direct its growth.

How is this to be done? We are even less sure of the answer than in any other aspect of social planning. How are societies to use symbolic communication not to destroy but to build; not as a weapon of war but as the chief means of achieving unity of thought, feeling, and action? How?

CHANGES IN THE PHILOSOPHY OF LANGUAGE

IT is a commonplace of the history of inventions that a new technique rarely appears suddenly, out of the blue. A technical invention is usually preceded by developments in scientific theory. In the case of language it is a striking fact that in the century preceding the growth of linguistic communication as a new social technique there was a parallel, but quite independent, change of direction in the philosophy of language. At the same time as language was becoming of greater actual importance in society, scholars were coming to recognize that the functions of language can be understood only if language is considered as a fact in society. This re-direction of interest has its sources, long before the beginnings of the Linguistic Revolution, in the middle of the eighteenth century. It is one of the waves of thought set in motion by the violent impact of the Renaissance—one of the remoter waves. The first effects of the Renaissance, in turning men to study the past, particularly the literature of the past, inevitably awoke some interest in language, but only in relation to literature. Later —in the seventeenth century—followed the study of the physical universe, and with it the beginning of the scientific study of man himself. It was only then, and in this roundabout way, that there began the study of language in relation to man. Philological learning, whose chief goal had long been the accurate establishment of texts of classical literature, now moved in a different direction. Concern with the classics gave way to concern with the nature of language itself.

Modern linguistic theory begins with an apparently casual discovery—the remark made by Sir William Jones in 1786 that the key to the history of language was Sanskrit.[1] Actually,

---

[1] In a lecture to the Bengal Asiatic Society : " No philologer could examine all three [Sanskrit, Latin, Greek] without believing them to have sprung from some common source."—Jones W (i) 26

of course, this discovery was no more an accident than, for instance, the invention of the gramophone. Edison was already deeply interested in the possibility of reproducing speech when " chance " led him to the gramophone. In the same way Sir William Jones's interest in Sanskrit was no doubt stimulated by the accident of his residence in India, but his discovery would have meant nothing to a generation not interested in the problems of the origin and history of language. To mention only one name : thirteen years earlier Lord Monboddo—much ridiculed by Dr. Johnson for his opinion that man is but a tailless ape and the ape a man in all but speech—had pointed out the close similarities between Greek and Sanskrit and postulated their common origin.[1]

At first sight, Jones's concern with Sanskrit may seem to be more remote from speaking man in society than even the study of classical literature ; in actual fact it incited students as never before to devote their attention to the spoken word. The study of Sanskrit showed irrefutably that the history and structure of languages were intelligible only through a knowledge of the sounds made by speakers. This rediscovery of the spoken word became the foundation of the modern study of language.

Within a few years of Jones's declaration the new " science of language " had begun its course as a specific field of study, independent of the study of literature. In the course of the following century its students had to work out for themselves both the form of its discipline and the technique of its methods. Three points of view emerged. There were some to whom the study of language was a natural science, with mechanical laws such as those of physics were supposed to be. There were those who believed that the chief clue to the understanding of the nature of language was psychology—to understand how language works we must study the mental processes of its speakers. And there were those who held that the study of language must be sociological, that language is a form of

[1] Monboddo OP (ii) 581

behaviour developed in the course of man's efforts to satisfy his needs in society.

The doctrine that language is a natural science, with laws analogous to those of physics, may now perhaps be regarded as one of the curiosities of the nineteenth century, but in its day it was widely accepted. The hint thrown out by Jones— that Sanskrit could explain the laws of change in Latin and Greek—was taken up by such men as Bopp and Grimm, whose masterly formulation of " sound-laws " seemed to lay down once and for all the lines on which the study of language should run. " Languages," said Bopp, " are to be considered organic natural bodies, which are formed according to fixed laws, develop as possessing an inner principle of life, and gradually die out." [1] It is true that the scholars who held this view accepted it as a metaphysical hypothesis rather than as a principle of method ; but in the outside world it was welcomed with acclamation, and at last became a commonplace of everyday thought when Max Müller made it the theme of one of his brilliant popularizations. The Royal Institution, hitherto the home of the physical sciences, opened its doors to him. Fashionable audiences were charmed into acquiescence with his doctrine that the method of the science of language " ought to be the same as that which has been followed with so much success in botany, geology, astronomy, and other branches of the study of nature." [2] With the easy perspicacity of a later generation we may now think of this as merely inevitable in the intellectual climate of that day, as a feature of the contemporary apotheosis of the physical sciences— Buckle, for instance, was making a similar claim for history, in his *History of Civilization* (1857).

Even the advent of Darwinism, which in the end was to bring a new outlook and a new method to the biological sciences, at first served to confirm rather than shake the confidence of those who held this view. Schleicher, for instance, followed hard on the appearance of *The Origin of Species* with a demonstration that languages are evolving organisms, in

---

[1] in 1827 ; from Jespersen LN 65   [2] Müller SL 22

origin independent of the human will ; they have lives of their own and are subject to growth, decay, and death.[1]

But in spite of the solid achievements of the German linguists and the brilliance of Max Müller, time was to show the barrenness of this doctrine. A more fruitful conception of language was destined to become dominant : that language is essentially a form of social behaviour, so that the study of language must draw upon psychology, biology, and sociology for its data and its methods.

A number of influences combined to bring about this truer understanding. First, perhaps, was that interest in psychology which had been so marked a feature of English thought from the time of Locke and which was to receive so great an accession of strength in the course of the century. Locke had re-established for the modern world the Platonic recognition of the interdependence between words and the processes of the mind,[2] and it was this above all which was to become the guiding principle in the study of language.

Not, however, without undergoing some aberrations. In the hands of Max Müller the recognition of interdependence of words and thoughts was shaped into an insistence on the primacy of words : " No thoughts without words." This dictum, as much because of its crudity as of its apparent novelty, became a centre of fierce controversy. Soon it fell into abeyance, to be revived in our own day with greater crudity by some, by others with a more subtle recognition of the truth that it conceals.

In the meantime a more gradual and more lasting effect on the study of language came from a converse inference of the relation between words and thoughts, that language is primarily communication—the behaviour of a speaker intending to convey his thoughts to others. It may seem strange that so commonplace a notion could ever have been neglected. But at the Renaissance, the early scholars of the modern world, absorbed in the restoration of the monumental remains of antiquity, tended to by-pass the fact that this literature was

[1] in 1863 ; from Seward DS 527 [2] Locke E 47

once the living utterance of living men. Later, with the discovery of Sanskrit, the prospect of language as an independent study was so alluring and the first fruits of this assumption so encouraging, that again the inherent relation of language with a living speaker was lost sight of.

Not by all, however. Those who approached the study of language through philosophy—Harris, Lowth, Monboddo, Stoddart—insisted one after another upon the pervasive effect of a speaker's thought throughout the language that he uses. A necessary preliminary to the consideration of language was therefore an analysis of the individual mind.[1] This was a notable advance, but in the infancy of modern psychology the analysis of mental processes presented so large and so complicated a task that it is not surprising to find a pause before the next step; the recognition that not only the speaker but the listener also is a primary factor in language. This recognition was naturally hardly ever wholly absent. We find it, for instance, in Monboddo,[2] but its full emphasis we owe above all to the genius of W. von Humboldt (1836).

When, therefore, Steinthal, von Humboldt's chief disciple among the linguists, said, " language can only be understood and explained through psychology," he meant not merely that men bring thought to the fashioning of language, but that language at every moment of its history is determined by the needs of man in society, and that in turn it determines his mind and behaviour. The name of the journal that in 1859 Steinthal founded with Lazarus is significant of his attitude, at once psychological and sociological : *Zeitschrift für Völkerpsychologie und Sprachwissenschaft.*

It was the very year of *The Origin of Species,* and the difference that Darwin made was this : in his hypothesis of evolution through natural selection he gave all biological study a centre of doctrine and method. Every form of living behaviour was

---

[1] For instance, Stoddart PL 5 : " In order to study Universal Grammar with effect, it is necessary to take a preliminary view of those faculties of the intellect and will on which the science of language depends."

[2] Monboddo OP 321-3

at once subjected to a new scrutiny. It is not surprising that fanciful analogies were soon luxuriating in every field of thought—that Schleicher, as we have seen, regarded a language as an organism subject to evolution. But after this first exuberance had died down, the more sober and deeply-rooted fruits of Darwin's thought began to appear. Since language is a biological process, a form of human behaviour, its history and present being must have been determined by the evolution of man. Thus at once the study of language was given a firm basis both of biology and of sociology.

For it must be remembered that Darwin's own hypothesis of evolution is not only biological but sociological. The spark that fired his thought—as well as that of Russell Wallace—came from Malthus. When in 1838 Darwin read the *Essay on Population* he suddenly realized that he " had at last got a theory by which to work." [1] Natural selection as conceived by him is a social process, the struggle among members of a community to secure command of natural resources. In spite, therefore, of Samuel Butler's denunciation that Darwin had " banished mind from the universe," natural selection is a psychological process, for it works in and through sexual and social competition and co-operation.

What Darwin's theory borrowed from psychology and sociology it returned in full measure ; [2] through these it gave a new direction to the modern study of language, by revealing its true psychological and sociological background, laying bare its roots in animal life and in primitive human society. The thought and feeling and therefore the language of man were shown to arise not only from his past history and present needs as an individual, but no less from the forgotten as well as the unforgotten past of men living in communities.

The linguist who achieved the widest acceptance of the social conception of language was Whitney, the chief antagonist of Müller. Before the stir aroused by the latter's *Lectures* had died down, Whitney entered the field to combat Müller's central doctrine of no thoughts without words, showing that

[1] Darwin LL (i) 83   [2] Flugel HP ch. i

it was a half-truth that led to a dangerously narrow conception of language itself. It was totally misleading, he urged, to regard language as expressing the mind of the individual in isolation ; the primary function of language is to promote intercourse within a society. " In all its stages of growth alike, speech is strictly a social institution. . . . The ideas of speech and of community are inseparable." [1]

Here, however, even Whitney stopped short. He would not take the next step with Darwin and recognize that language draws its being not only from man's present life in society but also from the past life of the species in evolution. He denied that there was continuity of development from the cries of animals to the language of men. " The essential characteristic of our speech is that it is arbitrary and conventional, that of the animals, on the other hand, is natural and instinctive." [2] " The human capacity to which the production of language is most directly due . . . is the power of intelligently . . . adapting means to ends." [3] It must have seemed to him as to others that Darwinism, in banishing mind from the universe, deprived us of the chief clue to understanding the nature of language. There seemed to be two opposing conceptions, not to be reconciled : Darwin's view that the language of men had grown with their evolution from speechless animal life, and Whitney's own view that language is an instrument consciously fashioned by men to fulfil their needs in society.

Since Whitney's day, however, it has become increasingly clear that these two views are far from irreconcilable. Our understanding of the nature of language has been enriched by evidence both from sociology and from psychology. We have surveys of the use of language in primitive communities—its relation to practical activities as well as to magic and religion : the work of Wundt, Frazer, Durkheim, Lévy-Bruhl, and Malinowski. The psychologists have given us detailed studies of the manner in which the growing child, moved by the urgencies of his life in society, fashions his own natural cries into the mother tongue. From the initial impetus which came from

[1] Whitney SL 437–8   [2] the same 438   [3] Whitney LG 303

Darwin himself as early as 1840,[1] the work expanded in the hands of such men as Preyer and Stern, who showed that while the child begins with cries as inarticulate as those of the other mammals, he is rapidly helped, by virtue of his innate endowment and the constant pressure of his everyday social life, to achieve the mastery of the language current in the group into which he is born. We see that there is a constant process of mutual adaptation between his primitive cries and the ordered system of conventional speech, and that the chief way in which social pressure acts upon him is to give him the daily experience of finding that language enables him to satisfy his needs in society.

Thus to-day we have reached the point at which the social nature of language is taken as a fundamental assumption by the professed linguist. Jespersen, for instance, is impelled to begin his book *Language* (1922) by saying " the only unimpeachable definition of a word is that it is a human act, an habitual act on the part of one human individual which has, or may have, the effect of evoking some idea in the mind of another individual." [2] Language is thus given its due place in the psychology of society. But psychology to-day is not confined to the study of thought. It is widely held that thought is a form of behaviour—or even " nothing but behaviour." A linguist such as De Laguna, after studying the development of language in the group-life of man, concludes therefore that " the essential function of speech is to influence the behaviour of others." [3] Thus the full dependence of the study of language upon sociology is at last recognized. In the words of Gardiner—an Egyptologist who came to the study of language in the effort to solve problems in his own field of interest—" the science to which linguistic theory ultimately owes its allegiance is neither logic nor psychology, but sociology." [4] In the words of Malinowski, "Any discussion of symbolism without its sociological context is futile." [5]

The wheel has come full circle. There is a convergence of

[1] Darwin BI (1877 ; from notes made in 1840)   [2] Jespersen LN 7
[3] De Laguna S 37   [4] Gardiner TS 33   [5] Malinowski ST 136

two doctrines that at their inception seemed diametrically opposed. Whitney no doubt thought he was moving in a direction entirely opposite to that of Max Müller when he urged that the function of words is rather to influence the thoughts of others than merely to act as the vehicle of thought. What now becomes clear is that by influencing the thoughts of others, language in fact becomes the vehicle of thought. The Behaviourists as critics of psychology, the logical Positivists as critics of logic and metaphysics, have to-day revived Müller's doctrine. In its cruder form it becomes the dogma that "thought is language"; but many who are unable to accept this will go so far as to admit that many of the apparent problems of the nature of thought are no more than problems of language. They will agree that logic and metaphysics and even mathematics are in essence social structures fundamentally linguistic in nature. The study of language is now a prominent feature in many fields of thought which hitherto have been hardly aware that it held any significance for them. And more and more it becomes clear that if in order to understand thought and the products of thought we must study language, in order to understand language we must study its working in society.

REFERENCES

Adamson EE	J. W. Adamson	*English Education* 1930
Alexander CP	S. Alexander	" Foundations of a Conational Psychology," *Br. J. Psy.* 1911
Allan CC	S. R. Allan	*Comrades and Citizens* 1938
Angyal SP	A. Angyal	*Foundations for a Science of Personality* 1941
Arnold ES	M. Arnold	*Reports on Elementary Schools* ed. 1910
Barker GT	E. Barker	*Greek Political Theory* 1918
Barker RG	E. Barker	*Reflections on Government* 1942
Bartlett R	F. C. Bartlett	*Remembering* 1932
Bell DM	E. T. Bell	*The Development of Mathematics* 1940
Bentham PL	J. Bentham	*Principles of Penal Law* (1832) ed. 1843
Bentham PM	J. Bentham	*Principles of Morals* (1789) Ed. 1823
Bergson H	H. Bergson	*L'Evolution Créatrice* (1907) Eng. tr. 1910
Bodmer LL	F. Bodmer and L. Hogben	*The Loom of Language* 1943
Bréal ES	M. Bréal	*Essai de Sémantique* (1897) Eng. tr. 1900
Bukharin HM	N. Bukharin	*Historical Materialism* 1925
Burt YD	C. Burt	*The Young Delinquent* 1927
Cajori HM	F. Cajori	*A History of Mathematics* 2nd ed. 1919
Carrington T	H. Carrington	*Telepathy* 1945
Cayton BM	H. R. Cayton and St. C. Drake	*Black Metropolis* 1946
Chuang EC	C. H. Chuang	*Education in China* 1922
Cohen RN	M. R. Cohen	*Reason and Nature* 1931
Cole SA	M. Cole	*Our Soviet Ally* 1943
Collingwood NL	R. G. Collingwood	*The New Leviathan* 1942
Cornford PT	F. Cornford	*Plato's Theory of Knowledge* 1935
Croce L	B. Croce	*Logic* Eng. tr. 1917
Darwin BI	C. Darwin	" Biography of an Infant," *Mind* 1877

REFERENCES

Darwin EE	C. Darwin	*The Expression of the Emotions* 1873
Darwin LL		*Life and Letters of Charles Darwin*, ed. F. Darwin 1887
Delacroix LP	H. Delacroix	*Le Langage et la Pensée* 1923
De Laguna S	G. A. de Laguna	*Speech* 1927
De Montmorency SI	J. E. G. de Montmorency	*State Intervention in English Education* 1902
Fisher HE	H. A. L. Fisher	*A History of Europe* (one vol. ed.) 1936
Flugel HP	J. C. Flugel	*One Hundred Years of Psychology* 1933
Flugel PS	J. C. Flugel	*The Psychology of Clothes* 1930
Fortescue HB	J. W. Fortescue	*A History of the British Army* 2nd ed. 1910
Freud EI	S. Freud	*The Ego and the Id.* Eng. tr. 1923
Freud IL	S. Freud	*Introductory Lectures.* Eng. tr. 1922
Gardiner TS	A. Gardiner	*The Theory of Speech and Language* 1932
Ginsburg PS	M. Ginsburg	*The Psychology of Society* 1921
Guillaume IE	P. Guillaume	*L'Imitation chez l'Enfant* 1925
Halbwachs CM	M. Halbwachs	*Les Cadres Sociaux de la Mémoire* 1925
Hitler MK	A. Hitler	*Mein Kampf* 1937
Hobbes L	T. Hobbes	*Leviathan* (ed. Pogson) 1909
Hogben MM	L. Hogben	*Mathematics for the Million* 1936
Hunt SS	J. L. Hunt and A. G. Pringle	*Service Slang* 1943
Jacobi PJ	J. Jacobi	*The Psychology of C. G. Jung* 1942
James PP	W. James	*Principles of Psychology* 1890
James RE	W. James	*Essays in Radical Empiricism* 1912
Janet MP	P. Janet	*Les Médications Psychologiques* 1919
Jast LC	L. S. Jast	*The Library and the Community* 1939
Jespersen LN	O. Jespersen	*Language, its Nature etc.* 1922

Jones W	W. Jones	*Works* 1804
Karlgren SS	B. Karlgren	*Sound and Symbol in Chinese* 1923
Layard SM	J. Layard	*Stone Men of Malekula* 1942
Leibniz NE	G. W. Leibniz	*New Essays on the Human Understanding*, ed. Langley 1896
Lewis IS	M. M. Lewis	*Infant Speech* 1936
Lewis LS	M. M. Lewis	*Language in School* 1942
Lippmann PO	W. Lippmann	*Public Opinion* 1922
Locke E	J. Locke	*Essay* (1690), ed. Fraser 1894
Malinowski AP	B. Malinowski	*Argonauts of the Western Pacific* 1932
Malinowski ST	B. Malinowski	*A Scientific Theory of Culture* 1944
Marriott EI	J. A. R. Marriott	*The English in India* 1932
Maynard RP	J. Maynard	*The Russian Peasant* 1942
McDougall GM	W. McDougall	*The Group Mind* 1920
McDougall OP	W. McDougall	*An Outline of Psychology* 1923
Mencken AL	H. L. Mencken	*The American Language*, 3rd ed. 1938
Mill OL	J. S. Mill	*On Liberty* 1859
Mill RG	J. S. Mill	*Representative Government* 1861
Miller SL	N. E. Miller and J. Dollard	*Social Learning and Imitation* 1941
Monboddo OP	J. B. Monboddo	*Of the Origin and Progress of Language* 1773
Mulcaster E	R. Mulcaster	*Elementarie* (1582), ed. Campagnac 1925
Müller SL	F. Max Müller	*Lectures on the Science of Language* 1861
Müller ST	F. Max Müller	*Lectures on the Science of Thought* 1887
Mumford CC	L. Mumford	*The Culture of Cities* 1938
Mumford TC	L. Mumford	*Technics and Civilization* 1934
Myrdal AD	G. Myrdal	*An American Dilemma* 1942
Ogden BF	C. K. Ogden	*Bentham's Theory of Fictions* 1932
Ogden MM	C. K. Ogden and I. A. Richards	*The Meaning of Meaning*, 2nd ed. 1927
Orwell TI	G. Orwell	*Talking to India* 1943
Pareto MS	V. Pareto	*The Mind and Society*. Eng. tr. 1934

REFERENCES

Pavlov CR	I. P. Pavlov	*Lectures on Conditioned Reflexes,* ed. Gantt 1928
PEP		*Report on the British Press.* P.E.P. London 1939
Piaget LP	J. Piaget	*Le Langage et la Pensée chez l'Enfant* 1923
Prince DP	M. Prince	*The Dissociation of a Personality* 1906
Richards BE	I. A. Richards	*Basic English and its Uses* 1943
Rickman SF	J. Rickman	*Sigmund Freud : a Selection* 1937
Rivers IU	W. H. R. Rivers	*Instinct and the Unconscious* 1920
Roberts HB	S. H. Roberts	*The House that Hitler Built* 1937
Rose IW	J. H. Rose	*The Indecisiveness of Modern War* 1927
Ruskin SL	J. Ruskin	*Sesame and Lilies* 1865
Russell AM	B. Russell	*The Analysis of Mind* 1921
Schonell BS	F. J. Schonell	*Backwardness in the Basic Subjects* 1942
Seth SC	G. Seth and D. Guthrie	*Speech in Childhood* 1935
Seward DS	A. C. Seward	*Darwin and Modern Science* 1909
Sheppard SH	E. W. Sheppard	*A Short History of the British Army,* 3rd ed. 1940
Smith WN	A. Smith	*The Wealth of Nations* 1776
Spearman NI	C. Spearman	*The Nature of Intelligence* 1923
Sprat RS	T. Sprat	*History of the Royal Society* 1667
Stoddart PL	J. Stoddart	*The Philosophy of Language* 1849
Stout AP	G. F. Stout	*Analytic Psychology* 1890
Stout MP	G. F. Stout	*Manual of Psychology,* 4th ed. 1929
Ure PM	A. Ure	*The Philosophy of Manufacture* (1835), Bohn's ed. 1861
von Hartmann PU	E. von Hartmann	*Philosophy of the Unconscious,* ed. Coupland 1884
Ward PP	J. Ward	*Psychological Principles* 1918
Watson PB	J. B. Watson	*Psychology from the Standpoint of a Behaviorist* 1919
Watson UB	J. B. Watson	" The Unverbalized in Human Behaviour," *Psy. Rev.* 1924
Webb SC	S. & B. Webb	*Soviet Communism* 1936
Wells A	H. G. Wells	*Anticipations* 1900

243

White PP	L. White and R. D. Leigh	*Peoples Speaking to Peoples* 1946
Whitehead IM	A. N. Whitehead	*Introduction to Mathematics* 1911
Whitney LG	W. D. Whitney	*The Life and Growth of Language* 1875
Whitney SL	W. D. Whitney	*Language and the Study of Language* 1867
Wilson SC	G. and M. Wilson	*The Analysis of Social Change* 1945
Woodward ER	W. H. Woodward	*Education in the Age of the Renaissance* 1906
Wright HC	T. Wright	*A History of Caricature* 1875
Young VE	G. M. Young	*Victorian England* 1936

INDEX

Adamson, J. W. 6
Adler, A. 79
affect 20, 30, 46, 74, 78
Africa 133, 182
Alexander, S. 74, 79, 87
Allan, S. 135
allusion, 92, 181, 193-5, 212, 214
American creed 201-2, 204-6, 211
Angyal, A. 93
anticipation 102, 115
armament 186
Armstrong, H. E. 38
Armstrong, W. G. 138
Army, British 143
  illiteracy in the 54
  New Model 137
Arnold, M. 39, 41
Ascham, R. 37
Attlee, C. R. 66
autism 30, 32
automatization 129, 134, 137, 139, 149

babbling 18
backwardness 3, 43, 55
Baldwin, Lord 187
Barker, E. 155, 163, 168
Barret, W. 141
Bartlett, F. C. 90, 101, 113
Basic English 61, 69, 168
behaviour, group 71, 96
Behaviourism 76, 79, 88
Bell, A. 6
Bell, E. T. 38
Bentham, J. 5, 90, 162, 224
Bergson, H. 87, 112
bilingualism, 63, 66
Bleuler, E. 30
Boche 192
Bodin, J. 28
Bodmer, F. 64
Bopp, F. 233
Breál, M. ii, 87
Brinsley, J. 37, 60, 64
Brougham, Lord 5
Bryce, Lord 207
Bukharin, N. 155-6, 163
Burt, C. 3, 32, 44, 54-5
Butler, S. 136, 236

Cajori, F. 38
canoe-launching 106

Carnegie Corporation 223
Carrington, H. 105
Carroll, Lewis 177
Cassell, J. 5
cathexis 83
Cayton, H. R. and Drake, St. C. 214
censorship 91, 183, 189, 197
China 46
  illiteracy in 52, 62, 67
Chuang, C. H. 63
Churchill, W. S. 61, 164, 168, 192
cinema 3, 34, 69, 185
cognition 30, 33, 74, 78, 81, 110, 115,
  153
cognitive reference 21
  functions of language 22
Cohen, M. R. 71
Collingwood, R. G. 84
Commonwealth, British 46, 60
communication, awareness of 123
  control of 227
  linguistic 2, 8, 234
  technique of 228
  world 68, 186
  and community 12, 19, 26, 68, 94,
    98, 161
  and conflict 216, 218-20, 222, 224,
    227
  and individuality 13
  and magic 108
  and mind 22, 28, 30-2, 37, 85
  and motives 177, 184
  and techniques 98, 100, 124, 126,
    129, 132, 135
  in politics 150, 159, 162, 164, 166
  in warfare 139, 142-4
Communist Party 155, 158
community, primitive 45
complex 83, 91
conation 20, 46, 74, 75, 78, 92
condensation 80, 91, 189-90, 195, 212,
  214
conflict, social 175, 216
consciousness, group 119, 122, 127, 135,
  140, 143, 145, 148-9, 153, 155, 160,
  170, 173, 186, 208, 216, 219, 223
  nature of 76, 86, 88, 90
Cornford, F. M. 84
Croce, B. 88
crowd stimuli 104, 121

INDEX

Darwin, C. 15, 23, 235, 237
declarative function 23-4, 39, 43, 45, 49, 52, 57-8, 65-6
Delacroix, H. 88
de Laguna, G. A. 238
democracy 158, 161, 164, 166, 168
depersonalization 209
Descartes, R. 74
dialectic, political 164, 167
discussion, group 160, 161, 163-4
disintegration, social 176, 184, 199
displacement 80, 91, 180, 190, 195, 212, 214
Dobuans 121
Dollard, J. and Miller, N. E. 16, 105, 121
Drake, St. C. and Cayton, H. R. 214
dreams 90-1, 181-2
Durkheim, E. 30

education 4, 7, 14, 26, 29, 41, 131-2, 165, 169, 208, 217
   Act 1870, 4, 7
   Act 1944, 132, 169
   linguistic 35
   political 155-6, 159, 184, 186, 194
egocentricity 30-2
Eisenhower, General D. D. 145
elections 155, 159
élite 43, 131
Elyot, T. 36
English 39, 46, 57, 59-60, 68
   Basic 61, 69, 168
Epstein, M. 44, 134
Erasmus, D. 36

family, functions of 34
Feltre, V. da 36
Fisher, H. A. L. 179, 187
Flugel, J. C. 51, 236
Fortescue, J. W. 141
franchise, extension of 4
Fraser, J. 6
freedom 158, 161
Freud, S. 30, 33, 77, 78, 80, 83, 89-90, 173, 180-1

Gardiner, A. H. 238
George III 181
Germany 9, 148, 165
ghost, group 71
"giantism" 132, 140, 168
Gillray, J. 181-2, 193, 195
Ginsburg, M. 72
Goebbels, J. 150, 152
gramophone 3
Grimm, J. L. 233

Guillaume, P. 16
Gulliver's Travels 181, 214
guns 137
Guthrie, D. and Seth. G. 17

Halbwachs, M. 101
Hansard 170, 188
Hazlitt, V. 32
history, group 112
Hitler, A. 9, 149, 151, 165, 177, 189, 194-5
Hobbes, T. 84
Hocart, A. M. 28
Hogben, L. 25
hormic 75
Hun 192
Hunt, J. L. and Pringle, A. G. 49
hunting 82, 98-9

ideals 174-5, 179, 205
illiteracy 2, 5, 52-4, 61, 140-1, 143, 157
imitation 16-17
incentives, group 202, 205
   individual 23, 178
India 52, 60
Industrial Revolution 127
information 167
initiation 13, 27, 29, 35, 45, 47, 60, 208
innovation, linguistic 49, 59
instinct 80, 88, 117
Isaacs, S. 32

Jacobi, J. 77, 90
James, W. 76
Jast, L. S. 2
"Jerry" 192
Jespersen, O. 238
Jews 204, 218
Johnson, J. W. 215
Jones, Sir W. 231
Jung, C. G. 76, 79, 90

Karlgren, B. 62
Kirk, Admiral 143

labour, division of 128-9
Lancaster, J. 6
language, artificial 63
   common 61-2, 168, 216
   semantic functions of 87, 228
   sex differences in 50, 55
   universal 47, 63-4, 68, 225
   and thought 86, 88
   as a natural science 233
   as an instrument 237
   as an organism 233
   as social behaviour 234
Laubach, F. 53

Layard, J. 104
Lazarus, M. 235
Leibniz, G. W. 38, 64, 77, 79, 85
Leigh, R. D. and White, L. 3, 53
Lenin, V. I. 8
Lévy-Bruhl, L. 30
Lewis, M. M. 15–16, 18–19, 43
libido 76
Lippmann, W. 167
literacy 4, 9, 63, 67, 129, 131–2, 134, 138, 142, 159, 165
    universal 1, 52, 133
literature, classical 36
    English 39, 43
Locke, J. 27, 77, 85, 234
Low, D. 193
Lowe, R. 6

machine, the 136
magic 107–8, 121
Malekula 104
Malinowski, B. 25, 28, 71, 102–3, 105, 108–10, 121–2, 175, 229, 238
mama 19–20
Manchester Guardian, The 167, 170
manipulative function 23–4, 39, 43, 45, 49, 51, 56, 58, 65–6
Marriott, J. A. R. 60
Mass Education, Report on 133
materialism 85
mathematics 25
Maynard, Sir John 62, 134, 155, 158, 160
McDougall, W. 75, 76, 81, 83, 105, 117, 163
meaning 15
mechanization in warfare 137
Melanesians, intuitive behaviour of 117
Mencken, H. J. 61, 213, 219
Mill, J. S. 162, 224
Miller, N. E. and Dollard, J. 16, 105, 121
Milton, J. 165
mind, nature of 73, 93
    unconscious 77–8, 80, 89
Monboddo, Lord 232, 235
mother 15, 21, 23
motives 120, 122, 174–5, 178–9, 185, 191, 206
    group 110
Mulcaster, R. 37, 65
Müller, F. Max 86, 88, 233–4
Mumford, L. 66, 68, 124, 132, 137, 140, 166, 169
Mussolini, B. 196
Myrdal, G. 200–2, 204, 207–13, 215, 217, 219, 221, 223

myth instead of history 112

Napoleon 181, 185
Nazi 189, 192, 196
" Negro " and " nigger " 212–14, 219
neologisms 49, 57–8
Newcastle Commission 6
New Order, Hitler's 194
news, transmission of 114
Newton, I. 38

Observer, The 143, 170
Ogden, C. K. and Richards, I. A. 64, 69, 91
orexis, definition of 20
    group 102–5, 108–10, 115, 120, 122, 149, 153, 170, 173, 179–80, 182, 184, 195–7, 200, 202, 205, 208–9, 214, 222, 226
    individual 22, 33, 80, 83, 191, 213
Orwell, G. 60

" paper state " 166
Paradise Lost 205
Pareto, V. 28, 177
Parliament, British 164, 167–8
Paul, H. 213
Pavlov, I. P. 156–7
" phatic communion " 25, 102
Piaget, J. 30–2
pictures, communication of 34
    " composite " 181, 212
pin, making of a 128
Plato 4, 84, 100
press, the 2, 8, 34, 123, 152, 157, 166, 184–5, 192, 217
Preyer, W. 238
Prince, M. 199
propaganda, importance of 150–1, 192
psycho-analysis 76, 89
Punch 57
purpose, reflex of 157

racial purity 206
radio 3, 8–9, 34, 52, 60, 69, 123, 135, 144–5, 152, 157, 169–70, 184–5
Reform Act 1832, 5
    1867, 7
remembering, group 100–2, 112–13
Renaissance, the 35, 231, 234
Report, Clarendon 39
    Mass Education 133
    Norwood 40
    Teaching of English 40
repression 208, 223–4
resistance, linguistic 17, 49–50, 55, 58, 62, 67

INDEX

Richards, I. A. and Ogden, C. K. 69
Rickman, J. 89
Rivers, W. H. R. 116, 119
Roberts, S. H. 150, 152
Roebuck, J. A. 5, 7
Rose, J. H. 139
Rousseau, J. J. 162
Ruskin, J. 39
Russell, B. 76, 89

Sanskrit, as key to languages 231-2
Sapir, E. 97
Schleicher, A. 233, 236
Schonell, F. J. 3, 44
semantic functions of language 87, 228
sentiment 83
Seth, G. and Guthrie, D. 17
Sheppard, E. W. 138
slang, nature of 48-51, 58
slave trade 201
Smith, Adam 127
social behaviour 109, 119
socialization, process of 12, 19, 26-7,
    31, 33, 49
Society, Royal 38
Spearman, C. 79
specialization in industry 130
    in politics 149
    in warfare 137, 140
speech 13, 17, 22, 24, 40, 42, 51, 53,
    133, 142
    approximation in 8, 22
    beginnings of 15, 238
    freedom of 10, 157, 162-3, 165
    therapists 44
Sprat, T. 38
Staff College 138, 142
Stalin, J. 154, 194, 196
    1936 Constitution 154, 165
Steinberg 53
Steinthal, H. 235
" stereotypes," Negro 210-11
Stern, W. 235, 238
Stoddart, J. 85
Stout, G. F. 74, 79, 86
Swazis 101, 114
symbols 28, 33, 76, 84, 89-90, 93, 97,
    115, 152, 185, 197
    pictorial 28, 33, 89-91, 109, 113, 119,
    174, 180, 193-4, 208, 210
    verbal 105

techniques, group 45, 106, 115-16, 118,
    124, 128, 135, 140, 147, 149, 153,
    165-6, 168, 175, 178, 230
telepathy 105

telephone, the 3
Tempest, The 37
Tennyson, A. 138
terms, technical 141
thinking, group 99, 102, 111, 162
    individual 75, 100
Times, The 3, 53-4, 56, 66
Tolstoy, L. 142
tool, definition of a 136
Treasury grant 1833, 5
Trobriand Islanders 102, 106, 109-10,
    115, 121

Uncle Tom's Cabin 214
unconscious, group 154, 183, 188, 207,
    210
UNO 66
Ure, A. 129-30, 151
U.S.A. 46, 61, 158, 168-9
    illiteracy in 52
U.S.S.R. 8, 46, 52-3, 61, 67, 133, 154,
    158-9, 165, 195-6

Vives, J. 36
von Hartmann, E. 77, 81
von Humboldt, W. 235
von Ribbentrop, J. 194

War, First World 139, 187, 191-2
    Napoleonic 179, 181
    Second World 52, 58, 143, 148, 167,
    185, 187, 219
Ward, J. 74, 79, 86
warfare 48, 104, 136, 140, 178
    in Malekula 104
    mechanization in 137, 141
    specialization in 137, 140
Watson, J. B. 76, 79, 88
Webb, S. and B. 8
Wells, H. G. 141
whale-boat 116
White, L. and Leigh, R. D. 2, 53
Whitehead, A. N. 25
Whitney, W. D. 236
Wilson, G. and M. 112
Woodward, W. H. 36
Wright, T. 181
xenophobia 58, 176, 191, 203-4, 206,
    215
Young, G. M. 141